MODERN LEGAL STUDIES

MISREPRESENTATION

AUSTRALIA AND NEW ZEALAND
The Law Book Company Ltd.
Sydney : Melbourne : Perth

CANADA AND U.S.A.
The Carswell Company Ltd.
Agincourt, Ontario

INDIA
N. M. Tripathi Private Ltd.
Bombay
and
Eastern Law House Private Ltd.
Calcutta and Delhi
M.P.P. House
Bangalore

ISRAEL
Steimatzky's Agency Ltd.
Jerusalem : Tel Aviv : Haifa

MODERN LEGAL STUDIES

MISREPRESENTATION

by

DAVID K. ALLEN
M.A. (Oxon.); LL.M. (McGill)
Of the Middle Temple, Barrister-at-law
Lecturer in Law, University of Leicester

LONDON
SWEET & MAXWELL
1988

Published in 1988 by
Sweet & Maxwell Limited of
11 New Fetter Lane, London.
Laserset by P.B. Computer Typesetting, Pickering, N. Yorks.
Printed and bound by
Adlard and Son Limited,
Dorking, Surrey, and Letchworth, Hertfordshire

British Library Cataloguing in Publication Data

Allen, David K.
Misrepresentation.
1. Fraud—England
I. Title
344.2063'6   KD1963

ISBN 0–421–34730–9 Pbk

for
Joan, Caroline, Nicholas and Richard

PREFACE

In writing this book I have sought to provide a clear exposition and analysis of the civil law of misrepresentation, which I hope will be of interest and assistance to students, teachers and practitioners of the law. In confronting this task, it seemed to me that clarity would best be served by examining in separate chapters the various strands that go to make up the general law of misrepresentation, reserving a more thematic analysis for an introductory chapter and a concluding chapter. Thus, Chapter 1 contains a brief historical introduction to the development of the general law of misrepresentation, together with an indication of the complexities to which that development has led. Chapter 2 examines the nature of misrepresentations (*i.e.* untrue statements which lead the representee to contract with the representor), and Chapter 3 describes the remedies available for such misrepresentations. I have included coverage of the action for deceit in this chapter, although it is not necessarily the case (though it is very frequent) that deceits induce representees to contract with representors, since Chapter 3 provided the most appropriate context for this coverage, and the same reason led me to describe the rules governing exclusion of liability for misrepresentation in this chapter. Chapter 4 in devoted to the purely tortious claim in negligent misstatement under *Hedley Byrne* v. *Heller*, and Chapter 5 examines the general law of misrepresentation in its contractual context, dealing with collateral warranties and collateral contracts. Chapter 6 is concerned with the role played by estoppel in this area of the law, and Chapter 7 examines the interrelationship of the various strands of the general law of misrepresentation examined in the previous chapters. I have used the term "the general law of misrepresentation" to denote the entire subject matter of the book, reserving the term "misrepresentation" for those untrue statements that induce the representee to contract with the representor, examined in Chapters 2 and 3.

I adopted a working definition of the topic as comprising an untrue statement made by one person to another which leads that other to act in reliance upon it to his detriment. Such a definition appears appropriate to cover warranties, misrepresentations, deceits and misstatements. In the case of estoppel by representation, its essence lies in an assertion that the representee be precluded from denying the truth of his statement, rather than in a claim for damages or equitable relief as is the case in actions for breach of warranty, misrepresentation, deceit and misstatement. However, the estoppel would not have been claimed but for the fact that the statement was untrue, and hence it also falls within the definition. Although the same is not true of promissory estoppel and proprietary estoppel, I have included brief coverage of those important topics for reasons which I hope will become apparent on reading Chapter 6.

My thanks are due to a number of people for assistance and advice in the writing of this book. Jon Holyoak was kind enough to read and comment valuably on drafts of Chapters 1 and 4. Edward Griew provided some illuminating insights into the topic as a whole. Thanks are also due to friends at the Universities of Sydney and Auckland (especially Francis Dawson) for listening to my views on some of the issues discussed in this book, and making me aware of many other dimensions of the subject. As a mere common lawyer adrift upon the limitless seas of equity (with apologies to Sir Robert Megarry) I have benefited considerably from a number of stimulating and informative discussions with Mark Thompson, whose generosity with his time has been vastly disproportionate to my ability to comprehend the mysteries of his trade. None of the above should be held responsible in any way for any misrepresentations, misstatements or warranties contained in the book, nor should they be estopped from denying any connection with it or its author.

I am also extremely indebted to Barbara Goodman who has succeeded superbly in the herculean task of reading my handwriting, and has produced the subsequent typescript with consummate skill and speed. Further, I am grateful to the editorial staff of Sweet & Maxwell for their continuing interest and encouragement, and also for preparing the tables of cases and statutes.

Finally, I should like to thank my wife and children, who have tolerated my frequent absences with their usual charm and patience.

David Allen
August 1987

CONTENTS

OTHER BOOKS IN THE SERIES

TABLE OF CASES

TABLE OF STATUTES

Chapter 1

INTRODUCTION

In this chapter we first examine the historical development of the various categories of liability for misrepresentation and then indicate some of the complexities in the law to which this ad hoc development has led.

1. HISTORICAL INTRODUCTION

The origins of liability for misrepresentation lie in the action of deceit on a warranty, which developed in the royal courts during the fourteenth century.[1] A seller of goods who made a false statement concerning the quantity or the quality of the goods would be held to have given a false warranty, which amounted to a deceit. This assimilation of the concepts of warranty and deceit reads oddly to a twentieth century lawyer, accustomed to a rigid classification of warranties as contractual and deceits as tortious. It is also contrary to our modern understanding of the action for deceit that such a claim would encompass both the seller of goods who was aware of the untruth of his statement and the seller who had given an express warranty, that is, had undertaken responsibility for the truth of his words,[2] albeit innocent of fraud. In fact, the courts gradually moved from insisting on an express warranty to imposing liability on the basis of a bare affirmation by the seller, that, for example, certain goods were his own.[3] The action was available if the plaintiff had been deceived by relying on the warranty, but not so if the untruth of the statement was obvious to him. The essence of the action was the deception of the plaintiff.

A claim in *assumpsit* could be made for breach of a promise to do something in the future, but the claim had to be in deceit if a false assertion (or warranty) of a present fact were made. However, by the latter half of the eighteenth century[4] actions in *assumpsit*, alleging that the warranty given by the defendant was

---

[1] Baker, *An Introduction to English Legal History* (2nd ed., 1979) p. 294.
[2] See *Chandelor* v. *Lopus* (1603) Cro.Jac. 4, 8 H.L.R. 282; *Furnis* v. *Leicester* (1618) Cro.Jac. 474; Stoljar, *Mistake and Misrepresentation* (1968), pp. 132–134; Greig (1971) 87 L.Q.R. 179 at 179–180.
[3] See *Crosse* v. *Gardner* (1689) Carth. 90, 1 Show.K.B. 68, 3 Mod. 361; *Medina* v. *Stoughton* (1700) 1 Salk. 210.
[4] See *Stuart* v. *Wilkins* (1778) 1 Doug. 18, where Ashurst and Buller L.JJ. referred to the long established practice of suing in *assumpsit* for breach of warranty.

false, were succeeding. The reason for framing the action in *assumpsit* was, according to Baker,[5] "to enable the joinder of actions. Thus, an action on the warranty if framed in *assumpsit* could be joined with an action to recover back the price for a total failure of consideration." However, the two claims were for a long time pleaded in the alternative.[6]

This assimilation of actions on a warranty into the law of contract had a number of consequences. For a start, the tort of deceit moved away from contract and became identified more with dishonest knowledge. The decision in *Pasley* v. *Freeman*,[7] whereby the deceit action was extended from contractual to non-contractual situations, was important in this respect. In holding the defendant liable for a knowingly false statement which did not benefit him,[8] the Court appeared to emphasise the *scienter* element of fraud and thereby the identification of deceit with dishonest knowledge.[9]

A further consequence was that, whereas the warranty rendering a defendant liable in an action on the case for deceit did not have to be part of the contract, the transfer of the remedy in cases of misrepresentation into contract required the courts to find a supporting consideration. This appears to be one reason why the courts began to speak of the need for the parties to have indicated their intention that the statements made by the defendant should form part of the contract. At the same time a further problem was posed by the parol evidence rule: could parol evidence be adduced to establish the existence of the prior warranty where the contract was in writing?[10] This also appears to have been a factor in the development of a requirement of an intention to warrant, which had not been a feature of the earlier case law, in that, as Greig notes[11]:

> "there was a confusing tendency to refer to the terms of the written contract in deciding whether a warranty had *previously* been given. This approach was only possible by distorting the concept of a warranty as an assertion of fact, and by relying upon the quite arbitrary test of intention."

This requirement of intention can be traced back to the judgment

---

[5] *Supra*, n. 1, p. 294. See also, *Williamson* v. *Allison* (1802) 2 East 446, 451.
[6] See *Jones* v. *Bright* (1829) 5 Bing. 533.
[7] (1789) 3 T.R. 51.
[8] *i.e.* that the plaintiff's buyer was a man to be trusted.
[9] See Stoljar *supra*, n. 2, pp. 133–4.
[10] See Greig *supra*, n. 2, at p. 181.
[11] *Ibid.*

of Buller J. in *Pasley* v. *Freeman*.[12] The possible reasons for the development, as noted above, are various,[13] the most likely reason in the particular case appears to be, as Greig suggests,[14] that Buller J. was speaking (albeit rather loosely) of an intention to make an affirmation, rather than an intention to warrant. In any event, the modern law is clear, as can be seen from the decision of the House of Lords in *Heilbut, Symons & Co.* v. *Buckleton*,[15] that "an affirmation at the time of the sale is a warranty, provided it appears on evidence to be so intended."[16]

As we have noted, the action for deceit focused increasingly upon fraud, while *assumpsit* took over the term "warranty" henceforth, therefore, covering both representations of fact[17] and promises. A consequence of this was that a certain category of case fell between the two, *i.e.* the case where a misrepresentation was neither made fraudulently nor did it become a term of the contract. To a certain extent this gap was filled by the fact that, as Atiyah notes[18]: " 'intent' to warrant is readily found by the courts when a seller makes statements of matters peculiarly in his knowledge." And this, as we shall see, was the technique frequently adopted until the 1960s in cases where the plaintiff sought damages at common law.

However, equity also had a role to play. First, it is clear that equity long had a jurisdiction, concurrent with that of the common law, in cases where a party had made a contract as a result of a fraudulent misrepresentation.[19] Indeed, this jurisdiction extended to the case, not actionable at common law prior to *Pasley* v. *Freeman*, where the perpetrator of the misrepresentation was not a party to the contract induced by his fraud.[20] The concurrent jurisdiction continued after the decision in *Pasley* v. *Freeman*.[21] It should be noted that this equitable jurisdiction was not restricted to what we would today regard as the available equitable remedies for misrepresentation: *i.e.* rescission and defence to an action for specific performance, but required the representor to make the

[12] (1789) 3 T.R. 51.
[13] See also, Atiyah, *Essays On Contract* (1986), pp. 277–278 and Greig *supra*, n. 2, at pp. 181–182.
[14] (1971) 87 L.Q.R. 182.
[15] [1913] A.C. 30.
[16] *Ibid.* at 44, *per* Lord Moulton.
[17] See, *e.g.* *Power* v. *Barham* (1836) 4 Ad. & E. 473.
[18] *Supra*, n. 13, at 278.
[19] See *Colt* v. *Woollaston* (1723) 2 P.Wms. 154 and Sheridan, *Fraud in Equity* (1957), p. 28.
[20] See *Hunt* v. *Carew* (1649) Nels.46; *Arnot* v. *Biscoe* (1743) 1 Ves.Sen. 95.
[21] See, *e.g.* *Sowerby* v. *Warder* (1791) 2 Cox 268; *Green* v. *Barrett* (1826) 1 Sim. 45.

representation good.[22] Early cases on making representations good illustrate that equity's jurisdiction also extended beyond knowledge of the falsity of a statement and recklessness as to its veracity to cases where a person made a deliberate statement to another with the intention that it be relied upon, irrespective of fraud. Equity would compel such a person, so far as it was in his power to do so, to make good the representation.[23] Thus, in *Burrowes* v. *Lock*[24] the defendant, a trustee, told the plaintiff that a share in the trust fund was unencumbered. As a consequence of this the plaintiff purchased the share. Having discovered that there were incumbrances, the plaintiff claimed against the defendant, whose argument that he had forgotten the existence of the incumbrances was of no avail, and he was required to make his representation good. In *Slim* v. *Croucher*[25] a person seeking to borrow money from the plaintiff offered as security a lease which he stated that he was entitled to have granted to him. The plaintiff asked the lessor, the defendant, about this, and was assured that the defendant was agreeable to granting a peppercorn lease of the property. In fact he had already granted the lease, and the borrower had mortgaged it, but he had forgotten this. The loan was duly made on the faith of the assurance. In the subsequent proceedings between the parties the lessor was held liable to make his representation good by repaying the money advanced, with interest. In *Pulsford* v *Richards*,[26] in which *Burrowes* v. *Lock* was approved, Sir John Romilly M.R. spoke of:

> "... that principle of equity which declares that the wilful representation of one contracting party, which draws another into a contract, shall, at the option of the person deceived, enable him to avoid, or enforce that contract ... applies not merely to cases where the statements were known to be false by those who made them, but to cases where statements, false in fact, were made by persons who believed them to be true, if in the due discharge of their duty, they ought to have known,

---

[22] See Dawson (1982) 1 Canta.L.R. 329, especially at 331–335.

[23] Alternatively, other remedies might be ordered, *e.g.* rescission (see *Pulsford* v. *Richards* (1853) 17 Beav. 87); injunction (see *Piggott* v. *Stratton* (1859) De G.F. & J. 33) or even that a representator's security be postponed to the representee (*Ibbotson* v. *Rhodes* (1706) 2 Vern. 554). See Dawson *supra*, n. 22 at pp. 361–366.

[24] (1805) 10 Ves. 470. See also, *Slim* v. *Croucher* (1860) 1 De G.F. & J. 518; *Higgins* v. *Samels* (1862) 2 J & H 460.

[25] (1860) 1 De G.F. & J. 518.

[26] *Supra*, n. 23, at 94.

or if they had formerly known and ought to have remembered the fact which negatives the representation made."

At the same time the remedy which today we associate perhaps most closely with misrepresentation, that of rescission, was available. Subject only to the overriding discretion of the court, rescission of the ensuing contract would be granted where there had been a material misrepresentation of fact which had induced the contract.[27] The question of which remedy was appropriate in any given case was canvassed by Sir John Romilly, M.R. in *Pulsford* v. *Richards*.[28] He said:

"The distinction between the cases where the person deceived is at liberty to avoid the contract, or where the Court will affirm it, giving him compensation only, are [sic] not very clearly defined. This question usually arises on the specific performance of contracts for the sale of property; and the principle which I apprehend governs the cases, although it is in some instances, of very difficult application, and leads to refined distinctions, is the following, viz., that if the representation made be one which can be made good, the party to the contract shall be compelled or may be at liberty to do so; but if the representation made be one which cannot be made good, the person deceived shall be at liberty, if he please, to avoid the contract."

By way of example, the Master of the Rolls contrasted the case of a person selling land which he represented as being within one mile of a particular town, whereas in fact it was several miles distant, with the case of sale of a property subject to a small rent which was not stated. In the former case the misrepresentation could not be made true, so the court, at the option of the deceived party, would annul the contract. In the latter case the court would not annul the contract, but would compel the seller to allow a sufficient deduction from the purchase money and thereby make his representation good.

As we have noted above,[29] the common law action for deceit after the decision in *Pasley* v. *Freeman* required proof of actual

---

[27] See *Reese Silver Mining Co.* v. *Smith* (1869) L.R. 4, H.L. at 79–80, *per* Lord Cairns L.C.; *Lamare* v. *Dixon* (1873) L.R. 6 (H.L.) 414 at 428, *per* Lord Cairns L.C. At common law, however, rescission was only possible where the misrepresentation was fraudulent or where there was a total failure of consideration: *Kennedy* v. *Panama etc. Royal Mail Co. Ltd* (1867) L.R. 2 Q.B. 580.

[28] *Supra*, n. 23, at 95.

[29] *Supra*, p. 2.

dishonesty. There was no room at common law for a claim for negligent misrepresentation, whereas

> "it was generally supposed to be settled in Equity that liability was incurred by a person who carelessly, although honestly, made a false representation to another about to deal in a matter of business upon the faith of such representation."[30]

In *Low* v. *Bouverie*,[31] however, it was held that this state of affairs in equity was quite inconsistent with the decision of the House of Lords in *Derry* v. *Peek*,[32] which had upheld the common law view that actual dishonesty had to be proved in order to establish deceit and "that in cases such as those of which that case was an instance, there is no duty enforceable at law to be careful in the representation which is made."[33] Hence, *Slim* v. *Croucher* was overruled: *Derry* v. *Peek*, it was said, had settled law and equity. It should be noted, however, that *Burrowes* v. *Lock* survived to the extent that it could be supported on the ground of estoppel. The Court of Appeal emphasised that estoppel was a rule of evidence only, not a cause of action, and it operated in a case such as *Burrowes* to preclude the trustee from denying the truth of his statement that the trust fund was unencumbered. *Slim* v. *Croucher* could not, however, be supported on the ground of estoppel. As Kay L.J. stated in *Low* v. *Bouverie*, the representation made by the lessor in *Slim* resembled a contract or promise rather than the statement of existing fact which must be shown to have been made in order to raise an estoppel by representation.[34]

The remedy of rescission, and also defence to an action for specific performance, for innocent (*i.e.* non-fraudulent) misrepresentation survived, however.[35] Thus, in *Redgrave* v. *Hurd*,[36] Sir George Jessel M.R. stated:

> "According to the decisions of Courts of Equity it was not necessary, in order to set aside a contract obtained by material false representation, to prove that the party who

---

[30] *Per* Lindley L.J. in *Low* v. *Bouverie* [1891] 3 Ch. 82 at 100, citing *Burrowes* v. *Lock* and *Slim* v. *Croucher*.

[31] [1891] 3 Ch. 82.

[32] [1889] 14 App.Cas. 337.

[33]. [1891] 3 Ch. 82 at 105, *per* Bowen L.J.

[34] *Jorden* v. *Money* (1854) 5 H.L.C. 185.

[35] As the equitable rule was made to prevail by the Judicature Acts, rescission was henceforth available for all misrepresentations, whether fraudulent, negligent or innocent.

[36] (1881) 20 Ch.D. 1.

obtained it knew at the time when the representation was made that it was false."[37]

Thus, the Court of Appeal ordered rescission of an agreement for the sale of the plaintiff's house to the defendant, as this was part of an arrangement whereby the defendant would come to join the plaintiff as his partner prior to the plaintiff's retirement, and the plaintiff had misrepresented the income and size of his practice, but fraud was not alleged. Of course, in cases of fraud it remained possible to obtain rescission.

By the end of the nineteenth century, therefore, misrepresentations might, depending upon the circumstances, give rise to a remedy in damages, in cases of warranty and deceit, to equitable remedies or to estoppel, which would give a representee relief from a claim which the representor might otherwise have had, or even, as in *Burrowes* v. *Lock*, by removing what would otherwise be a defence for a representor, allow the representee himself to claim. The main gap, which, as we shall see, took until the 1960s to fill, was the absence of a remedy in damages for a careless misrepresentation, explicable, at least in part, by a concern that to allow such a claim would be to breach the doctrine of consideration.[38]

In accordance perhaps with the laissez-faire notions of the age, the circumstances in which a representee could obtain damages for misrepresentation were strictly limited, in cases of warranty, by the requirement of an intention to warrant and in cases of deceit by the rather narrow definition of deceit adopted by the House of Lords in *Derry* v. *Peek*. Equitable relief was not so limited, but it was subject to the restrictions that it afforded only limited[39] compensation for positive losses and that it was not automatically available, being discretionary and therefore subject to the vagaries of conduct and circumstance.[40]

2. ENSUING COMPLEXITIES OF THE GENERAL LAW OF MISREPRESENTATION: AN OUTLINE

As we shall see in subsequent chapters, the modern era has ushered in an expansion in the range and ambit of remedies for misrepresentation. The ad hoc nature of the development of

---

[37] *Ibid.* at 12; see also, *Adam* v. *Newbigging* (1888) 13 App.Cas. 308.
[38] See the judgment of Lord Devlin in *Hedley Byrne & Co. Ltd* v. *Heller & Partners Ltd* [1964] A.C. 465 at 525–528.
[39] See Chap. 3 *infra* (indemnity), pp. 31–32.
[40] See Chap. 3 *infra* (limits on the right to rescind), pp. 32–39.

remedies for misrepresentation has, no doubt, increased rather than diminished the complexities of the general law of misrepresentation, but, it may be argued, this state of affairs is necessitated by the variety of ways in which statements may be made which induce persons to contract or otherwise act in a way which they anticipate will be to their advantage, but turn out not so to be.

So, with regard to the common situation of a statement made in the course of negotiations leading to a contract, it may, for example, take the form of a simple statement of fact about the subject matter of the contract ("it's a good little bus"), or it may be an assurance ("take my word for it, it's a good little bus"), or a guarantee related explicitly to the contract which the representor seeks to induce the representee to make ("if it'll help you make up your mind to buy it, I'll guarantee it's a good little bus"). At the other end of the scale there may simply be an expression of opinion about the merits or suitability of the subject matter of the contract ("I think it'll be good for a few thousand miles yet"). As we shall see, the differences between these statements may assume considerable significance if it transpires that it is not a "good little bus," or not good for the indicated mileage. And, of course, untrue statements along a similar range from guarantee to puff may be made, as a result of reliance upon which the representee may suffer a detriment other than the entering into a disadvantageous contract with the representor. Thus, I may persuade you to buy shares in the Megalitherium Company by assuring you of its profitability, or by emphasising my expertise as an investment adviser or, without any statement concerning my skills or the merits of the company, simply by advising you to buy shares in it.

In all these cases, the legal consequences attached to such statements may vary considerably, taking account not only of the different degrees of seriousness with which the statements, assessed objectively, are made, but frequently also of such factors as the state of mind and knowledge of the representor (whether fraudulent, negligent or innocent) and the conduct of the representee in the light of the surrounding circumstances. Small wonder then that the law of misrepresentation is usually regarded as being so complex.

The fact that the subtle but important distinctions between the various types of statement are reflected in the available remedies makes the characterisation of the particular statement in question crucial. If the representee is content simply to have rescission of the contract induced by the misrepresentation, he will not usually need to concern himself as to whether the statement was made fraudulently, negligently or innocently, and indeed it may be sufficient for him to sit back and resist specific performance rather than actively seek rescission. If he has suffered financially as a result of the misrepresentation then, depending upon the nature of his losses, he may seek to characterise the misrepresentation as a warranty so as to obtain compensation for expectation losses or he may simply wish to be compensated for his reliance losses, in which case a tortious claim will suffice. This is not to say that the law permits the representee to determine the juridical nature of the misrepresentation, but the difference between, for example, a representation and a warranty may, as we shall see, be so fine that there is considerable room for argument and persuasion.

The question of measure of damages is, as will be seen, of some significance in the general law of misrepresentation. In the preface we spoke of misrepresentation as being essentially reliance based. It might be assumed, therefore, that damages for misrepresentation will be awarded so as to compensate the representee to the extent of his detrimental reliance; to the extent of putting him in the position he would have been in if the misrepresentation had not been made rather than awarding him his expectation interest: *i.e.* putting him in the position he would have been in if the representation had been true. However, if it can be established that the representor's statement amounts to a warranty, or if the representation can be used as the basis of an estoppel, the effect of the available remedies may be to put the representee in as good a position as if the representation had been true. To the extent that it is possible to generalise, the law of contract is very frequently seen as protecting the expectation interest[41] and the law of tort as protecting the reliance interest. The general law of misrepresentation may, therefore, be regarded as occupying a kind of no man's land between the two, and this autonomous status is a major source of difficulty in expounding and comprehending this area of the law, especially bearing in mind the significant role that equity still plays in cases of misrepresentation.

The following five chapters seek to describe and analyse the various strands of the general law of misrepresentation, and the concluding chapter examines their interrelationship.

---

[41] See, *e.g. Robinson* v. *Harman* (1848) 1 Exch. 850 at 855; *Wertheim* v. *Chicoutimi Pulp Co.* [1911] A.C. 301 at 307. But note cases where the reliance interest is appropriate where the expectation loss cannot be proved; *e.g. McRae* v. *Commonwealth Disposals Commission* (1950) 84 C.L.R. 377; *Anglia Television Ltd* v. *Reed* [1972] 1 Q.B. 60.

Chapter 2

THE NATURE OF MISREPRESENTATION

1. Introduction

In this chapter we shall examine the essential characteristics of a misrepresentation, that is, an untrue statement which induces the representee to enter into a contract with the representor. Discussion of the remedies available to the representee, equitable, common law and statutory, is reserved for Chapter 3, as is an analysis of the extent to which liability for misrepresentation can be excluded.

As we saw in Chapter 1, the rules concerning rescission of a contract, the basic remedy for misrepresentation, differed at common law and in equity, prior to the Judicature Acts (1873–75).[1] The rule in equity was that it was not necessary, in order to set aside a contract induced by a misrepresentation, to prove that the representor knew that his representation was false.[2] The common law rule was ultimately[3] narrower, in that, for rescission to be available the statement had to be fraudulent or reckless and without care as to whether it was true or false.

In the event, the rules of equity were made to prevail by the Judicature Act. Consequently, a contract may be rescinded for misrepresentation whether the representor is aware of the untruth of his representation or not. Before we examine what we mean by a representation and the circumstances in which liability may be imposed, and, thereafter in Chapter 3, the available remedies to the representee, it is important to note that three states of mind in the representor may be identified, and the remedies other than rescission will depend upon which state of mind he is held to have been in at the time of the misrepresentation. The three categories of misrepresentation are fraudulent, negligent and innocent. Prior to the 1960s negligent misrepresentations were subsumed within the category of innocent misrepresentation and when the courts speak of innocent misrepresentation in the earlier cases they may well be dealing with a case where the misrepresentation was made

---

[1] See p. 6 and the remarks of Sir George Jessel M.R. in *Redgrave* v. *Hurd* (1881) 20 Ch.D. 1 at 12–13.
[2] See *Reese River Silver Mining Co. Ltd* v. *Smith* (1869) L.R. 4 H.L. 64 at 79–80, *per* Lord Cairns.
[3] Earlier cases did not always require knowledge of the representation's falseness.

carelessly. The characteristics of a misrepresentation that we shall now examine are characteristics which in general[4] any statement must have in order to be treated in law as a misrepresentation, though, as noted above, the extent to which remedies other than rescission will be available to the representee will depend upon the state of mind of the representor and indeed, as we shall see, rescission itself, as an equitable remedy, will not always be available.

2. ESSENTIAL ELEMENTS OF MISREPRESENTATION

(a) Statement of fact

The statements made by parties in the course of pre-contractual negotiations are broadly categorised into three groups by the law. One group consists of those statements which are held to have been intended by the parties to have contractual effect, and are categorised as warranties collateral to the ensuing contract or as separate collateral contracts. These are distinguished from 'mere' representations, the second group, essentially by the lack of contractual intention in the latter category, and this distinction is examined in detail in Chapter 5. We are here concerned rather with the distinction between the second group and the third, which consists of statements which do not even amount to representations and are, therefore, without effect in law. At the outset it should be noted that a primary requirement of an actionable misrepresentation is that it must be a statement of existing fact. One aspect of this requirement is that such a statement is to be distinguished from a promise to do something in the future, which must be shown to be part of a contract in order to be actionable.[5] It is, however, perfectly possible for liability to attach to a statement of intention if the implication that the intention exists is in fact untrue. Hence the famous remark of Bowen L.J. in *Edgington* v. *Fitzmaurice*[6]:

> "The state of a man's mind is as much a fact as the state of his digestion. It is true that it is very difficult to prove what the state of a man's mind at a particular time is, but if it can be ascertained it is as much a fact as anything else. A misrepre-

---

[4] Slight differences exist between the rules concerning fraudulent misrepresentations and those governing other misrepresentations, and these differences are explained in the course of this chapter. See also, Chap. 3 pp. 30 n. 8, 33, 35.

[5] See *Beattie* v. *Lord Ebury* (1872) 7 Ch.App 777 at 804, *per* Mellish L.J.; *Maddison* v. *Alderson* (1883) 8 App.Cas 467.

[6] (1885) 29 Ch.D. 459 at 483.

sentation as to the state of a man's mind is, therefore, a misstatement of fact."

Thus, in *Edgington* a statement by the directors of a company in a prospectus that money which they invited the public to lend them would be used to improve the buildings and extend the business, was held to amount to an actionable (fraudulent) misrepresentation, since in fact they intended to use the money to discharge certain outstanding liabilities.

Statements of opinion. Similarly, a statement of opinion is prima facie not actionable as a misrepresentation, unless it can be shown that the person making the statement did not in fact hold the opinion expressed, or that a reasonable man equipped with his knowledge could not honestly have held the opinion. Two cases may be contrasted. In *Bisset* v. *Wilkinson*[7] the respondents wished to purchase land for sheep-farming, and negotiated with the appellant for the sale of his land, which had never been used for sheep-farming. The appellant estimated that the land would carry two thousand sheep, the respondents bought the land but were unable to make a success of sheep-farming there, and fell into arrears on the payment of interest on the unpaid purchase money. The appellant claimed these arrears from them, and the respondents counterclaimed, alleging, *inter alia*, misrepresentation. It was held that the appellant's statement was an honest statement of his opinion of the farm's capacity and not a representation of its actual capacity.

By contrast, in *Smith* v. *Land and House Property Corporation*[8] the plaintiffs put up a hotel for sale, including in the particulars that the hotel was let to "Mr. Frederick Fleck (a most desirable tenant) at a rental of £400 per annum . . . for an unexpired term of 27 years, thus offering a first class investment." This statement was made in August 1882. In fact, on May 1st the Lady Day quarter's rent was entirely unpaid and had only thereafter been paid in instalments under duress, and none of the Midsummer quarter's rent had been paid. The defendants agreed to purchase the hotel, but Fleck went into liquidation before completion, and the defendants refused to complete. The plaintiffs sued for specific performance and the defendants counterclaimed for rescission. The court agreed with the defendants. The description of Fleck was not merely a statement of opinion, but amounted to an assertion that nothing had occurred in the relations between the

[7] [1927] A.C. 177.
[8] (1885) 28 Ch.D. 7. See also, *Brown* v. *Raphael* [1958] Ch. 636.

plaintiffs and Fleck which could be considered to make him an unsatisfactory tenant. Bowen L.J. said:

"... if the facts are not equally known to both sides, then a statement of opinion by the one who knows the facts best makes very often a statement of material fact, for he impliedly states that he knows facts which justify his opinion."[9]

Thus, an honest statement of opinion will fall into the third category mentioned above, *i.e.* those statements which, if untrue are nevertheless not actionable, unless such a statement is held to carry the implication that the maker of the statement knew facts which justified the opinion.

"Mere puffs." A misrepresentation must also be distinguished from what is known as a "mere puff," *i.e.* a vague, imprecise, eulogistic statement such as a salesman may employ in describing his wares. Such a statement will not be actionable. For example, in *Scott* v. *Hanson*[10] land was described in the particulars of sale as a lot consisting of 14 acres of uncommonly rich water meadow. The defendant, who agreed to purchase the land, refused to complete, on the ground that the land was in fact very imperfectly watered. Lord Lyndhurst L.C. held that the land was accurately described as water meadow and the description was not such as to amount to a misrepresentation. In the apt phrase of the Solicitor-General, appearing for the plaintiff, the descriptive words were "vague flourishes of the auctioneer." The more specific a statement is concerning the qualities of the subject matter of the contract, the more likely it is to be regarded as a misrepresentation.[11] If, for example, it had been claimed in *Scott* v. *Hanson* that specific benefits would enure to the purchaser as a consequence of purchasing such rich water meadow, the court would probably have held such a claim, if untrue, to amount to a misrepresentation.

(b) Misrepresentation of law not actionable

Beyond the straightforward proposition that a misrepresentation of law is not actionable lies a number of complexities. A few

---

[9] (1885) 28 Ch.D. 7 at 15. See also, *Esso Petroleum Co. Ltd* v. *Mardon* [1976] Q.B. 801 at 817–8, *per* Lord Denning M.R.

[10] (1829) 1 Russ. & M. 128. See also, *Dimmock* v. *Hallett* (1866) 2 Ch.App. 21 at 27.

[11] See, in a slightly different context, *Carlill* v. *Carbolic Smoke Ball Co. Ltd* [1893] 1 Q.B. 256; *cf. Lambert* v. *Lewis* [1982] A.C. 225 at 262.

examples may serve to illustrate these complexities.[12] For a start, as we have noted above, a statement of opinion may be a misrepresentation if the maker of the statement does not in fact hold that opinion, and since a statement of law is a statement of opinion it too may amount to a misrepresentation if a proposition of law is wilfully misstated.[13] In general though, the fact that a misrepresentation of law is not actionable leads to the need to distinguish between such a representation and a representation of fact. In many cases, of course, no problem will arise. A statement that a car is a good little motor is clearly a representation of fact; a statement that a misrepresentation renders a contract voidable, not void, is clearly a statement of law.

It is with statements of mixed law and fact that the greatest difficulty has been experienced. A number of different situations may be identified. Thus a statement as to private rights is treated as a representation of fact, as in *Cooper* v. *Phibbs*[14] where the plaintiff's agreement to rent a salmon fishery in Ireland in ignorance of the fact that it already belonged to him (as tenant under a settlement) was set aside. A statement as to the effect of a document is treated as a representation of fact.[15] As regards the position where a statement is made that a rule of law applies to a particular situation, two cases may be contrasted. In *Solle* v. *Butcher*[16] the parties agreed a rental on the erroneous basis that the property in question, a flat which had been reconstructed, had been so changed that it was no longer controlled by the Rent Restriction Acts. This was held to be a misrepresentation of fact. However, in *Territorial & Auxiliary Forces Association* v. *Nichols*[17] a statement was made that a house, known to be in the occupation of the Crown, was governed by the Rent Restriction Acts. This was held to be a misrepresentation of law, as the Rent Restriction Acts did not bind the Crown, and therefore was not actionable. In the former case the proposition of law was perfectly accurate: the misrepresentation lay in the statement about the changed nature of the flat. In the latter case it was the proposition of law that was inaccurate.

---

[12] See Treitel *The Law of Contract* (7th ed.) pp. 257–9.
[13] *Supra*, p. 13.
[14] (1867) L.R. 2 (H.L.) 149. See also, *Mackenzie* v. *Royal Bank of Canada* [1934] A.C. 468; *Lyle-Mellor* v. *Lewis* [1956] 1 W.L.R. 29.
[15] *Hirshfeld* v. *L.B. & S.C. Ry* (1876) 2 Q.B.D. 1; *Wauton* v. *Coppard* [1899] 1 Ch. 92.
[16] [1950] 1 K.B. 671.
[17] [1949] 1 K.B. 35.

(c) Must induce representee to contract with representor

In the course of his important judgment in *Pulsford* v. *Richards*[18] Sir John Romilly said:

> "With respect to the character or nature of the misrepresenta-
> tion itself, it is clear that it may be positive or negative; that it
> may consist as much in the suppression of what is true as in the
> assertion of what is false; and it is almost needless to add that it
> must appear that the person deceived entered into the contract
> on the faith of it. To use the expression of the Roman law ... it
> must be a representation *dans locum contractui* that is, a repre-
> sentation giving occasion to the contract: the proper interpre-
> tation of which appears to me to be the assertion of a fact on
> which the person entering into the contract relied, and in the
> absence of which, it is reasonable to infer, that he would not
> have entered into it; or the suppression of a fact, the knowledge
> of which it is reasonable to infer, would have made him abstain
> from the contract altogether."

Though, as we shall see, this statement rather overstates the position as regards the extent to which silence can constitute misrepresentation, otherwise it still holds good today. Perhaps the most
important aspect of an actionable misrepresentation is that it must
induce the representee to contract with the representor. Thus, if the
representee is never aware of the existence of the misrepresentation, it will have no legal effect. An example of this principle can be
seen in *Re Northumberland and Durham District Banking Co. ex p.
Bigge*,[19] in which the plaintiff, who claimed that he had been persuaded to acquire shares by a misrepresentation as to the condition
of the company, failed in his action for rescission since he was able
to show neither that he had read one syllable of the false reports
which contained the alleged misrepresentation, nor that anybody
had told him what the reports contained.

Again, if the plaintiff is aware of the misrepresentation, but does
not allow it to affect his judgment, he will not obtain relief. Thus, in
Smith v. *Chadwick*[20] the plaintiff bought shares in a company on the

---

[18] (1853) 17 Beav. 87 at 96.
[19] (1859) 28 L.J.Ch. 50. See also, *Horsfall* v. *Thomas* (1862)1 H. & C. 90. Also, if the
    representee is aware of the untruth of the representation, or if he relies upon his
    own information he will have no remedy: *Jennings* v. *Broughton*(1854) 5 De G.M.
    & G. 126. See also *Strover* v. *Harrington*, *The Times*, December 8, 1987, where it
    was held that knowledge of the plaintiffs' solicitors, which had not been communi-
    cated to the plaintiffs personally, was sufficient to prevent them from suing on a
    misrepresentation contained in the particulars of sale of vendors from whom they
    bought a property.
[20] (1884) 9 App.Cas. 187. See also, *Attwood* v. *Small* (1838) 6 Cl. & Fin. 232.

faith of a prospectus which included the false statement that a certain Grieve was a director of the company. In fact, the plaintiff had never heard of Grieve, and his claim for damages was dismissed. If the plaintiff tests the accuracy of the representation, he will be unable to claim relief for innocent misrepresentation,[21] even if he does not in fact discover the truth.[22] But if he is given an opportunity to check the truth of the representation but chooses not to do so, he will not be denied relief. Thus, in *Redgrave* v. *Hurd*[23] the plaintiff, an elderly solicitor, offered to sell his practice and house. The defendant was interested, and the plaintiff represented that his business brought in £300–£400 per year. The defendant was given an opportunity to examine the practice accounts, but did not do so. The defendant subsequently agreed to purchase the house and took possession, but, on discovering that the business was worth materially less than the amount claimed, refused to complete. The plaintiff sought specific performance and the defendant counterclaimed for, *inter alia*, rescission. It was held that the defendant was entitled to succeed. In the words of Sir George Jessel M.R.:

> "If it is a material representation calculated to induce him to enter into the contract, it is an inference of law that he was induced by the representation to enter into it, and in order to take away his title to be relieved from the contract on the ground that the representation was untrue, it must be shown either that he had knowledge of the facts contrary to the representation, or that he stated in terms, or shewed clearly by his conduct, that he did not rely on the representation."[24]

It is of interest to note that in the above case the Court of Appeal saw no reason to deny relief to a representee, even where he had been negligent himself (and may therefore have been no less culpable than the representor).[25] In such a case today, if damages were sought it would be possible for the award to be reduced on account of the contributory negligence of the

[21] But if the misrepresentation is fraudulent this rule does not apply. See *S. Pearson & Son Ltd.* v. *Dublin Corporation* [1907] A.C.351, especially at 353–4 ('Now it seems clear that no one can escape liability for his own fraudulent statements by inserting in a contract a clause that the other party shall not rely upon them," *per* Lord Loreburn L.C.).

[22] See *Clarke* v. *Mackintosh* (1862) 4 Giff. 134; *Attwood* v. *Small* (*supra*, n. 20).

[23] (1881) 20 Ch.D.1. See also, *Laurence* v. *Lexcourt Holdings Ltd.* [1978] 1 W.L.R. 1128, especially at 1137.

[24] (1881) 20 Ch.D. 1 at 21. But, see the words of Bowen L.J. in *Smith* v. *Land and House Property Corporation* (1884) 28 Ch.D. 7 at 16.

[25] *Ibid.* at 13–14.

representee,[26] though the Law Reform (Contributory Negligence) Act does not affect rescission, (the remedy sought in *Redgrave*).[27]

(d) Need not be sole inducement

The representation need not be the sole inducement to contract in order to be actionable. Thus, in *Edgington* v. *Fitzmaurice*[28] the directors of a company issued a prospectus inviting subscriptions for debentures. They stated that the object of the debenture issue was to carry out alterations in the company's buildings and to develop trade. In fact, the object of the loan was to enable the directors to pay off pressing liabilities. The plaintiff was induced to take debenture bonds to the amount of £1500, partly because of the misrepresentation and partly because he mistakenly believed that he would have a charge on the company's property. The company became insolvent, and the plaintiff sought repayment of his £1500 in an action in deceit. The Court of Appeal held that it was not necessary to show that the misrepresentation was the sole inducement; it was enough that the misrepresentation was *an* inducement. Accordingly he was held entitled to succeed.

Sometimes a representation may be made by one person to another and relied on subsequently by a third party, who contracts with the representor. If the representor intended his representation to have this effect, he may be liable to the third party if the statement was untrue. Thus, in *Pilmore* v. *Hood*[29] the defendant, wishing to sell his public house, represented to X, who had agreed to purchase it, that the receipts were £180 per month. X, to the defendant's knowledge, communicated this information to the plaintiff, who thereafter became the purchaser as X was unable to complete. In fact, the representation was false, and the plaintiff was held entitled to succeed in an action for deceit against the defendant. However, in *Peek* v. *Gurney*,[30] where untrue statements were contained in the prospectus of an intended company,

---

[26] See Law Reform (Contributory Negligence) Act 1945; Treitel, *The Law of Contract* (7th ed.) p. 262, n. 74.

[27] Possibly a representor in such a case, where the representee seeks rescission, could attempt to persuade the court to exercise its discretion to award damages in lieu of rescission, under s.2(2) of the Misrepresentation Act 1967 (see *infra* p. 52). Assuming that the representee's damage is the fault of both parties, the prima facie award of damages could thus be reduced, so as to reflect the relative culpability of the parties.

[28] (1885) 29 Ch.D. 459.

[29] (1883) 5 Bing N.C.97. See also, *Langridge* v. *Levy* (1837) 2 M. & W. 519.

[30] (1873) L.R. 6 H.L. 377. See also, *Cross* v. *Lewis Hillman Ltd.* [1970] Ch. 445 at 461.

the House of Lords held that liability of the directors for such misrepresentations did not follow the shares beyond their transfer from allottee to his purchaser, unless the purchaser could show some direct connection between them and himself in the communication of the prospectus. In such a case now it may be possible to claim in negligent misstatement, and argue that it was reasonably foreseeable that the representation would be passed on.[31]

(e) Must be material

A further element of an actionable misrepresentation is that it must be material. This means that it must be of a kind that would affect the judgment of a reasonable man in deciding whether to contract with the representor or, if so, on what terms. For example, in an insurance contract, it is material that a previous proposal for insuring the subject-matter has been declined, and failure to disclose this will entitle the insurer to rescind.[32] Again, in an insurance contract it is material that the subject-matter has been considerably over-valued.[33] In truth the illustrations of the requirement of materiality are largely to be found in the context of insurance. As Chitty notes,[34] a requirement of materiality is a necessary part of a rule requiring disclosure, but it is not a necessary part of a rule affording relief for active misrepresentation. However, earlier cases of high authority certainly regarded it as a necessary element,[35] and, as has been remarked, a representation that was not material would by definition be of such a trivial nature that its untruth would cause but little loss to the representee.[36] It should be noted that the perpetrator of a fraudulent misrepresentation will not be allowed to argue that his representation was immaterial,[37] though whether the same would be true for the perpetrator of a negligent misrepresentation remains an open question. It should further be noted that, if the contract so provides, any representation, however trivial, will be

---

[31] See *Yianni* v. *Edwin Evans and Sons* [1981] Q.B. 438; *Shankie-Williams and others* v. *Heavey* (1986) 279 E.G. 316, *infra* Chap. 4, p. 80.
[32] *Locker and Woolf Ltd.* v. *Western Australian Insurance Co. Ltd* [1936] 1 K.B. 408.
[33] *Ionides* v. *Pender* (1874) L.R. 9 Q.B. 531
[34] *Chitty on Contracts* (25th ed., 1983), Vol. 1, p. 2224, n. 2.
[35] See *Smith* v. *Chadwick* (1882) 20 Ch.D. 27 at 44 (C.A.) and (1884) 9 App.Cas. 187 at 196 (H.L.).
[36] See Treitel, *op. cit.* n. 26 p. 260.
[37] *Smith* v. *Kay* (1859) 7 H.L.C. 750 at 759.

material, and again the insurance context provides the most frequent examples of this.[38]

A distinction must be drawn between the requirement of materiality and the need to establish that the representee relied upon the representation. The requirement of materiality imports an essentially objective standard, whereas the question whether or not the representee was induced to rely upon the misrepresentation depends upon its effect on the particular individual. The need to distinguish is emphasised in the judgment of Bowen L.J. in *Smith* v. *Land and House Property Corporation*[39] where he said:

> "I cannot quite agree with the remark of the late Master of the Rolls in *Redgrave* v. *Hurd*, that if a material representation calculated to induce a person to enter into a contract is made to him it is an inference of law that he was induced by the representations to enter into it . . . "

In other words, the fact that a statement is one that would affect the judgment of a reasonable man does not mean that it necessarily persuaded the particular representee to contract, and conversely the fact that the representee was persuaded to contract does not mean that a reasonable man would have been.

(f) Must be unambiguous

A further requirement sometimes said to exist is that the misrepresentation, to be actionable, must be unambiguous. If the words used by the representor are genuinely capable of more than one meaning, the onus is on the representee to establish the sense in which he understood it and that in that sense it was false.[40] Even if the representee is able so to establish, the representor will not be guilty of fraud,[41] provided he honestly believed in what he represented, though the representee may have a defence to an action for specific performance.[42] However, if the court takes the view that the ambiguity is a deliberate device employed by the representor, he may be liable, and it will be no defence that the

---

[38] See, *e.g. Anderson* v. *Fitzgerald* (1853) 4 H.L.C. 484; *London Assurance* v. *Mansel* (1879) 11 Ch.D. 363.

[39] (1884) 28 Ch.D. 7 at 16.

[40] See *Schroeder* v. *Mendl* (1877) 37 L.T. 452; *Arkwright* v. *Newbold* (1881) 17 Ch.D. 301; *Smith* v. *Chadwick* (1884) 9 App.Cas. 187.

[41] *Akerhielm* v. *De Mare* [1959] A.C. 789.

[42] *New Brunswick & Canada Railway and Land Co.* v. *Muggeridge* (1860)1 Dr. & Sm. 363.

statement on its true construction carries a meaning that is in fact true.[43]

3. NON-DISCLOSURE

The general rule is that non-disclosure does not amount to a misrepresentation, for there is no general duty to disclose material facts.[44] Thus, a failure by the vendor to inform the would-be purchaser of his house of the existence of dry rot will not amount to misrepresentation, even if the vendor is aware of the purchaser's misapprehension,[45] unless, of course, the misapprehension has been caused by a positive misrepresentation made by the vendor. However, in a number of exceptional situations non-disclosure will amount to a misrepresentation.

(a) Partial non-disclosure

Liability for a partial non-disclosure may arise in a number of ways. For example, a statement may be made which is true at the time, but which later ceases to be true, before the contract is entered into, to the knowledge of the representor. In such a case his failure to inform the representee of the true state of affairs will amount to a misrepresentation. Thus, in *With* v. *O'Flanagan*[46] the would-be vendor of a medical practice represented to a potential purchaser during negotiations that the takings of the practice were at the rate of £2,000 per annum. By the time the contract was made several months later, however, receipts had fallen off considerably owing to the illness of the vendor and the employment of several *locum tenentes*. The vendor's failure to communicate this change of circumstances to the purchaser was held to entitle the latter to rescission.

A statement that is literally true but misleading, in the sense that it implies the existence of other facts which are untrue, may

---

[43] See *Piggott* v. *Stratton* (1859) 1 De G.F. & J. 33 at 50; *The Siboen and the Sibotre* [1976] 1 Lloyds Rep. 293 at 318.

[44] See, *e.g. Keates* v. *Cadogan* (1851) 10 C.B. 591; *Turner* v. *Green* [1895] 2 Ch. 205.

[45] Unless he has concealed the dry rot (see n. 51 *infra*). In appropriate circumstances the court might, however, find that there had been an operative mistake; see *Smith* v. *Hughes* (1871) L.R. 6 Q.B. 597. Also, failure to disclose the existence of a latent defect of whose existence the seller of goods is aware may render him liable to negligence to a buyer who is caused loss or injury by the defect: *Hurley* v. *Dyke* [1979] R.T.R. 265, 303.

[46] [1936] Ch. 575. See also, *Davies* v. *London and Provincial Marine Insurance Co.* (1878) 8 Ch.D. 469. As regards the question whether there is a duty to disclose a change in a stated intention, there are conflicting decisions; *cf. Traill* v. *Baring* (1864)4 D.J. & S. 318 and *Wales* v. *Wadham* [1977] 1 W.L.R. 199. See also, Financial Services Act 1986, ss.147, 164.

be actionable. Thus, in *Nottingham Patent Brick and Tile Co.* v. *Butler*,[47] when asked by the purchaser of land if there were restrictive covenants, the vendor's solicitor replied that he was not aware of any. This was held to imply that he had read the deeds, which was not in fact true, and his reply therefore amounted to a misrepresentation. Again, if the representor omits facts which falsify the statements (true in themselves) which he has made, he will be liable for misrepresentation.[48] Thus, in *Curtis* v. *Chemical Cleaning and Dyeing Co.*[49] an employee of the defendants informed the plaintiff, who had taken her dress to the shop to be cleaned, that a receipt which she was asked to sign excluded the defendants' liability for damage to the beads and sequins on the dress. In fact the receipt excluded liability for all damage. The employee's statement was held to amount to a misrepresentation.

The question whether the Misrepresentation Act 1967 applies to cases of partial non-disclosure is examined later in this chapter.

(b) Misrepresentation by conduct

Most of the cases of misrepresentation by conduct are cases of criminal liability, but it is thought that the principles are applicable, *mutatis mutandis*, to civil liability. Thus, in the old case of *R.* v. *Barnard*[50] the defendant wore a commoner's cap and gown in order to persuade an Oxford bootmaker to supply him with bootstraps. The fact of his appearing so dressed was held to amount to a sufficient false pretence. There seems no reason why an action in deceit should not be brought in such circumstances. In *Walters* v. *Morgan*[51] Lord Campbell L.C. emphasised that the absence of a fiduciary relationship between vendor and purchaser had the consequence that the purchaser was not bound to disclose the existence of material facts within his knowledge. He went on to say:

"Simple reticence does not amount to legal fraud...But a single word, or (I may add) a nod or a wink, or a shake of the head, or a smile from the purchaser intended to induce the vendor to believe the existence of a non-existing fact, which might influence the price of the subject to be sold, would be

---

[47] (1886) 16 Q.B.D. 778; see also, *Goldsmith* v. *Rodger* [1962] 2 Lloyds Rep. 249.
[48] See *Dimmock* v. *Hallett* (1866) 2 Ch.App. 21.
[49] [1951] 1 K.B. 805.
[50] (1837) 7 C. & P. 784.
[51] (1861) 3 D.F. & J. 718. See also, *Gordon and Texeira* v. *Selico Ltd and Select Management Ltd* (1986) 11 H.L.R. 219 (concealment of dry rot held to amount to deceit). See Gleeson and McKendrick [1987] Conv. 121. See also, Financial Services Act 1986, s.133.

sufficient ground for a Court of Equity to refuse a decree for a specific performance of the agreement."[52]

(c) Fiduciary relationship

Where the relationship between the parties is of a confidential or fiduciary nature, a duty of disclosure to likely to exist. The category of fiduciary relationships is not closed, but the essential principle can be gleaned from remarks of Lord Chelmsford L.C. in *Tate* v. *Williamson*,[53] in which the defendant, having become financial adviser to a profligate Oxford undergraduate, bought his estate at half its value. Lord Chelmsford said:

"Wherever two persons stand in such a relation that while it continues confidence is necessarily reposed by one, and the influence which naturally grows out of that confidence is possessed by the other, and this confidence is abused, or the influence is exerted to obtain an advantage at the expense of the confiding party, the person so availing himself of his position will not be permitted to retain the advantage, although the transaction could not have been impeached if no such confidential relation had existed."[54]

The transaction was accordingly set aside.

Examples of the kind of relationship regarded as fiduciary include trustee and beneficiary, solicitor and client, principal and agent and parent and child. In many of these cases the duty can be satisfied by making full disclosure, for example, in cases of principal and agent,[55] but in cases where the relationship is one to which the doctrine of undue influence[56] applies, such as trustee and beneficiary and solicitor and client, the duty may be more extensive, and will very frequently require that the weaker party had independent advice prior to entering into the transaction,[57] that the advice is competent and based on knowledge of all the

---

[52] (1861) 3 D.F. & J 718 at 723–724.
[53] (1866) L.R. 2 Ch.App. 55.
[54] *Ibid.* at 61.
[55] *Armstrong* v. *Jackson* [1917] 2 K.B. 822.
[56] See *Chitty on Contracts* (25th ed., 1983) paras. 502–515; Treitel *The Law of Contract* (7th ed. 1987) pp. 314–323; *Lloyds Bank Ltd* v. *Bundy* [1975] Q.B. 326; *National Westminster Bank plc* v. *Morgan* [1985] A.C. 686; Sealy [1962] C.L.J. 69; [1963] C.L.J. 119.
[57] *Allcard* v. *Skinner* (1887) 36 Ch.D. 145; *Lloyds Bank Ltd.* v. *Bundy* [1975] Q.B. 326 at 342.

salient facts, and, in some cases, that the independent adviser must approve the transaction and that his advice is followed.[58]

(d) Contracts uberrimae fidei

In certain contracts one of the parties is in an especially strong position to know the material facts and consequently he is placed under a duty to make a full disclosure of those facts. This duty of utmost good faith (*uberrima fides*) is seen in cases of insurance contracts and contracts involving family arrangements. Certain other cases, to be considered briefly, involve a limited duty of disclosure, and are, therefore, very much akin to contracts *uberrimae fidei*.

Insurance contracts. All contracts of insurance involve a requirement of utmost good faith.[59] A person will be in breach of this duty if he withholds material facts from the insurer,[60] and such a failure to disclose will entitle the insurer to rescind the contract of insurance. A fact is material if it "would influence the judgment of a prudent insurer in fixing the premium, or determing whether he will take the risk."[61] Thus, a policy of marine insurance can be avoided if the insured greatly overvalues the cargo,[62] or fails to declare that the ship carrying the cargo had already been stranded.[63] Again, a life insurance policy is voidable if the insured fails to disclose that several other insurance companies have declined proposals to assure his life,[64] and a house insurance policy may be avoided if the insured has a previous conviction for robbery.[65]

---

[58] *Powell* v. *Powell* [1900] 1 Ch. 243 at 247; see also, *Inche Noriah* v. *Shaik Allie Bin Omar* [1929] A.C. 127; *cf. Re Coomber* [1911] 1 Ch. 723. See Treitel *op. cit.* n. 56, p. 318.

[59] Though most of the cases concern the duty of the insured, it is clear that a duty of utmost good faith is equally incumbent upon the insurer: *Carter* v. *Boehm* (1766) 3 Burr. 1905; *Banque Keyser Ullmann S.A.* v. *Skandia (U.K.) Insurance Co. Ltd.* [1987] 2 All E.R. 923.

[60] See *London Assurance Co.* v. *Mansel* (1879) 11 Ch.D. 363 at 367–368; *Rozanes* v. *Bowen* (1928) 32 Lloyds L.R. 98 at 102.

[61] Marine Insurance Act 1906, s.18(2), held to be applicable to all classes of insurance in *Locker and Woolf Ltd* v. *Western Australian Insurance Co.* [1936] 1 K.B. 408 at 415. See also, *Lambert* v. *Co-operative Insurance Society Ltd.* [1975] 2 Lloyds Rep. 485.

[62] *Ionides* v. *Pender* (1874) L.R. 9 Q.B. 531. Similarly if the vessel itself is over-insured: see *Thames and Mersey Marine Insurance Co.* v. *Gunford Ship Co. Ltd.* [1911] A.C. 529.

[63] *Proudfoot* v. *Montefiore* (1867) L.R. 2 Q.B. 511.

[64] *London Assurance Co.* v. *Mansel* (1879) 11 Ch.D. 363.

[65] *Woolcott* v. *Sun Alliance and London Insurance Ltd* [1978] 1 W.L.R. 493.

It is not, in general, necessary to disclose facts which are known or ought to be known to the insurer, similarly, where the facts reduce the risk. Facts may be held to be irrelevant and therefore not material: in *Dawsons Ltd* v. *Bonnin*[66] the place at which a lorry which the appellants insured with the respondent was usually garaged was misstated on the proposal. The misstatement was held not to be material. However, the policy made the truth of the statements made in the proposal, apart from the condition of materiality, a condition of the insurers' liability, and hence the claim failed.[67] Though the general rule is that the duty of disclosure is limited to those facts which the insured knows or ought to know, by providing that the insured's declarations shall form the basis of the contract, the contract may thus increase the obligation of the insured by extending the insurer's option to rescind to cases where the failure to disclose results from ignorance of a fact or a reasonable belief that the fact was not material. In such cases the courts will put a strict burden of proof on the insurer,[68] but this has not always relieved an insured from the harsh consequences of making an insignificant misstatement or failing to disclose a perfectly trivial matter, and reforms have been proposed by the Law Commission.[69]

Family arrangements. A duty to make full disclosure exists in the case of certain family arrangements, such as divisions of property or an agreement to vary the terms of a valid will. In *Gordon* v. *Gordon*[70] a division of property was made, based upon an assumption that the elder son was illegitimate. This was set aside 19 years afterwards upon proof that the younger son had concealed knowledge of a marriage ceremony that had taken place between his parents prior to his brother's birth. In *Wales* v. *Wadham*[71] a failure by a wife to disclose to her husband during negotiations for a financial settlement after divorce that she planned to remarry was held not to invoke a breach of the duty of *uberrima fides*. This was because the basis of the negotiations was

---

[66] [1922] 2 A.C. 413.
[67] See also, *Condogianis* v. *Guardian Assurance Co.* [1921] 2 A.C. 125.
[68] See, *e.g. Anderson* v. *Fitzgerald* (1853) 4 H.L.C. 484; *Joel* v. *Law Union and Crown Insurance Co.* [1908] 2 K.B. 863.
[69] Report on Insurance Law, Non-disclosure and Breach of Warranty (Law Com. 104) (1980). Insurance contracts are exempted from the relevant provisions of the Unfair Contract Terms Act 1977.
[70] (1816–19) 3 Swan. 400. See also, *Greenwood* v. *Greenwood* (1863) 2 De J. and S. 28.
[71] [1977] 2 All E.R. 125.

that neither party was making a full disclosure (for example, the husband did not disclose his income).

(e) Contracts where there is a limited duty of disclosure

A couple of examples may be given here. Contracts of suretyship or guarantee (where they can be distinguished from contracts of insurance)[72] seem not to be contracts of utmost good faith, though the point is not entirely settled.[73] A contract of suretyship appears to require disclosure of unusual circumstances known to the creditor which the surety would not normally expect.[74]

Contracts for the sale of land involve a limited duty of disclosure in that the vendor has a general duty to disclose the existence of latent defects in title.[75]

A partner owes a duty of utmost good faith to his partners[76] and statute requires disclosure of a large number of matters in a prospectus, hence placing a heavy duty upon promoters and company directors.[77]

4. MISREPRESENTATION ACT

The provisions of this Act are examined in detail elsewhere.[78] For the purposes of our present discussion it is relevant to mention that the Act in several places employs the phrase "after a misrepresentation has been made"[79] and this phrase, together with the absence of a definition of the word "misrepresentation" in the Act has raised the question whether its ambit is restricted to active misrepresentations only, and does not extend to cases where the law imposes a duty of disclosure.

It is thought that the previous law as to the meaning of "misrepresentation" applies to misrepresentations governed by the Act.[80] It also seems likely that the expression "a misrepresen-

---

[72] See *Seaton* v. *Heath* [1899] 1 Q.B. 782 at 792–793; *Chitty on Contracts* (25th ed., 1983) paras. 470–471.

[73] *Cf. Wales* v. *Wadham* [1977] 2 All E.R. 125 at 139 and *Davies* v. *London & Provincial Marine Insurance Co.* (1878) 8 Ch.D. 469 at 475.

[74] See *National Provincial Bank of England Ltd* v. *Glanusk* [1913] 3 K.B. 335 at 338. See also, *London General Omnibus Co.* v. *Holloway* [1912] 2 K.B. 72.

[75] See *Yandle & Sons* v. *Sutton* [1922] 2 Ch. 199.

[76] See Partnership Act 1890, ss.28, 29, 30.

[77] Financial Services Act 1986, s.163. See also, ss.146, 144(2)(*a*) and 162(1).

[78] *Infra,* pp. 36–39; 45–58.

[79] See s.1, s.2(1), s.2(2), and also, s.3 ("any misrepresentation made by him").

[80] See *Andre & Cie S.A.* v. *Ets. Michel Blanc & Fils* [1979] 2 Lloyds Rep. 427 at 435, *per* Geoffrey Lane L.J.; Atiyah & Treitel (1967) 30 M.L.R. 369.

tation has been made" will cover cases of partial non-disclosure as exemplified by cases such as *With* v. *O'Flanagan* and *Nottingham Patent Brick and Tile Co.* v. *Butler* discussed above,[81] and also will cover cases of misrepresentation by conduct.[82] In such cases it does not seem to strain the meaning of the word "made" unduly to hold that a misrepresentation has been made. Certainly it may be argued that in the case of a representation, originally true, but later becoming false, there was no "misrepresentation made" at the time when the representation was made, but the court is likely to regard such a representation as a continuing one,[83] and hence it would become a misrepresentation on the occurrence of the falsifying event. Greater difficulties occur in cases of complete non-disclosure such as contracts *uberrimae fidei*. It has been argued that "failure to disclose the existence of a material fact is equivalent to affirmation of its non-existence,"[84] but it seems unduly artificial to regard a misrepresentation as having been made in such a situation.

---

[81] *Supra*, pp. 21–22.
[82] Treitel *op.cit.* n. 56 *supra*, p. 310.
[83] See *Smith* v. *Kay* (1859) 7 H.L.C. 750 at 769, *per* Lord Cranworth; *Briess* v. *Woolley* [1954] A.C. 333 at 354, 358; Hudson (1969) 85 L.Q.R. 524–525.
[84] Cheshire, Fifoot & Furmston's *Law of Contract* (11th ed., 1986) pp. 287–288. See also, Hudson *op. cit.* n. 83 *supra*, pp. 526, 529, citing the judgment of Vaughan Williams L.J. in *London General Omnibus Co.* v. *Holloway* [1912] 2 K.B. 72 at 80. ("... I think that the non-disclosure by the plaintiffs of the fact that to their knowledge the clerk had been guilty of defalcations in their service before the bond was executed constituted a representation that he had not been guilty of such dishonesty.")

Chapter 3

REMEDIES FOR MISREPRESENTATION

In this chapter we examine the remedies for misrepresentation, and also consider to what extent liability for misrepresentation can be excluded or limited.

As we saw in Chapter 1[1] the rules concerning the availability of rescission at common law and in equity were effectively assimilated by the Judicature Acts, in that the equitable rule prevailed thereafter. Thus, a contract may now be rescinded if it was induced by an actionable misrepresentation, whether fraudulent, negligent or innocent. We shall now examine what is meant by rescission, when the remedy is available and what its effects are.

The basic rule is that misrepresentation renders the ensuing contract voidable at the option of the representee. Thus, in *Clough* v. *London and North Western Railway Co.*[2] Mellor J. said:

"The fact that the contract was induced by fraud did not render the contract void, or prevent the property from passing, but merely gave the party defrauded a right, on discovering the fraud, to elect whether he would continue to treat the contract as binding, or would disaffirm the contract and resume his property."[3]

It is, therefore, up to the representee to indicate in some positive way that he will not be bound by the terms of the contract. If he does nothing, the contract will remain valid and binding. It should be noted that the option is that of the representee alone. It is not open to the representor, in a situation where the representee has decided not to rescind as he see the contract benefiting him, to claim that the contract is void. As we shall see,[4] the fact that

[1] See p. 6 *supra.*
[2] (1871) L.R. 7 Ex. 26. It should, however, be noted that if the misrepresentation is such as to cause a mistake as to the identity of the person contracting (see, *e.g.* *Cundy* v. *Lindsay* (1878) 3 App.Cas 459) or fundamentally misrepresents the nature and effect of the contract itself (see, *e.g.* *Saunders* v. *Anglia Building Society* ([1971] A.C. 1004), the representee may be entitled to treat the contract as void. However, this is the result of the mistake, not of the misrepresentation.
[3] (1871) L.R. 7 Ex. 26 at 34.
[4] *Infra*, pp. 32–39.

misrepresentation renders the contract voidable may affect the availability of rescission, and in addition, the fact that the remedy is equitable means that it is discretionary and is therefore not available as of right.

The right to rescind, once exercised, is a final act.[5] The representee cannot later affirm. Nor having affirmed can he later rescind.[6] It is necessary for the representee to inform the representor of his decision to rescind. This may be done by instituting proceedings, or less formally by simply giving notice to the representor.[7] Alternatively, he may act defensively and plead misrepresentation as a defence to a suit for specific performance.[8] However, in an exceptional case the requirement of notice may be waived. In *Car and Universal Finance Co. Ltd* v. *Caldwell*[9] the defendant sold his car to a certain Norris, who paid by cheque. The cheque was dishonoured when the defendant presented it the following morning, and he immediately informed the police and the Automobile Association. Subsequently Norris sold the car to a firm of dealers, Motobella Co. Ltd., who had notice of the defect in title, and the car passed through the hands of other purchasers and ultimately was bought by the plaintiffs.

The Court of Appeal considered that where a representor, by absconding, deliberately makes it impossible for the representee to communicate his intention to rescind, which the representor knows he will almost certainly want to do, the representor can no longer insist on his right to be informed of the election to rescind. In such a case the representee might evince his intention to rescind by overt means falling short of communication or repossession. In informing the police and the Automobile Association the defendant had clearly declared his intention. Since he had done so prior to the sale to Motobella, their later sale vested no title in the plaintiffs. The Court did not commit itself to a view as to the position of the representee in such a case if the misrepresentation were innocent. It is suggested that the *Caldwell* principle should be

---

[5] See *Clough* v. *London and North Western Railway Co.* (1871) L.R. 7 Ex. 26 at 34.
[6] *Ibid.* at 36.
[7] If goods have been obtained by fraud, rescission may be effected by repossessing them: *In re Eastgate* [1905] 1 K.B. 465.
[8] See, *e.g.* *Redgrave* v. *Hurd* (1881) 20 Ch.D. 1, *supra* p. 17. The principles governing misrepresentation as a defence and as a ground for rescission appear to be the same, except in certain cases of fraud. See *Feise* v. *Parkinson* (1812) 4 Taunt. 639, 641; *Barker* v. *Walters* (1844) 8 Beav. 92; Treitel, *The Law of Contract* (7th ed., 1987) pp. 286–287. In such cases the representee who acts defensively may not be required to return what he obtained under the contract, whereas he would be so required if he took positive action to rescind.
[9] [1965] 1 Q.B. 525.

treated as a narrow exception and restricted to cases of fraud. It may be argued that a person who agrees to transfer his car to a stranger in exchange for a cheque is less deserving of relief than a bona fide purchaser of the subject matter of the contract and Sellers L.J. accepted that legislation might be necessary to do justice between the victims of fraud.[10]

(a) Indemnity

The effect of rescission is to nullify the contract *ab initio*. The parties must, therefore, be restored to their original positions, and this requires *restitutio in integrum* to be effected. This requirement is mutual: *i.e.* as rescission is an equitable remedy both parties, and not just one, must be reinstated. One aspect of this requirement is that the defendant is bound to indemnify the plaintiff against obligations incurred as a consequence of the misrepresentation. To this extent monetary compensation is available for an innocent misrepresentation, but its ambit is narrower than that of the statutory remedy in damages which is available for a negligent misrepresentation[11] and that of the common law remedy in damages for a negligent misstatement.[12] As the decision in *Whittington* v. *Seale-Hayne*[13] demonstrates, the indemnity is limited to obligations necessarily created by the contract. In that case the plaintiffs took a lease of the defendant's premises with a view to breeding poultry and on the strength of the defendant's innocent misrepresentation that the premises were in a sanitary condition. In fact, the water supply was poisoned and as a consequence the manager of the farm became ill and the poultry died. The Urban District Council declared the premises to be unfit for habitation and required the plaintiffs to renew the drains. The plaintiffs sought rescission of the agreement, plus an indemnity to cover the value of the lost stock, loss of profit on sales, loss of breeding season, rent and removal of stores, medical expenses, rates paid and the cost of repairing the drains. It was held that the

---

[10] *Ibid.* at 552. This suggestion has not as yet been taken up. However, in their 12th Report (1966) Cmnd. 2958, the Law Reform Committee recommended the reversal of the rule in *Caldwell* (para. 16), and the Court of Session in *Macleod* v. *Ker* 1965 S.C. 253 decided a similar case in favour of the third party.

[11] Misrepresentation Act 1967, s.2(1). Discussed in detail *infra* pp. 49–52.

[12] See *Hedley Byrne & Co. Ltd.* v. *Heller & Partners Ltd.* [1964] A.C. 465. Discussed in detail in Chap. 4 *infra*.

[13] (1900) 82 L.T. 49. *Cf. Newbigging* v. *Adam* (1886) 34 Ch.D. 582, where Fry L.J. appeared to espouse a broader view of the ambit of the indemnity (at p. 596) though this is explained by Treitel (*op. cit*, n. 8 *supra* at p. 281) as explicable in the context of the facts of *Newbigging* v. *Adam*.

indemnity covered only the last two items. The obligations to pay rates and to carry out the repairs were obligations imposed by the lease, and as such, once the agreement had been entered into, the plaintiffs were bound to carry them out. They were not bound to use the premises as a poultry farm, and hence, the loss of profits, medical expenses etc., though no doubt reasonably foreseeable, were not recoverable. If a claim in negligence could have succeeded in 1900 such losses would have been recoverable, assuming that breach of a duty of care could have been proved, on the ordinary principles of remoteness of damage. The fact that such a claim may now be brought greatly improves the position of the representee, but there will still be cases where a misrepresentation is made without fraud or fault on the part of the representor and in such cases the monetary compensation that accompanies rescission will be limited to an indemnity.

(b) Limits on the right to rescind

Restitutio in integrum. At common law a precise *restitutio in integrum* was required. Thus in *Clarke* v. *Dickson*[14] the plaintiff was induced by the defendant's fraud to take shares in a partnership. Several years later, during which time dividends had been declared and the partnership had become a limited liability company, the company was in bad circumstances and was in the process of being wound up when the plaintiff discovered the fraud and sought to rescind. It was held that he could not rescind, as he was not able to effect an exact restitution. The nature of the corporate body, and of his shares in it had changed,[15] and the object of rescission is compensation in so far as that can be effected. Unjust enrichment of the representee cannot be permitted.

The position was, however, more flexible in equity. Lord Blackburn explained the position thus in *Erlanger* v. *New Sombrero Phosphate Co.*[16]

---

[14] (1858) E.B. & E. 148, see especially at pp. 154–155. See also, *Sheffield Nickel Co. Ltd.* v. *Unwin* (1877) 2 Q.B.D. 215.

[15] It was in this case that Crompton J. gave the example (at p. 155) of a butcher who bought cattle as a result of fraud, killed them and sold the meat. Precise *restitutio in integrum* in such a case would plainly be impossible. In such a case (and this is equally true of the facts of *Clarke*) there is, prima facie, no reason why the representee should not claim damages in deceit, and the existence now of a remedy in damages under s.2(1) of the Misrepresentation Act makes those cases where today the right of rescission is lost less harsh on the representee than was hitherto the case.

[16] (1878) 3 App.Cas. 1218. See also, *Adam* v. *Newbigging* (1888) 13 App.Cas. 308.

"a Court of Equity ... can take account of profits, and make allowance for deterioration. And I think the practice has always been for a Court of Equity to give this relief whenever, by the exercise of its powers, it can do what is practically just, though it cannot restore the parties precisely to the state they were in before the contract."[17]

Thus, in *Erlanger* the company had bought a phosphate mine, which they had worked. They later wished to rescind the sale for breach of fiduciary duty by one of their promoters. It was held that they could do so on the terms that they were required to return the mine and account for their profits in working it. More recently, a deterioration in the subject matter of the contract has not been regarded as disentitling the representee to rescind, indeed: "if mere deterioration of the subject matter negatived the right to rescind, the doctrine of rescission would become a vain thing."[18] So, in *Armstrong* v. *Jackson*[19] a stockbroker, in response to an instruction from the plaintiff to buy shares, in fact sold the plaintiff his own (*i.e.* the broker's) shares. At the date of purchase in 1910 the shares were worth nearly £3. In 1915 the plaintiff became suspicious, discovered the truth and instituted proceedings. By that time the shares were worth five shillings only. It was held that he could rescind, provided he returned the shares and the dividends that he had received. It may be appropriate for the court to order the representee to pay compensation on account of any deterioration. Rigby L.J. in *Lagunas Nitrate Co.* v. *Lagunas Syndicate*[20] put the matter thus: "If substantially compensation can be made, rescission with compensation is *ex debito justitiae.*"[21] A final point to note is that the courts seem more inclined to exercise their discretion to order restitution in cases where fraud is involved than in cases where the misrepresentation is innocent.[22]

---

[17] (1878) 3 App.Cas. 1218 at 1278–1279.
[18] *Per* McCardie J. in *Armstrong* v. *Jackson* [1917] 2 K.B. 822 at 829.
[19] [1917] 2 K.B. 822.
[20] [1899] 2 Ch. 392
[21] *Ibid.* at 457.
[22] See, *e.g. Spence* v. *Crawford* [1939] 3 All E.R. 271: " . . . the court will be more drastic in exercising its discretionary powers in a case of fraud than in a case of innocent misrepresentation . . . A case of innocent misrepresentation may be regarded rather as one of misfortune than as one of moral obliquity. There is no deceit or intention to defraud. The court will be less ready to pull a transaction to pieces where the defendant is innocent, whereas in the case of fraud the court will exercise its jurisdiction to the full." *per* Lord Wright at 288. See also, *Hulton* v. *Hulton* [1917] 1 K.B. 813.

Affirmation. If the representee affirms the contract, then provided he has full knowledge of the true facts, he loses the right to rescind. For example, continued use of goods obtained as a result of a misrepresentation after knowledge of the falseness of the misrepresentation will bar the right to relief. Thus, in *United Shoe Machinery Co. of Canada* v. *Brunet*[23] the respondents were allegedly induced by misrepresentations by the appellants that they were patentees of certain machines to lease the machines from them. However, since the respondents did not repudiate the leases after discovering the alleged false representations but continued to work the machines and pay royalties, they had in effect affirmed the contracts and could not thereafter avoid them. Many of the examples of this rule are contained in cases where shareholders, having purchased shares as a result of a misrepresentation, discover the truth and yet receive dividends[24] or attempt to sell the shares,[25] and are thereby held to have affirmed, as such acts are entirely inconsistent with an intention to rescind, but indicate a desire to keep the contract alive. Much will depend upon the facts of the particular case as to whether affirmation is deemed to have taken place. Factors such as the nature of the contract, the effect upon third parties and indeed even the question whether the representor has changed his position as a result of the representee's failure to rescind[26] may be relevant. Affirmation may be inferred in certain cases where the representee fails to rescind. Thus, in *First National Reinsurance Co. Ltd* v. *Greenfield*[27] where the company claimed against the defendant for unpaid calls on shares, it was held to be no defence for him to have given the company notice that he repudiated the shares: it was necessary for him to take active steps to remove his name from the register.

Lapse of time may be evidence of affirmation. In *Clough* v. *London and North Western Railway Co.*[28] Mellor J. said:

> "And lapse of time without rescinding will furnish evidence that he has determined to affirm the contract; and when the

---

[23] [1909] A.C. 330.
[24] See *Western Bank of Scotland* v. *Addie* (1876) L.R. 1 Sc & Div. 145 at 163; *Scholey* v. *Central Railway Co. of Venezuela* (1870) L.R. 9 Eq. 266 n.
[25] *Re Hop and Malt Exchange and Warehouse Co., ex p. Briggs* (1866) L.R. 1 Eq. 483.
[26] See *Clough* v. *London and North Western Railway Co.* (1871) L.R. 7 Ex. 26 at 34 and 35.
[27] [1921] 2 K.B. 260. See also, *Deposit and General Life Assurance Co.* v. *Ayscough* 6 E. & B. 761 at 763.
[28] *Supra*, n. 26 at 35.

lapse of time is great, it probably would in practice be treated as conclusive evidence that he has so determined."

Again, much will depend upon the facts of the case[29]; the same period of delay might or might not amount to a lapse of time in different cases. Thus, in the case of share allotments speedy action is required once the representee is aware of the misrepresentation. In *Re Russian (Vyksounsky) Ironworks Co. (Taite's Case)*[30] a delay of a month was held to be fatal. On the other hand, in a series of cases against the Mutual Reserve Life Insurance Co. plaintiffs succeeded, despite considerable delay in rescinding insurance contracts the size of whose premiums had been misrepresented to them.[31]

Lapse of time. There may be a difference between cases involving fraud or breach of fiduciary duty and cases where the misrepresentation is innocent. In the former category lapse of time does not *per se* bar rescission; it is evidence of affirmation. But in the latter category lapse of time may itself bar rescission. In *Leaf* v. *International Galleries*[32] the plaintiff bought a painting, represented as having been painted by John Constable, from the defendants in 1944 for £85. In 1949 he tried to sell the painting at Christie's and discovered that in fact it was not a Constable. He informed the defendants, who continued to contend that the painting was a Constable. He therefore claimed rescission of the contract and the return of his £85. The Court of Appeal held that, assuming the equitable remedy of rescission were available to a buyer of goods,[33] it was not open to the plaintiff in this case, as he had not acted within a reasonable time. It had been held by the trial judge, with whom the Court of Appeal agreed, that there had been no laches, so the delay could not be said to be evidence of affirmation. Jenkins L.J. said: "... it behoves the purchaser either to verify or, as the case may be, to disprove the representation within a reasonable time."[34] This reasoning seems open to question. Why should a buyer, on an assurance from a presumably reputable dealer, be required to verify that assurance after

---

[29] See *Aaron's Reefs Ltd.* v. *Twiss* [1896] A.C. 273 at 294, *per* Lord Davey.
[30] (1876) L.R. 3 Eq. 795.
[31] *Mutual Reserve Life Insurance Co.* v. *Foster* (1904) 20 T.L.R. 715; *Cross* v. *Mutual Reserve Life Insurance Co.* (1904) 21 T.L.R. 15; *Menno* v. *the Same* (1904) 21 T.L.R.167; *Molloy* v. *the Same* (1905) 22 T.L.R. 59.
[32] [1950] 2 K.B. 86.
[33] It seems clear that it would be so available today. See Treitel, *The Law of Contract* (7th ed., 1987) pp. 287–288.
[34] [1950] 2 K.B. 86 at 92.

purchase? At least, it may be argued, if the representor is negligent in such a case (it does not appear from the report whether this was the case in *Leaf*), he is the person who should suffer, to the extent of not being permitted to resist rescission.

Third Party Rights. Although the representee is entitled (subject to his delay being taken to be evidence of affirmation, or of excessive delay under *Leaf*) to take his time over rescission, he does this at the risk of the intervention of third party rights. Since the misrepresentation renders the contract voidable rather than void, its continuing validity prior to rescission means that, to take a typical instance in this context, a representor who has acquired goods as a result of his misrepresentation can pass a good title to a third party if he transfers the goods before the representee rescinds, provided that the third party acts in good faith and provides consideration. Consequently, it is always advisable for the representee to act swiftly once he is aware that there has been a misrepresentation.[35] If the ensuing contract were void, no good title could pass from representor to third party. Hence in cases such as *Lewis* v. *Averay*[36] one sees the representee arguing that the misrepresentation of identity by a rogue was of such a kind as to make the case one of unilateral mistake, and as such void *ab initio*. Again, a representee cannot rescind an allotment of shares in a company after the company has gone into liquidation, as third party rights intervene at that juncture.[37]

Misrepresentation Act 1967. Prior to the enactment of the Misrepresentation Act 1967, which followed a report by the Law Reform Committee on Innocent Misrepresentation[38] there existed certain other bars to the right to rescind. There was uncertainty concerning the effect of a pre-contractual representation which was incorporated into the contract.[39] This uncertainty was

---

[35] See *Car & Universal Finance Co. Ltd.* v. *Caldwell* [1965] 1 Q.B. 525. *Supra*, pp. 30–31.

[36] [1972] 1 Q.B. 198. See also, *Phillips* v. *Brooks Ltd.* [1919] 2 K.B. 243; *Ingram* v. *Little* [1961] 1 Q.B. 31.

[37] See *Oakes* v. *Turquand and Harding* (1867) L.R. 2 H.L. 325; *In re Scottish Petroleum Co.* (1883) 23 Ch.D. 413. *Cf.* the rules concerning an individual's bankruptcy, *e.g. Load* v. *Green* (1846) 15 M. & W. 216.

[38] 10th Report (1962) Cmnd. 1782.

[39] Dicta in *Pennsylvania Shipping Co.* v. *Compagnie Nationale de Navigation* [1936] 2 All E.R. 1167 suggested that rescission was no longer possible after incorporation. In *Compagnie Francaise des Chemins de Fer Paris-Orleans* v. *Leeston Shipping Co.* (1919) 1 Lloyds L.R. 235 the opposite view was favoured.

resolved by section 1(*a*) of the Act which provides that a person who has entered into a contract after a misrepresentation has been made to him, and that misrepresentation has become a term of the contract, is entitled to rescind the contract, provided that he would otherwise be entitled to rescind the contract (for example, rescission would not be possible if any of the bars existed[40]) without alleging fraud.[41] Thus, if you are induced to contract with me for the purchase of my car by my untrue statement concerning the roadworthiness of the car, the fact that the contract itself contains a term attesting to the car's roadworthiness does not prevent you from rescinding the contract for the misrepresentation if you are so minded, and if rescission is still otherwise possible. This will be equally true whether the misrepresentation has become a warranty or a condition. Thus, even though, as a warranty, the misrepresentation which has been incorporated as a term would give a right to damages only, the representee has the option of rescinding and therefore causing *restitutio in integrum* to be effected. Conversely, he may elect to keep the contract alive and claim damages for the breach of warranty.

It has been pointed out[42] that the use of the words "rescission" "rescind" and "rescinded" in the Act raises a possible confusion, in that the term "rescission" has two possible meanings: "rescission for misrepresentation," where, as we have seen,[43] the contract is set aside for all purposes and *restitutio in integrum* is effected; and "rescission for breach" whereby, on account of the other party's breach of contract the innocent party repudiates his obligations by refusing to perform, or refusing to accept performance. If, as seems more likely, the former meaning is intended, a potential problem might exist in the case of a representee who rescinds out of court for an incorporated misrepresentation. He might well thereby lose his right to claim damages if (as seems likely) the effect of rescission for misrepresentation is to destroy all outstanding liabilities for breach of contract.[44] As we shall see, however,[45] section 2(2) of the Misrepresentation Act empowers the court in cases of innocent and negligent misrepresentation to declare the contract subsisting and award damages in lieu of rescission. It is possible that the effect of this, in addition to

---

[40] *Supra*, pp. 32–36.
[41] If there has been fraud it has long been clear that a contract may be rescinded after execution. See *Gillett* v. *Peppercorne* (1840) 3 Beav. 78.
[42] Atiyah and Treitel (1967) 30 M.L.R. 369 at 370–372.
[43] *Supra*, p. 29.
[44] By contrast to "rescission for breach" which does not have this effect.
[45] *Infra*, pp. 52–54.

allowing the representee the monetary equivalent of his lost right to rescind, would be to revive the claim for breach of contract.[46]

A further bar to rescission that existed in certain cases of misrepresentation prior to the enactment of the Misrepresentation Act was that the ensuing contract had been executed. This rule had been clearly established with regard to sales or other dispositions of interests in land since the decision in *Wilde* v. *Gibson*.[47] Authority for the application of this principle to contracts not relating to land was found in *Seddon* v. *North Eastern Salt Co. Ltd*,[48] which concerned a contract for the sale of shares. This, for various reasons,[49] was somewhat dubious authority for a general principle that there could be no rescission following execution of a contract, and had been the object of intermittent criticism, especially by Denning L.J. (as he then was).[50]

The Law Reform Committee recommended that, in the case of contracts other than those for the sale or other disposition of an interest in land, the fact that the contract had been executed should of itself be no bar to rescission. The Committee favoured the retention of the rule in *Wilde* v. *Gibson* and *Angel* v. *Jay* with the exception that in the case of leases taking effect in possession for a term not exceeding three years, execution of the lease or tenancy agreement should not be a bar to rescission. The legislature, however, preferred a broad general rule, and consequently, it is provided by section 1(*b*) of the Misrepresentation Act that in any case where the contract has been performed, rescission, subject to the same limitations as section 1(*a*), may be effected.[51] It is, therefore, possible for a contract for the sale of land to be rescinded after conveyance. Again, as we shall see, the fact that section 2(2) empowers the court to grant damages in lieu of rescission provides an alternative remedy in cases where rescission would cause hardship.

---

[46] See Treitel *op. cit.* n. 33 p. 289.

[47] (1848) 1 H.L.C. 605 (a conveyance). See also, *Angel* v. *Jay* [1911] 1 K.B. 666 (a lease).

[48] [1905] 1 Ch. 326.

[49] See the Law Reform Committee 10th Report (*supra*, n. 38) para. 8.

[50] In *Solle* v. *Butcher* [1950] 1 K.B. 671; *Leaf* v. *International Galleries* [1950] 2 K.B. 86 and especially in *Curtis* v. *Chemical Cleaning & Dyeing Co.* [1951] 1 K.B. 805.

[51] It may be noted that a possible consequence of the view expressed above (*supra*, p. 27) that the use of the phrase "misrepresentation made" in s.1 does not cover non-disclosure would be to prevent an insurer from rescinding, after the contract of insurance had been executed, following a failure to disclose a material fact by the insured.

It should finally be noted that the fact that, as we have noted, in cases of innocent and negligent misrepresentation, the court is empowered by section 2(2) of the Act to grant damages in lieu of rescission requires that the "right to rescind" must be seen as being a qualified right only, and the court may take account of the consequences of rescission to representee or representor in exercising its discretion.

2. DAMAGES

(a) Deceit

Nature of deceit. As we saw in Chapter 1,[52] an untrue statement of fact, *i.e.* a false warranty, was originally actionable on the case for deceit. It became established that an action would lie provided that the plaintiff could establish that the defendant knew that his words were untrue[53] or that the defendant had given an express warranty.[54] As actions on warranties began to be framed in *assumpsit*, so the action in deceit increasingly emphasised the element of the defendant's knowledge of his statement's falsity. This trend was a a particular consequence of the decision in *Pasley* v. *Freeman*[55] in which, as a result of a knowingly false representation made by the defendant to the plaintiff that a third party's credit was good, the plaintiff entered into a contract with the third party and suffered loss. In previous cases the action in deceit had succeeded in circumstances which today would be regarded as involving either a breach of contract or a misrepresentation which induced the plaintiff to contract with the defendant. The extension of liability for deceit to a non-contractual situation, in which the defendant did not benefit from the fraud, was novel, and, in founding liability upon the knowledge of falsity, the case laid the basis for the modern law of deceit. In the subsequent case of *Langridge* v. *Levy*[56] Parke B. summed up the principle incorporated in *Pasley* v. *Freeman* as follows: "...a mere naked falsehood is not enough to give a right of action; but if it be a falsehood told with an intention that it should be acted upon by the party injured, and that act must produce damage to him..."[57]

---

[52] *Supra*, p. 1.
[53] See, *e.g. Furnis* v. *Leicester* (1618) Cro.Jac. 474.
[54] See, *e.g. Chandelor* v. *Lopus* (1603) Cro.Jac. 4.
[55] (1789) 3 T.R. 51.
[56] (1837) 2 M & W 519.
[57] *Ibid.* at 531.

The meaning of fraud was adverted to in *Pasley* v. *Freeman* by Buller J. when he said "knowledge of the falsehood of the thing asserted is fraud and deceit."[58] A number of subsequent cases have examined further the state of mind that the plaintiff must be shown to have had in order to be liable for deceit. Thus in *Foster* v. *Charles*[59] Tindal C.J. said: "It is fraud in law if a party makes representations which he knows to be false, and injury ensues, although the motives from which the representation proceeded may not have been bad." Liability would therefore ensue even though the representor was seeking neither to benefit himself nor to harm the representee by his statement. In *Taylor* v. *Ashton*[60] Parke B. emphasised that gross negligence was not enough to amount to deceit. He also said:

> "It is not necessary to show that the defendant knew the facts to be untrue; if they stated a fact which was untrue for a fraudulent purpose, they at the same time not believing that fact to be true, in that case it would be both a legal and moral fraud."[61]

Recklessness would suffice. Thus, according to Bowen L.J. in *Edgington* v. *Fitzmaurice*[62] " ... it is immaterial whether they made the statement knowing it to be untrue, or recklessly, without caring whether it was true or not, because to make a statement recklessly for the purpose of influencing another person is dishonest."

These and other cases decided during the previous 100 years, were considered and applied by the House of Lords in *Derry* v. *Peek*.[63] By a special Act of Parliament a tramway company was authorised to make certain tramways. The Act provided that the carriages to be used in the tramways might be moved with animal power and, if the Board of Trade consented, by steam or mechanical power. The directors issued a prospectus which stated that the company had the right to use steam or mechanical power instead of horses. They honestly believed this statement to be true. The respondent bought shares on the faith of the statement, but the Board of Trade consent was never forthcoming, and the company was subsequently wound up. The respondent brought an

[58] (1789) 3 T.R. 51 at 57.
[59] (1830) 7 Bing. 105 at 107. See also, *Polhill* v. *Walter* (1832) 3 B. & Ad. 114.
[60] (1843) 11 M. & W. 401. See also, *Collins* v. *Evans* (1844)5 Q.B. 820.
[61] (1843) 11 M. & W. 401 at 415.
[62] (1885) 29 Ch.D. 459 at 481–482.
[63] (1889) 15 App.Cas. 337. See now, Financial Services Act 1986, ss.150, 166.

action in deceit against the directors. Lord Herschell stated the law as follows:

> "First, in order to sustain an action of deceit, there must be proof of fraud, and nothing short of that will suffice. Secondly, fraud is proved when it is shewn that a false representation has been made (1) knowingly, or (2) without belief in its truth, or (3) recklessly, careless whether it be true or false... To prevent a false statement being fraudulent, there must, I think, always be an honest belief in its truth... Thirdly, if fraud be proved, the motive of the person guilty of it is immaterial. It matters not that there was no intention to cheat or injure the person to whom the statements were made."[64]

The honest belief of the directors in the truth of their statement prevented the claim from succeeding.

In general the type of statement that amounts to a misrepresentation as discussed in Chapter 2 will also amount to the type of statement that is actionable in deceit (provided, of course, that fraud can be proved). Indeed, many of the cases discussed in Chapter 2 are deceit cases. Thus, the statement must be a representation of fact, not of opinion, and as to the present rather than the future, though of course a misrepresentation of present intention may be actionable,[65] as may a dishonest statement that the representor holds a particular opinion. As regards ambiguity, if the representor makes a statement with the intention that it should be understood in the sense in which the representee is able to prove that he understood it, the statement will be actionable.[66] However, where the representor honestly believes his statement to be true in the sense in which he understands it, the statement will not be actionable merely because it is understood by the representee in a different sense, and in that sense it is false to the knowledge of the representor.[67] Such will be the case even if the sense in which the representee understood the statement is the meaning which on its proper construction it should bear.[68]

---

[64] *Ibid.* at 374.

[65] See *Edgington* v. *Fitzmaurice* (1885) 29 Ch.D. 459 at 481–482.

[66] See *Smith* v. *Chadwick* (1884) 9 App.Cas. 187.

[67] *Akerhielm* v. *De Mare* [1959] A.C. 789.

[68] *Ibid.* Treitel (*The Law of Contract*, 7th ed., 1987, p. 259 n. 45) questions whether liability in such a case could not be imposed under *Hedley Byrne* v. *Heller* or under s.2(1) of the Misrepresentation Act 1967. In principle there seems no reason why liability should not be so imposed, assuming the existence of a special relationship in the former case and an ensuing contract in the latter. Both elements existed in *Akerhielm*.

The statement need not be material, but it must induce reliance by the representee. Such reliance, as *Pasley* v. *Freeman* shows, need not necessarily amount to the entering into a contract with the representor,[69] though this will very frequently be the case. A difficult question that can arise concerns the position where the representation is made by an agent. If the agent is aware that his statement is false, the principal will be liable for his fraud,[70] but the principal will in general not be liable where he is aware of the untruth of the statement but the agent who makes it is not,[71] unless, aware that the false statement was being made, he stood by.[72]

As a consequence of the enactment of section 2(1) of the Misrepresentation Act 1967[73] and the fact that, as noted in the previous paragraph, most cases of deceit involve an ensuing contract, the statutory remedy, with its reversed burden of proof, makes it more attractive to a plaintiff than the action in deceit. As the constituents of deceit and the section 2(1) claim in terms of the nature of the statement made are effectively identical, the difficulties of proving that the defendant lacked an honest belief in the truth of his statement are likely to persuade the plaintiff to pursue the statutory remedy. The main factor (perhaps the sole one other than the fact that if no contract ensues the statutory remedy is not available) in favour of the action in deceit concerns the way in which damages are assessed.

Measure of damages in deceit. As regards the measure of damages in cases of deceit, it was held by the Court of Appeal in *Doyle* v. *Olby (Ironmongers) Ltd*[74] that the object is to place the representee in the position he would have been in if the representation had not been made. This emphasises the tortious nature of the cause of action.[75] Thus, in a case such as *Doyle* where the plaintiff was induced by the defendant's fraud to purchase a business from him, the prima facie measure of damages is the difference between the price paid and the fair value of the property. However, in that case it was held that the defendant was liable to compensate the

---

[69] See *Mafo* v. *Adams* [1970] 1 Q.B. 548 (plaintiff deceived into giving up protected tenancy).

[70] *S. Pearson & Son Ltd.* v. *Dublin Corporation* [1907] A.C. 331; *Briess* v. *Woolley* [1954] A.C. 333.

[71] *Cornfoot* v. *Fowke* (1840) 6 M & W 358; *Armstrong* v. *Strain* [1952] 1 K.B. 232.

[72] *The Siboen and the Sibotre* [1976] 1 Lloyds Rep. 293 at 321.

[73] Discussed *infra*, pp. 45–52.

[74] [1969] 2 Q.B. 158.

[75] *Ibid.* at 166, *per* Lord Denning M.R.

plaintiff for all the losses flowing directly from his representation unless they were rendered too remote by the plaintiff's own conduct. Thus, the plaintiff was entitled to recover his overall loss up to his final disposal of the business, less any benefits he had received. He was, therefore, able to recover for such items as interest, rates and an overdraft. At the time the court was not prepared to award damages in such cases for worry and anxiety, but subsequently it has been accepted that such an award may be made in an appropriate case.[76]

The effect of this may be to compensate a plaintiff to the same extent that would have been the case had the measure of damages been contractual. Such was the situation in *Archer* v. *Brown*,[77] a case whose facts were not dissimilar to those in *Doyle* v. *Olby*. The plaintiff was induced by the defendant to purchase for £20,000 half of the shares in a company, at the time an employment agency, but due to be expanded into an insurance and holiday travel business. The plaintiff raised the £20,000 by means of a bank loan secured by a first charge on his son's house and a mortgage on his own house, and the defendant was informed of this. At the same time as the sale agreement, the plaintiff entered into a service agreement with the company whereby, together with the defendant, he was to be joint managing director. Problems arose very soon after the sale, and the plaintiff was induced to purchase the rest of the shares in the company for £10,000, financed by an unsecured bank loan. Soon afterwards it transpired that the defendant had sold the shares in the company several times over, and by the time the plaintiff's deceit action against him was heard he was already appealing against his conviction on fraud charges.[78]

The plaintiff's claim for damages included the £30,000 paid for nothing, interest of over £13,000 on the bank loans, his loss of earnings, expenses while seeking a new job, and exemplary damages or in the alternative aggravated damages in respect of the disappointment that he suffered. His claim succeeded except as regards the exemplary damages. In *Mafo* v. *Adams*[79] the Court of Appeal had considered that exemplary damages might be awarded in a deceit action, but Lords Hailsham and Diplock in *Broome* v. *Cassell & Co.*[80] did not agree, though Lord Hailsham accepted

---

[76] *Shelley* v. *Paddock* [1979] Q.B. 120 (£500), affirmed [1980] Q.B. 348. See also, *Archer* v. *Brown* [1985] Q.B. 401 (£500), but note *Saunders* v. *Edwards* [1987] 2 All E.R. 651 at 661.

[77] [1985] Q.B. 401.

[78] An interesting illustration of the relative speed of criminal and civil justice.

[79] [1970] 1 Q.B. 548.

[80] [1972] A.C. 1027 at 1080 and 1130–1131 respectively.

that the matter had not been finally determined. In *Archer* Peter
Pain J. accepted that "the door, on the authorities, is open,"[81] but
considered that the punitive function of such an award had already
been fulfilled by the time the defendant had spent in prison. On
this aspect of a deceit action the possibility exists of a clear
distinction between the award of damages in such a case and that
under section 2(1) of the Misrepresentation Act 1967, for it is clear
that a punitive award is not available in a case of negligence.[82]

The defendant's argument that the plaintiff's liability to pay
interest on the bank loans was the result of his impecuniosity
rather than the deceit of the defendant was understandably
castigated as "brazen" by Peter Pain J. who, having accepted the
directness test, went on to speak in terms of reasonable foreseeability: thus it was reasonably foreseeable that the defendant's
deceit would cause the plaintiff's impecuniosity as the former had
been informed at the time of how the latter proposed to finance
the transaction. Had this not been the case, since Lord Denning's
judgment in *Doyle* v. *Olby* would suggest that *all* consequential
losses are recoverable, the defendant's lack of knowledge would
have made no difference to the extent of his liability. This remains
a potentially significant distinction between damages in deceit and
damages under section 2(1), and represents perhaps the main
reason for a plaintiff electing to sue in deceit rather than under the
statute.[83]

If a contract does ensue from the fraudulent misrepresentation,
rescission may be sought in addition to damages for deceit. The
two are not alternatives,[84] but the plaintiff must not duplicate his
claim. Thus, in *Archer* v. *Brown* the plaintiff could recover the
£30,000 paid for nothing either as damages for deceit or as part of
the *restitutio in integrum* process which rescission demands, but
obviously he could not recover it twice over. But he could formally
have the contract with the defendant rescinded as well as
recovering the £30,000. It has long been established that rescission
for fraudulent misrepresentation is available even if the contract
has been completely performed or executed.[85] However, the later

---

[81] [1984] 2 All E.R. 267 at 281; [1985] Q.B. 401 at 423.
[82] See, *e.g. Broome* v. *Cassell & Co.* [1972] A.C. 1027 at 1131, *per* Lord Diplock.
As we shall see, damages under s.2(1) are measured on a tortious basis.
[83] Though note *McGregor on Damages* (14th ed., 1980) para. 1473.
[84] See *Archer* v. *Brown* [1984] 2 All E.R. 267 at 275; [1985] Q.B. 401 at 415.
[85] See, *e.g. Edwards* v. *M'Leay* (1818) 2 Swan. 287; *Hart* v. *Swaine* (1877) 7 Ch.D.
42. By contrast it is only since the enactment of the Misrepresentation Act 1967
(s.1) that rescission after execution has been available in cases of non-
fraudulent misrepresentation. See p. 38 *supra*.

rescission is sought, the greater is the risk that third party rights may have intervened, thus rendering rescission impossible.[86]

(b) Section 2(1) of the Misrepresentation Act 1967

In its Report on Innocent Misrepresentation[87] the Law Reform Committee addressed itself to a particular criticism levelled against the existing law: that there was no right to damages to compensate for loss caused by a negligent misrepresentation. Of course, as the Committee reported in 1962, its conclusions were arrived at prior to the decision of the House of Lords in *Hedley Byrne & Co. Ltd.* v. *Heller & Partners Ltd.*[88] and thus, we shall never know whether it would have considered the tortious remedy of damages for negligent misstatement sufficient to remedy the problem posed by the absence in general of a remedy in damages. In any event, the Committee, agreeing that the present law was inadequate, proposed that a person who made an untrue representation, by himself or his agent, should be liable to compensate his co-contractors for loss suffered as a consequence of the misrepresentation unless he could prove that, up to the time when the contract was made, he (or his agent, if the representation was made by him) had reasonable grounds for believing that the representation was true.

Section 2(1) of the Misrepresentation Act largely follows this recommendation. It reads as follows:

> "Where a person has entered into a contract after a misrepresentation has been made to him by another party thereto and as a result thereof he has suffered loss, then, if the person making the misrepresentation would be liable to damages in respect thereof had the misrepresentation been made fraudulently, that person shall be so liable notwithstanding that the misrepresentation was not made fraudulently, unless he proves that he had reasonable ground to believe and did believe up to the time the contract was made that the facts represented were true."[89]

This introduces a further factor in addition to those contained in the Law Reform Committee's recommendations: the so-called

---

[86] See p. 36 *supra*.
[87] (1962) Cmnd. 1782. For discussion of other aspects of this report see *supra*, pp. 36, 38.
[88] [1964] A.C. 465. See Chap. 4 *infra*.
[89] The relationship between s.2(1) and *Hedley Byrne* v. *Heller* is considered in Chap. 4 *infra*. *Cf.* Financial Services Act 1986, ss.150, 166.

"fiction of fraud."[90] This clumsy concept, requiring a plaintiff to establish that the defendant would have been liable in damages if the statement had been made fraudulently, has fortunately not so far (subject to the question of the measure of damages, discussed below)[91] led to any of the potential consequences adverted to by Atiyah and Treitel[92] as a result of this flirtation with the law of deceit. For example, one possible consequence is that the rule contained in section 32 of the Limitation Act 1980 applies to section 2(1). This provides that, where an action is "based upon" or "concealed by" the defendant's fraud, time does not begin to run until the plaintiff discovers the fraud or could with reasonable diligence have discovered it. This might be unfortunate since, as Lord Reid noted during the debate on the Bill,[93] though it is right that everything is presumed against a fraudulent person, it would be harsh to allow a claim to be raised after 10 or 20 years against an innocent mirepresentor and then put him to the proof of not only belief but reasonable grounds for belief. One indication that the courts will not treat the fiction of fraud as requiring the applicability of the rules developed in the context of deceit can be seen in *Gosling* v. *Anderson*[94] where it was held that a principal may be liable under section 2(1) for his agent's misrepresentation although the kind of shared responsibility that the law requires to render the principal liable in cases of fraud[95] is absent.

The courts have tended to assume that if the statement made by the defendant amounted to an actionable misrepresentation, then the reversed burden of proof comes into play. Thus, in *Howard Marine & Dredging Co. Ltd.* v. *A. Ogden & Sons (Excavations) Ltd.*,[96] where the plaintiffs' marine manager, a Mr. O'Loughlin, misquoted the capacity of certain sea-going barges to the defendants, who wished to tender (and on the strength of the quote did successfully tender) for an excavation contract, Bridge L.J. considering the applicability of section 2(1), said[97]:

> "The first question then is whether Howards would be liable in damages in respect of Mr. O'Loughlin's misrepresentation

---

[90] See Atiyah and Treitel (1967) 30 M.L.R. 369 at 373.
[91] See *infra.*, p. 49.
[92] (1967) 30 M.L.R. 369 at 373–375. See also, Treitel *op. cit*, n. 33 *supra*, pp. 268–269.
[93] 274 H.L. 936.
[94] [1972] E.G.D. 709. See also, *infra*, pp. 49–50. See Treitel *op. cit*, n. 33 *supra*, pp. 268–269.
[95] *Supra*, p. 42.
[96] [1978] Q.B. 574. See also, the remarks of Lord Denning M.R. in *Gosling* v. *Anderson* [1972] E.G.D. 709 at 713.
[97] [1978] Q.B. 574 at 596. Shaw L.J. agreed with the views expressed by Bridge L.J. on the operation and effect of the Act (*ibid.* at 601). See also, the judgment of Lord Denning M.R. (*ibid.* at 592–593).

if it had been made fraudulently, that is to say, if he had known that it was untrue. An affirmative answer to that question is inescapable. The judge found in terms that what Mr. O'Loughlin said about the capacity of the barges was said with the object of getting the hire contract for Howards, in other words with the intention that it should be acted upon by Ogdens. It follows, therefore, on the plain language of the 1967 Act that, although there was no allegation of fraud, Howards must be liable unless they proved that Mr. O'Loughlin had reasonable ground to believe what he said about the barges' capacity."

The Court of Appeal also indicated the correct approach once the fiction of fraud is established. The trial judge had asked himself whether the innocent misrepresentation was negligent. However, Bridge and Shaw L.JJ. agreed that once the fiction is made out, the onus passes immediately to the representor to prove that he had reasonable grounds to believe the facts represented, and this is not the same thing as being under a duty of care whose extent may vary with the circumstances. In the words of Bridge L.J.[98]: "In the course of negotiations leading to a contract the statute imposes an absolute obligation not to state facts which the representor cannot prove he had reasonable ground to believe."[99]

This imposes a heavy burden upon a representor (justifiable, in the eyes of the Law Reform Committee, on the basis that the representor would normally be in a better position than the representee to know the true facts), especially bearing in mind that the reasonable grounds of belief must continue up to the time when the contract is made. There is thus a continuing obligation, of a kind which does not necessarily exist under common law liability for negligent misstatement.[1] The difficulties of discharging the burden can be seen in the *Howard Marine* case itself, where the marine manager's misquotation was based upon his recollection of the figure given in Lloyd's Register. His recollection was accurate but the figure in the Register was erroneous: the correct figure was contained in shipping documents which he had seen, but did not remember, and which were kept at the plaintiffs' London office (he was in the north-east of England when he gave the information).

[98] [1978] Q.B. 579 at 596.
[99] For convenience's sake we have used the term "negligent misrepresentation" to denote the claim under s.2(1), but this should be read bearing in mind the important words of Shaw and Bridge L.JJ. quoted above.
[1] See, *e.g. Argy Trading Development Co. Ltd.* v. *Lapid Developments Ltd.* [1977] 3 All E.R. 785, and pp. 77–78 *infra*.

A question that provoked some uncertainty until comparatively recently was, where the misrepresentation was made by an agent, whether or not the agent was personally liable under section 2(1). The matter was clarified in *The Skopas*[2] where Mustill J. held that the liability attaches to the principal only, as the Act was concerned with parties to a contract and with representations made in the particular context of a contract. Neither an agent nor a person acting on behalf of an agent could, therefore, be liable under section 2(1), though liability at common law for negligent misstatement could certainly attach to such persons under *Hedley Byrne & Co. Ltd.* v. *Heller & Partners Ltd..*[3]

The relatively straightforward nature of the task of establishing the fiction of fraud, together with the benefits of the reversed burden of proof once that initial hurdle has been surmounted, makes section 2(1) an attractive remedy for the representee. It should further be noted that damages under section 2(1) and rescission of the contract may be awarded. Thus, in *F. & H. Entertainments Ltd.* v. *Leisure Enterprises Ltd.*[4] the plaintiffs took assignments of the leases of certain premises from the defendants for £23,100 in reliance upon an innocent misrepresentation by the defendants that they had not received notices from their landlords, under the rent review clauses in the leases, of the landlords' desire to increase the rents. In fact, the defendants had received valid notices requesting substantial increases. The plaintiffs went into occupation and spent £4,000 equipping the premises for use. Shortly afterwards they learned of the increases, and sought rescission, repayment of the deposit and damages. It was held that they were entitled to all of these, as the defendants were unable to discharge the burden of proof imposed upon them by section 2(1). An inquiry was directed into damages, which were to cover all expenditure properly and not extravagantly incurred (and would therefore comprise most, if not all, of the £4,000). In such a case it is, of course, open to the court to award damages in lieu of rescission under section 2(2) of the Misrepresentation Act, and this power is discussed below.[5]

---

[2] *Resolute Maritime Inc. and another* v. *Nippon Kaiji Kyokai and others* [1983] 1 W.L.R. 857.

[3] [1964] A.C. 465. *Infra*, Chap. 4.

[4] (1976) 120 S.J. 331.

[5] *Infra*, pp. 52–54.

Measure of damages under section 2(1). The measure of damages under section 2(1) is said to be the same as the measure for fraud[6]: *i.e.* that the plaintiff must be put in the position he would have been in if the representation had not been made. This was emphasised in the *F. & H. Entertainments* case, where, as we have seen, Walton J. stated that the proper measure of damages covered all expenditure properly and not prematurely or extravagantly incurred. In *Andre & Cie* Ackner J. stated that the appropriate measure of damages for the victim of an innocent misrepresentation was tortious. In *McNally*, where the plaintiff suffered loss when the defendant misrepresented to him that his (*i.e.* the plaintiff's) qualifications and experience were appropriate for a job in Libya which the defendants offered to him, Sir Douglas Frank, following *Doyle* v. *Olby (Ironmongers) Ltd.*[7] held that all the damages flowing from the defendants' tortious act were recoverable, thereby apparently permitting a more extensive test for remoteness of damage than exists in cases of negligence.[8] This possible consequence of the fiction of fraud does not appear to have been taken up in any of the subsequent cases. In any event it is clear that the cause of action was regarded as tortious by the learned judge.

Nevertheless, a line of cases in the early years of the Act's life lends support to the notion that the measure of damages under section 2(1) is contractual rather than tortious, *i.e.* that the plaintiff is entitled to be put in the position in which he would have been if the representation had been true, and these will be examined before the most recent cases are discussed. In *Gosling* v. *Anderson*[9] the seller of a house stated erroneously to the purchaser that planning permission had been obtained for a garage on a part of the premises described in the contract as a "parking area." The buyer claimed damages under section 2(1) for the cost of storing her car elsewhere and travelling to collect it. To compensate such losses on a tortious basis would be quite unremarkable, but in addition the plaintiff sought to amend by claiming the difference in value of the property with and without planning permission for the garage. This would appear to reflect

---

[6] See *F. & H. Entertainments Ltd.* v. *Leisure Enterprises Ltd.* (1976) 120 S.J. 331 (Walton J.) *supra*, p. 48; *Andre & Cie S.A.* v. *Ets-Michel Blanc & Fils* [1977] 2 Lloyds Rep. 166 (Ackner J.); affirmed without reference to this point [1979] 2 Lloyds Rep. 427; *McNally* v. *Welltrade International Ltd.* [1978] I.R.L.R. 497 (Sir Douglas Frank).
[7] [1969] 2 Q.B. 158.
[8] *Cf.* the test in *Doyle* and that in *The Wagon Mound* [1961] A.C. 388.
[9] [1972] E.G.D. 709.

the contractual rather than the tortious measure, putting her in the position she would have been in if the statement had been true. Lord Denning M.R. was nevertheless prepared to permit this, and ordered an inquiry as to damages with the pleadings being amended so as to ascertain the difference in value.

In *Jarvis* v. *Swan's Tours*[10] Lord Denning M.R., in discussing the liability of a firm of travel agents for misrepresentations contained in their brochure said: "It is not necessary to decide whether they were representations or warranties: because since the Misrepresentation Act 1967 there is a remedy in damages for misrepresentation as well as for breach of warranty."[11] If Lord Denning meant no more by this statement than to underline the existence of the statutory remedy, as an alternative rather than an equivalent to the contractual remedy, his words are unexceptional. However, they are open to the interpretation that the measure of damages under section 2(1) is contractual, the same as those for breach of warranty, thereby admitting a claim for loss of bargain which the tortious measure would disallow.

More problematical still is the decision of Graham J. in *Watts* v. *Spence*.[12] The defendant and his wife were joint owners of a house which the plaintiff wished to purchase. The defendant, without his wife's knowledge, agreed to sell the house to the plaintiff. Subsequently, the wife having refused to join in the sale, the plaintiff sued for specific performance and alternatively damages for loss of bargain, either in breach of contract or under section 2(1). The claim for specific performance was unsuccessful, as, since the husband had no authority from his wife to sell her share of the house, she could not be compelled to convey. Under the rule in *Bain* v. *Fothergill*,[13] in the absence of fraud or bad faith, a claim for damages for failure to make good title to land is limited to the return of the deposit and the expenses of investigating title. Hence damages for loss of bargain in breach of contract could not be awarded. However, Graham J. held that the rule in *Bain* v.

[10] [1973] Q.B. 233.

[11] *Ibid.* at 237. In *Davis & Co.* v. *Afa-Minerva* [1974] 2 Lloyds Rep. 27, Judge Fay (sitting as a Deputy Judge) expressly relied on Lord Denning's dictum in *Jarvis*, in a case where the defendants had misrepresented the abilities of a burglar alarm system which they supplied to the plaintiffs. Damages were awarded for loss of stock which burglars took a considerable time to collect, a state of affairs which would have been obviated if the system had functioned as represented. However, such an award is consistent with either the tortious or the contractual measure of damages.

[12] [1976] Ch. 165.

[13] (1874) L.R. 7 (H.L.) 158. The Law Commission has recommended the abolition of the rule in *Bain* v. *Fothergill* Law Com. 166 Cm. 192 (1987).

Fothergill had nothing to do with the statutory action under section 2(1), and as a consequence held that damages for loss of bargain could be awarded under section 2(1).[14]

This seems[15] to have been based on the erroneous assumption that damages for loss of bargain can be recovered in a deceit action. It has been clear since the decision of the Court of Appeal in *Doyle* v. *Olby (Ironmongers) Ltd.*[16] that this is not the case, but that such damages are awarded on a *restitutio in integrum* basis. The reaction of commentators to the judgment in *Watts* v. *Spence* has been mixed,[17] but it was followed by Latey J. in *Errington* v. *Martell-Wilson (dec'd).*[18] Most recently, however, Mervyn Davies J. in *Sharneyford Supplies Ltd.* v. *Edge*[19] expressed his agreement with the comments in McGregor and said:

> "An action on the new statutory right is an action in which damages will be measured as in tort, not contract, and in tort, as I understand, loss of bargain damages may not, in every case, be recoverable."[20]

In *Sharneyford* the plaintiff brought a claim in breach of contract and misrepresentation against the defendant for failure to give vacant possession of a maggot farm that the defendant had agreed to sell to him. A preliminary issue was tried as to whether, if the plaintiff was entitled to damages, such a claim was limited to his expenses, under the rule in *Bain* v. *Fothergill*. The question of whether he was entitled to damages under section 2(1) also arose. It was held that he was entitled to his expenses only, applying *Bain* v. *Fothergill* to the contract claim, and to damages on a tortious basis under section 2(1).

It appears, therefore, that, subject on the one hand to the apparent approach of Lord Denning M.R. in two early cases under

---

[14] Curiously, however, Graham J. did not in fact adopt the true contractual measure of damages in *Watts*. He ordered an inquiry, to arrive at the value of the house at the dates of contract and completion, with the plaintiff being entitled to damages equal to the rise in value, if any, of the house between those dates. But the contract measure in a case of failure to convey comprises the difference between the price and the value of the house at the time fixed for completion.

[15] [1976] Ch. 165 at 174 and see also, *McGregor on Damages* (14th ed., 1980), para. 1487.

[16] [1969] 2 Q.B. 158.

[17] Compare McGregor *supra*, n. 15 paras. 1486–1489 with *Chitty on Contracts* (25th ed., 1983) para. 419.

[18] (1980) 130 N.L.J. 545.

[19] [1985] 1 All E.R. 976. Agreement with the criticism in McGregor of *Watts* v. *Spence* was also expressed by Balcombe L.J. in the Court of Appeal ([1987] Ch. 305 at 323).

[20] [1985] 1 All E.R. 976 at 990.

the Act and on the other hand to a seeming misunderstanding by Graham J. of the measure of damages in a deceit action, the proper measure of damages under section 2(1) is tortious. The Denning approach has largely been disregarded,[21] and the judgment of Mervyn Davies J. in *Sharneyford* has exposed the flaws of *Watts*.

(c) Section 2(2) of the Misrepresentation Act 1967

As a consequence of its recommendations concerning the availability of rescission after execution of the contract,[22] the Law Reform Committee was concerned to give greater flexibility to the court in granting rescission, so as to enable it to take account of the relative importance or insignificance of the facts represented.[23] It would be unfortunate and potentially unfair on the representor if rescission were the inevitable consequence of even the most trivial misrepresentation, and, as the Committee noted[24] the conflict between the remedies for misrepresentation and those for breach of contract would be exacerbated.

The Committee, therefore, recommended that wherever the court had the power to order rescission it should be empowered to award damages in the alternative if satisfied that this would provide adequate compensation to the plaintiff, bearing in mind the nature of the misrepresentation and the minor nature of the injury to him in comparison with the consequences of rescission, if awarded. This recommendation was given effect in section 2(2) of the Act, which reads as follows:

> "Where a person has entered into a contract after a misrepresentation has been made to him otherwise than fraudulently, and he would be entitled, by reason of the misrepresentation, to rescind the contract, then, if it is claimed, in any proceedings arising out of the contract, that the contract ought to be or has been rescinded, the court or arbitrator may declare the contract subsisting and award damages in lieu of rescission, if of opinion that it would be equitable to do so, having regard to the nature of the misrepresentation and the loss that would be caused by it if the contract were upheld, as well as to the loss that rescission would cause to the other party."

---

[21] See, as well as the cases cited at n.6 *supra*, the decision of the Court of Appeal in *Chesneau* v. *Interhome Ltd.* (*The Times*, June 7, 1983).

[22] *Supra*, p. 38

[23] Cmnd. 1782, para. 11.

[24] *Ibid.*

A number of comments on the subsection may be made. First, it should be noted that where the misrepresentation is made fraudulently section 2(2) does not apply and damages and rescission can be claimed. If the misrepresentation is made negligently, damages may be claimed under section 2(1) in accordance with the principles discussed above,[25] but if the representee wishes to rescind, his claim to do so will be subject to the exercise of the court's discretion under section 2(2). If the misrepresentation is wholly innocent, the representee's remedy will be entirely at the discretion of the court: either rescission (plus indemnity)[26] or damages in lieu.

A question that arises out of the wording of section 2(2) is whether "would be entitled, by reason of the misrepresentation, to rescind the contract" means that the right to rescind must have continued to exist until the date of the "proceeding arising out of the contract" or whether it is enough that the right existed after the representation was made. This matter was considered in *Alton House Garages (Bromley) Ltd.* v. *Monk*,[27] a case concerning the sale of a Rolls Royce, purportedly with its full service history. In fact, after the sale it transpired that the history provided related to another car. *Inter alia* the plaintiffs sought damages in lieu of rescission under section 2(2). Cantley J. noted that the wording of section 2(2) was "would be entitled . . . to rescind the contract" not "would have been entitled," and that the court's power arose if it was claimed that the contract "ought to be . . . rescinded" not "ought to have been or could have been rescinded." Consequently, it seemed to him that the sub-section was dealing with the situation at the time when the court was being asked to exercise its discretion to declare the contract subsisting and award damages in lieu of rescission, and if the party claiming rescission was not entitled to rescission, this option was not available to the court. In this particular case the plaintiffs had resold the car and thus their right to rescind was lost. Consequently, the court had no power to award damages in lieu of rescission.[28]

Measure of damages under section 2(2). The question of the measure of damages under section 2(2) has exercised the ingenuity of commentators without, as yet, troubling the courts. An important clue is contained in section 2(3) which reads:

---

[25] *Supra,* pp. 45–52.
[26] *Supra,* pp. 31–32.
[27] Lexis transcript. Hearing 31.7.81.
[28] *Cf.* Chitty *op. cit,* n. 17 *supra,* para. 435.

"Damages may be awarded against a person under subsection (2) of this section whether or not he is liable to damages under subsection (1) thereof, but where he is so liable any award under the said subsection (2) shall be taken into account in assessing his liability under the said subsection (1)."

This seems to imply that damages under section 2(2) will be less than those awarded under section 2(1), which, given that the representor in a section 2(2) case will be innocent, and in a section 2(1) case negligent, seems appropriate. Some kind of sub-tortious[29] measure of damages appears, therefore, to be applicable. There is no further clue in the Act as to how this is to be measured, save that damages under section 2(2) are in lieu of rescission and, therefore, are presumably designed to compensate the representee for the fact that the contract is not being rescinded: the monetary equivalent of the lost right to rescind is therefore at issue. The distinction between this and the tortious measure may lie in the extent to which consequential losses are to be compensated.[30] All reasonably foreseeable losses are compensated in tort, whereas rescission plus indemnity[31] is restricted to compensation for expenditure necessarily incurred as a result of entering into the contract. On this basis, the difference between section 2(1) damages and section 2(2) damages may be illustrated by considering the facts of a case such as *Whittington* v. *Seale-Hayne*.[32] Suppose that the plaintiff enters into a lease on the basis of innocent misrepresentations as to the state of sanitation of the premises, and incurs the expense of rates and rent under the provisions of the lease, and suffers illness because of the insanitary condition of the premises. The tortious measure of damages (*e.g.* if the misrepresentation had been made carelessly) would allow compensation for the illness as well as the obligations of the lease; the rescission plus indemnity measure would cover the latter only. In sum therefore, the representee in a section 2(2) claim would receive, in McGregor's words, "the difference between the value transferred and the value received, with the value received arrived at in the light of the obligations taken on . . . with no recovery being possible for consequential losses."[33]

---

[29] On the assumption that the measure of damages under s.2(1) is tortious: see pp. 49–52 *supra*.
[30] See *McGregor on Damages* (14th ed.) paras. 1491–1492.
[31] See, *e.g.* *Whittington* v. *Seale-Hayne* (1900) 82 L.T. 99 *supra*. pp. 31–32.
[32] (1900) 82 L.T. 49. *Supra*, pp. 31–32.
[33] *McGregor on Damages* (14th ed.) para. 1492.

3. EXCLUSION OF LIABILITY FOR MISREPRESENTATION

Clearly, the representor may seek to exclude or limit his liability for misrepresentation. His attempt to do so will be subject to section 3 of the 1967 Act.[34] This provides as follows:

> "If a contract contains a term which would exclude or restrict—
>
> (a) any liability to which a party to a contract may be subject by reason of any misrepresentation made by him before the contract was made; or
> (b) any remedy available to another party to the contract by reason of such a misrepresentation,
>
> that term shall be of no effect except in so far as it satisfies the requirement of reasonableness as stated in section 11(1) of the Unfair Contract Terms Act 1977; and it is for those claiming that the term satisfies that requirement to show that it does."

The requirement of reasonableness is as follows:

> 11. (1) "In relation to a contract term, the requirement of reasonableness for the purposes of this Part of this Act, section 3 of the Misrepresentation Act 1967 and section 3 of the Misrepresentation Act (Northern Ireland) 1967 is that the term shall have been a fair and reasonable one to be included having regard to the circumstances which were, or ought reasonably to have been, known to or in the contemplation of the parties when the contract was made."

Section 3 applies to both business and non-business liability (by contrast with attempts to exclude liability for collateral contracts or warranties and for negligent misstatement under *Hedley Byrne* v. *Heller*[35]). It should be noted that it will apply both to attempts to exclude or limit liabilities and to attempts to exclude or limit remedies. Thus, a purported barring of rescission would be covered, even though there was no attempt to exclude or restrict liability in damages. It has been argued[36] that the court may uphold the clause to the extent that it satisfies the requirement of

---

[34] Substituted by s.8 of the Unfair Contract Terms Act 1977. The essential difference between the old and the new s.3 is that under the former it was reliance upon the exempting term which had to be shown to be reasonable, whereas under the latter it is the term itself which must be shown to be reasonable.

[35] *Infra*, pp. 87–93; 118–121. For the definition of "business liability," see Chap. 5 p. 89 *infra*.

[36] See *Chitty on Contracts* (25th ed., 1983) para. 458.

reasonableness, and thus, in a case where it considered that it would be fair and reasonable to exclude damages but not fair and reasonable to exclude rescission, uphold to that extent a clause which purported to exclude both remedies.

As yet there has been little caselaw on section 3 (and that mainly on the section as originally drafted) but some indications of its ambit have emerged. An early decision was *Overbrooke Estates Ltd.* v. *Glencombe Properties Ltd.*[37] where conditions of sale at an auction provided that the vendors did not make representations and the auctioneers (the vendor's agent) had no authority to make representations. Brightman J. held that this was not a clause which excluded or restricted liability, but rather a public limitation of the otherwise ostensible authority of the agent, and consequently, the statutory control was inapplicable. Subsequently, in *Cremdean Properties Ltd.* v. *Nash*[38] Bridge L.J., while agreeing with the reasoning in *Overbrooke*, examined the general question of distinguishing between clauses which exclude liability and clauses which prevent liability from arising. In considering a clause in the form "notwithstanding any statement of fact included in these particulars the vendor shall be conclusively deemed to have made no representation within the meaning of the Misrepresentation Act 1967," he said:

> "I should have thought that that was only a form of words the intended and actual effect of which was to exclude or restrict liability, and I should not have thought that the courts would have been ready to allow such ingenuity in forms of language to defeat the plain purpose at which section 3 is aimed."[39]

The court is, therefore, likely to interpret restrictively attempts to elude liability by means of elaborate drafting. Thus, attempts to circumvent the statutory controls by means of clauses which require the representee to satisfy himself as to the correctness of representations have met with short shrift when examined in the light of the requirement of reasonableness. In *Howard Marine and Dredging Co. Ltd.* v. *A. Ogden & Sons (Excavations) Ltd.*,[40] the relevant clause stated:

---

[37] [1974] 1 W.L.R. 1335. This decision was on the original version of s.3, but is equally applicable to the section substituted by s.8 of the Unfair Contract Terms Act. See also, *Collins* v. *Howell-Jones* (1981) 259 E.G. 331.
[38] (1977) 244 E.G. 547.
[39] *Ibid.* at 551.
[40] [1978] Q.B. 574. For the facts of this case, see pp. 46–47 *supra*. Again this is a decision on the old s.3, but, at least on the majority view, this would appear to make no difference.

" . . . charterers acceptance of handing over the vessel shall be conclusive that they have examined the vessel and found her to be in all respects seaworthy, in good order and condition and in all respects fit for the intended and contemplated use by the charterers and in every other way satisfactory to them."

Bridge L.J. considered that such a clause was to be narrowly construed and could only be relied upon as conclusive evidence that the charterers were satisfied about such aspects of the vessel as would be apparent on an ordinary examination. As the misrepresentation concerned the deadweight capacity of the vessel, the clause failed, though, even if it could have been construed so as to cover the misrepresentation, it would not have been fair and reasonable. Shaw L.J. agreed.[41]

The court's critical approach to such clauses is likely to be especially manifest where the representee is a private person dealing with a corporate representor. In *South Western General Property Co.* v. *Marton*[42] the defendant (a builder purchasing a site on which to build a home for himself) purchased land at an auction. The agreement included the following statement: "any intending purchaser must satisfy himself by inspection or otherwise as to the correctness of each statement contained in the particulars." Again, this was held not to satisfy the requirement of reasonableness,[43] especially given that the defendant was a householder buying for his own purposes, rather than a property speculator, *vis-à-vis* whom the clauses might well have been reasonable.

Even the fact that the clause is a common-form clause will not necessarily protect it. In *Walker* v. *Boyle*[44] condition 17 of the National Conditions of Sale (19th ed.) was held to be unreasonable under section 3. The relevant wording of the condition was as follows: "no error, mis-statement or omission in any preliminary answer concerning the property . . . shall annul the sale, nor (. . .) shall any damages be payable, or compensation allowed by either party, in respect thereof." As Dillon J. noted, the National

---

[41] Lord Denning M.R. however regarded reliance on the clause as being fair and reasonable, as the charterers had had full inspection and examination of the vessel. See Yates and Hawkins, *Standard Business Contracts* (Sweet & Maxwell, 1986) pp. 141–142.

[42] (1982) 263 E.G. 1090.

[43] It may be that the judge did not, in any event, consider that the statement formed part of the contract: this does not emerge clearly from the judgment.

[44] [1982] 1 W.L.R. 495.

Conditions of Sale were not the product of negotiations between the conflicting interests in a house purchase transaction, and in his view condition 17's precarious survival over the years did not qualify it for the title of fairness and reasonableness. Dillon J. also made short shrift of the following words appearing above the replies on the form of preliminary enquiries: "These replies on behalf of the Vendor are believed to be correct but accuracy is not guaranteed and they do not obviate the need to make appropriate searches, enquiries and inspections." These words could not be used to negative a representation of fact made in a reply to preliminary enquiries, and Dillon J. thus ignored them. The courts have, therefore, proved resistant thus far to purported exclusions of liability for misrepresentation, both on the question of whether such a clause forms part of the agreement between the parties and on the question of whether, if part of the contract, the clause satisfies the requirement of reasonableness.

Fraud

Spencer Bower and Turner take the view[45] that it would be difficult to persuade a court to allow an agreement to nullify the effect of a fraudulent misrepresentation. This view is borne out by the decision of the House of Lords in *S. Pearson & Son Ltd.* v. *Dublin Corporation.*[46] The plaintiff contractors were induced to enter into a contract for the construction of sewage works by statements by the defendants that an old wall existed. This led them to tender at a lesser sum than would otherwise have been the case. The defendants' statements were made in the knowledge of their falsity, or recklessly. The contracts contained clauses to the effect that the contractors should not rely on any representation made in plans or elsewhere but should ascertain and judge the facts for themselves. Lord Loreburn L.C. said: "Now it seems clear that no one can escape liability for his own fraudulent statements by inserting in a contract a clause that the other party shall not rely upon them."[47] Lord James agreed emphatically:

> "When the fraud succeeds, surely those who designed the fraudulent protection cannot take advantage of it. Such a clause would be good protection against any mistake or miscalculation, but fraud vitiates every contract and every clause in it."[48]

---

[45] *Actionable Misrepresentation* (3rd ed., 1974), p. 221.
[46] [1907] A.C. 351.
[47] *Ibid.* at 353–354.
[48] *Ibid.* at 362.

As the latter quotation indicates, it was possible at common law to exclude liability for mistake and innocent misrepresentation, as was emphasised in *Boyd and Forrest* v. *Glasgow and South Western Rail Co.*,[49] but as that decision also indicates, public policy militates very strongly against allowing liability in deceit to be excluded.

---

[49] 1915 S.C. 20. Also, see Law Reform Committee 10th Report, *Innocent Misrepresentation* Cmnd. 1782 (1962) para. 23.

Chapter 4

NEGLIGENT MISSTATEMENT[1]

Twenty years ago the House of Lords held that in certain circumstances tortious liability could exist for a carelessly made untrue statement that caused pure economic loss. Before we examine the various elements of this liability, its role in the law of tort and in the law of obligations generally, and its implications, it is worth considering briefly the background against which this decision was reached.

1. The Law Prior to Hedley Byrne v. Heller

If fraud could be established against the maker of an untrue statement, it had long been clear that an action for damages would lie in the tort of deceit. *Derry* v. *Peek*[2] underlined the difficulties of establishing the necessary state of mind in the representor and the paucity of case law over the years further evidences these difficulties. In addition it was argued that *Derry* v. *Peek* denied the possibility of liability for a negligent misrepresentation. This interpretation was adopted in *Le Lievre* v. *Gould*,[3] where the Court of Appeal held that a surveyor, not contractually bound to the plaintiff mortgagees of a builder's interest under a building agreement, owed no duty of care to them in relation to certificates attesting that certain specified stages in the progress of the buildings had been reached. Bowen L.J. said[4]:

> "Negligent misrepresentation does not amount to deceit, and negligent misrepresentation can give rise to a cause of action only if a duty lies upon the defendant not to be negligent, and in that class of case of which *Derry* v. *Peek* was one, the House of Lords considered that the circumstances raised no such duty . . . the law of England . . . does not consider that what a man writes on paper is like a gun or other dangerous instrument, and, unless he intended to deceive, the law does

[1] For the sake of clarity the tortious claim under *Hedley Byrne* v. *Heller* will hereafter be referred to as "negligent misstatement": the claim under s.2(1) of the Misrepresentation Act is referred to as "negligent misrepresentation."
[2] (1889) 14 App.Cas. 337. See Chap. 3 *supra*, pp. 40–41.
[3] [1893] 1 Q.B. 491.
[4] *Ibid.* at 501, 502.

not, in the absence of contract, hold him responsible for drawing his certificate carelessly."

The decision of Chitty J. in *Cann* v. *Willson*.[5] holding a valuer liable to a mortgagee for careless misstatements in a valuation for mortgage purposes, where the valuer himself put the valuation before the mortgagee's solicitor, was overruled as being inconsistent with *Derry* v. *Peek*.

However, the problem posed by the inability of plaintiff representees to establish the absence of honest belief in the truth of their statements on the part of representors was slightly mitigated by the decision of the House of Lords in *Nocton* v. *Lord Ashburton*[6] where it was held that, in the absence of fraud, damages could be awarded for breach of duty arising out of a fiduciary relationship such (as was the case in *Nocton*) as that between a solicitor and his client. Otherwise, outside the law of contract,[7] the representor was immune from liability in damages.

The decision of the House of Lords in *Donoghue* v. *Stevenson*[8] might have been thought of as affording assistance to the representee. In that case Lord Atkin said[9]:

> "You must take reasonable care to avoid acts or omissions which you can reasonably foresee would be likely to injure your neighbour. Who then in law is my neighbour? The answer seems to be—persons who are so closely and directly affected by my act that I ought reasonably to have them in contemplation as being so affected when I am directing my mind to the acts or omissions which are being called in question."

These words might have appeared to provide a basis for a claim against the maker of a negligent misstatement.

Such, though, was not the view of the majority of the Court of Appeal in *Candler* v. *Crane, Christmas & Co.*[10] The plaintiff was considering the investment of a sum of money in a company. He wished to see the accounts, and the defendants, the company's accountants, were informed of this. The accounts were duly prepared and shown to the plaintiff. In fact, the accounts had been prepared carelessly and gave an entirely misleading impression of

---

[5] (1889) 39 Ch.D. 39. *Cann* v. *Willson* was decided after the decision of the Court of Appeal in *Derry* v. *Peek* but before the hearing in the House of Lords.
[6] [1914] A.C. 932.
[7] See Chap. 5 *infra*.
[8] [1932] A.C. 562.
[9] *Ibid.* at 580.
[10] [1951] 2 K.B. 164.

the state of the company. The plaintiff, who invested £2,000 in the company, subsequently lost his money when the company was wound up in the following year. He sued the accountants for negligence, based on the misstatements contained in the accounts. The Court of Appeal considered that if the House of Lords in *Donoghue* had intended to overrule *Le Lievre* v. *Gould* they would have said so. Asquith L.J. said[11]:

> "The inference seems to me to be that Lord Atkin continued to accept the distinction between liability in tort for careless (but non-fraudulent) misstatements and liability in tort for some other forms of carelessness, and that his formula defining 'who is my neighbour' must be read subject to his acceptance of this overriding distinction."

Denning L.J., in a notable dissenting judgment, considered that the decisions in *Donoghue* and *Nocton* entitled the Court of Appeal to examine the law afresh. He considered that persons, such as accountants, who exercised professional skills and had special knowledge, owed a duty of care to those who were closely and directly affected by their work, even in the absence of a contract. This duty was owed only to those persons to whom, to take the example of accountants, the accounts were shown by the accountants or to whom the accountants knew their employer would show the accounts. This covered the facts of the instant case, and consequently he was prepared to find the defendants liable.

However, the majority view continued to prevail, at least as regards negligent misstatements resulting in economic loss. The statement of Asquith L.J. quoted above appeared broad enough to exclude recovery for physical damage to persons or property consequent upon a negligent misstatement. However, this view was not accepted by Salmon J. in *Clayton* v. *Woodman & Son (Builders) Ltd.*[12] and he held a firm of architects liable for injuries sustained by the plaintiff bricklayer as a consequence of negligent instructions given by them to him. It has been accepted since then that Salmon J's view that such cases fall within the general principles of *Donoghue* v. *Stevenson* is the correct one.

The problem, as Denning L.J. recognised in his judgment in *Candler*, is that of the need to restrict the range of potential

---

[11] *Ibid.* at 190.
[12] [1962] 2 Q.B. 533 (reversed on the facts [1962] 2 Q.B. 546). See also, *Clay* v. *A. J. Crump & Sons Ltd.* [1964] 1 Q.B. 533; *Wyong Shire Council* v. *Shirt* (1980) 20 A.L.J.R. 217. However, if a misstatement were to create a risk of potentially indeterminate physical damage, the court might seek to delimit the duty of care.

plaintiffs and potential defendants. As Lord Reid stated in the landmark decision of the House of Lords, *Hedley Byrne & Co. Ltd.* v. *Heller & Partners Ltd.*[13]

> "...the law must treat negligent words differently from negligent acts... Quite careful people often express definite opinions on social or informal occasions even when they see that others are likely to be influenced by them; and they often do that without taking that care which they would take if asked for their opinion professionally in a business connection... But it is at least unusual casually to put into circulation negligently made articles which are dangerous."

Lord Reid went on to say[14]:

> "Another obvious difference is that a negligently made article will only cause one accident and so it is not very difficult to find the necessary degree of proximity or neighbourhood between the negligent manufacturer and the person injured. But words can be broadcast with or without the consent or the foresight of the speaker or writer."

Both these factors relate to the nature of statements, as distinct from acts,[15] as indicating the need for, at best, a duty of care which is in some way narrower than the neighbour principle stated in *Donoghue* v. *Stevenson*. Another relevant factor is the nature of the loss. Liability for pure economic loss in the law of negligence had not been admitted prior to *Hedley Byrne* v. *Heller*. We shall have to consider the policy reasons behind this restriction and the relationship between statements and acts in detail later on in this chapter. For now it may be enough to quote Lord Pearce[16]:

> "Economic protection has lagged behind protection in physical matters where there is injury to person and property. It may be that the size and the width of the range of possible claims has acted as a deterrent to extension of economic protection."

2. THE DECISION IN HEDLEY BYRNE V. HELLER

Thus, if liability were to be imposed for a negligent misstatement, some way would have to be found of delimiting the duty of care so

[13] [1964] A.C. 465 at 482–483.
[14] *Ibid.* at 483. See also, the judgment of Lord Pearce at 534.
[15] On the question whether such a distinction can validly be made, see Craig (1976) 92 L.Q.R. 213 and *infra* pp. 93–94.
[16] [1964] A.C. 465 at 536–537.

as to take account of these factors. The House of Lords took advantage of the opportunity to do so presented to them in the case of *Hedley Byrne & Co. Ltd.* v. *Heller & Partners Ltd.*[17] The appellants were advertising agents who were instructed by Easipower Ltd. to book television and newspaper advertising space on their behalf. This would have to be done on the basis that the appellants were liable on the contracts.[18] In order to satisfy themselves as to Easipower's creditworthiness, Hedley Byrne contacted their bankers and asked them to inquire as to Easipower's financial position. The bankers contacted Hellers, who were the bankers of Easipower. When asked whether Easipower would be good for an advertising contract for £8,000–£9,000 Hellers stated that they believed Easipower to be respectably consolidated and good for its normal business engagements. Three months later, in response to an inquiry from Hedley Byrne's bankers as to whether Easipower was trustworthy in the way of business to the extent of £100,000 per annum advertising contract, Hellers repeated that Easipower was respectably consolidated and considered good for its ordinary business engagements. They added that the figures were larger than they were accustomed to see. In the case of each response by Hellers the information was said to be given "without responsibility." In reliance upon the references, Hedley Byrne placed orders which resulted in a loss of over £17,000. They claimed damages from Hellers on the basis of breach of a duty of care.[19]

The decision of the House of Lords went against Hedley Byrne on the basis that the giving of the information "without responsibility" precluded the possibility of liability. However, their Lordships held that in appropriate circumstances there could be liability in tort for a negligent misstatement. *Chandler* was overruled. *Le Lievre* was explained and not followed. In the words of Lord Devlin[20]: "It may be that the decision on the facts was correct even though the reasoning was too wide." *Derry* v. *Peek* was explained as not authorising the proposition that, in the absence of contract there could be no liability for a negligent misstatement. *Nocton* v. *Lord Ashburton* clearly indicated that there might be circumstances in which a duty could be

---

[17] [1964] A.C. 465.
[18] The television companies insisted that agents such as Hedley Byrne had to become *del credere* agents. See Stevens (1964) 27 M.L.R. 121 at 123.
[19] An allegation of fraud was abandoned at an early stage in the proceedings.
[20] [1964] A.C. 465 at 519.

imposed. Lord Reid quoted[21] Lord Haldane, in *Robinson* v. *National Bank of Scotland Ltd.*[22]:

> "I think, as I said in *Nocton's* case, that an exaggerated view was taken by a good many people of the scope of the decision in *Derry* v. *Peek*. The whole of the doctrine as to fiduciary relationships, as to the duty of care arising from implied as well as express contracts, as to the duty of care arising from other special relationships which the courts may find to exist in particular cases, still remains, and I should be very sorry if any word fell from me which should suggest that the courts are in any way hampered in recognising that the duty of care may be established when such cases really occur."

Lord Reid took up the "special relationships" point, and went on to say[23]:

> "...I can see no logical stopping place short of those relationships where it is plain that the party seeking information or advice was trusting the other to exercise such a degree of care as the circumstances required, where it was reasonable for him to do that, and where the other gave the information or advice when he knew or ought to have known that the inquirer was relying on him."

Lord Morris, who agreed with his colleagues that the Court of Appeal in *Le Lievre* v. *Gould* was wrong to overrule *Cann* v. *Wilson*, also quoted Lord Haldane as indicating the existence of a duty, quite apart from a fiduciary or a contractual duty, to exercise care in the making of a statement. After reviewing the authorities he went on to say[24]:

> "My lords, I consider that it follows and that it should now be regarded as settled that if someone possessed of a special skill undertakes, quite irrespective of contract, to apply that skill for the assistance of another person who relies upon such skill, a duty of care will arise ... Furthermore, if in a sphere in which a person is so placed that others could reasonably rely upon his judgment or his skill or his ability to make careful inquiry, a person takes it upon himself to give information or advice to, or allows his information or advice to be passed on to, another person who, as he knows or should know, will place reliance upon it, then a duty of care will arise."

[21] *Ibid.* at 486.
[22] 1916 S.C. (H.L.) 154, 157.
[23] [1964] A.C. 465 at 486.
[24] *Ibid.* at 502–503.

Lord Hodson agreed with his colleagues that the duty should be expressed in general rather than specific terms. He agreed with Lord Morris that reasonable reliance upon judgment, skill or ability to make careful inquiry was the essence of the duty, but did not "think it is possible to catalogue the special features which must be found to exist before the duty of care will arise in a given case."[25]

Lord Devlin agreed that the effect of *Nocton* v. *Lord Ashburton* was that, outside contract, there could be a special relationship between parties which imposed a duty to give careful advice and accurate information. It was open to the House in the instant case to say to what cases, beyond the breach of a fiduciary obligation that was the situation in *Nocton*, this principle applied. In his view the problem created by the facts of *Hedley Byrne* was a by-product of the doctrine of consideration. A nominal charge by the respondents for their advice would have had the effect of rendering them liable in contract. However, his Lordship did not accept that it followed that there was no liability for the careless performance of a gratuitous service. In his view there was:

"... ample authority to justify your Lordships in saying now that the categories of special relationships which may give rise to a duty to take care in word as well as in deed are not limited to contractual relationships or to relationships of fiduciary duty, but include also relationships which in the words of Lord Shaw in *Nocton* v. *Lord Ashburton* are 'equivalent to contract,' that is, where there is an assumption of responsibility in circumstances in which, but for the absence of consideration, there would be a contract.... It is a responsibility that is voluntarily accepted or undertaken, either generally where a general relationship, such as that of solicitor and client or banker and customer, is created, or specifically in relation to a particular transaction."[26]

The fact that there had to be a voluntary undertaking to assume responsibility was of great importance, as the disclaiming of responsibility in the particular case was the reason for the dismissal of the appeal. He went on to say[27]:

"I shall therefore content myself with the proposition that whenever there is a relationship equivalent to contract, there is a duty of care.... Where there is a general relationship [*e.g.*

[25] *Ibid.* at 514.
[26] *Ibid.* at 528–529.
[27] *Ibid.* at 530.

of solicitor and client]...it is unnecessary to do more than prove its existence and the duty follows. Where, as in the present case, what is relied on is a particular relationship created ad hoc, it will be necessary to examine the particular facts to see whether there is an express or implied undertaking of responsibility."

Lord Pearce considered that, for a duty to arise, "the representation must normally, I think, concern a business or professional transaction whose nature makes clear the gravity of the inquiry and the importance and influence attached to the answer."[28] This seems to emphasise the notion of a special skill and the circumstances in which such a skill is exercised. He regarded the form of the inquiry and the answer as being of especial significance.

But for the disclaimer it is very likely that liability would have been imposed in *Hedley Byrne*. Hellers were professionals possessed of a special skill, who knew that Hedley Byrne would be the recipients of their information, even though it was not immediately addressed to them. The reliance of Hedley Byrne upon such information was clearly reasonable[29] and they suffered loss as a result. Though the relationship was "particular," in the sense in which Lord Devlin used the word, rather than "general," the circumstances, in the absence of a disclaimer, would surely have been such that the court would have found an implied undertaking of responsibility. The only possible restriction upon this lies in the judgments of Lord Morris[30] and Lord Hodson[31] where it is suggested that the only duty accepted and therefore owed by a banker giving a reference as to credit-worthiness is that of honesty.

The words of Lord Reid quoted above[32] on the rationale for the distinction between words and acts were echoed by Lord Pearce[33]:

"Words are more volatile than deeds. They travel fast and far afield. They are used without being expended and take effect in combination with innumerable facts and other words. Yet they are dangerous and can cause vast financial damage.... If the mere hearing or reading of words were held to create proximity, there might be no limit to the persons to whom the

---

[28] *Ibid.* at 539.
[29] Though see Weir [1963] C.L.J. 216 at 218.
[30] [1964] A.C. 465 at 504.
[31] *Ibid.* at 513.
[32] *Supra*, p. 64.
[33] [1964] A.C. 465 at 534. But *cf.* Lord Morris at p. 496.

speaker could be liable. Damage by negligent acts to persons or property on the other hand is more viable and obvious."

Given the general acceptance by the House of Lords of this rationale, it was clear that the general "neighbour" test in *Donoghue* v. *Stevenson* could not serve. A narrower, yet sufficiently flexible test was necessary: the "special relationship" provided the necessary control device whereby the floodgates could remain closed,[34] and yet did not unduly restrict the categories of persons who could be liable for negligent misstatements.

3. LIABILITY FOR NEGLIGENT MISSTATEMENT AFTER HEDLEY BYRNE

We now have to consider the application and development of this doctrine over the ensuing 20 years. As we have seen[35] the enactment of the Misrepresentation Act in 1967 has had a significant impact upon the law of misrepresentation generally, and, as we shall see, the development of liability for economic loss resulting from careless words has had implications for claims where economic loss has resulted from a careless act. These matters aside, the courts have had many misstatement cases before them since *Hedley Byrne* and these provide a good opportunity to analyse the doctrine and attempt to indicate its limits.

An early decision was that in *W. B. Anderson & Sons Ltd.* v. *Rhodes (Liverpool) Ltd. and others.*[36] The defendants were importers and wholesalers in the Liverpool fruit and vegetable market. In addition they sometimes carried on business as commission agents. The plaintiffs were companies carrying on similar importing and wholesale businesses to that of the defendants. The defendants did business with T. Ltd., to whom they sold vegetables on credit. The defendants did not realise, as time went by, that T. Ltd.'s. account was excessively overdue. This unawareness was due to the great slackness of the defendants' accounting system. The considerable state of indebtedness continued, and the defendants began to act as commission agents for T. Ltd., *i.e.* they effected contracts on the market between T. Ltd.

---

[34] The spectre of liability "in an indeterminate amount for an indefinite time and to an indeterminate class" (*per* Cardozo C.J. in *Ultramares Corporation* v. *Touche* (1931) 255 N.Y.Rep. 170) still tends to haunt the judiciary, with particular reference to liability for pure economic loss. But see the judgment of Lord Roskill in *Junior Books Ltd.* v. *Veitchi Co. Ltd.* [1982] A.C. 520 at 545–546.

[35] *Supra.* Chap. 3.

[36] [1967] 2 All E.R. 850.

and other suppliers, receiving a commission from T. Ltd. The plaintiffs asked them whether T. Ltd. were reliable, the defendants inferred that they were creditworthy. T. Ltd. later became insolvent, and were unable to pay for potatoes purchased and delivered to them by the plaintiffs.

Cairns J. held the defendants liable. The representation, though not made by professional advisers, concerned a business transaction whose nature made clear the seriousness of the inquiry and the importance and influence attached to the answers. There was reasonable reliance upon the judgment and skill of the defendants. The learned judge did not consider, on the authority of *Hedley Byrne*, that the duty of care could arise only in the case of professional men, and consequently, he held the defendants liable.

This decision seems perfectly consistent with the decision in *Hedley Byrne*. A commentator on the decision identified five factual elements which made the case a clear one for extending the principle beyond the professional adviser:

> "(1) a serious business inquiry (2) concerning an immediate identified transaction (3) in which the defendants had a direct financial interest (4) about which the defendants, who were respected traders, were in a position to know more than the plaintiffs, and (5) where it was obvious to all concerned that the answers given by the defendants were going to be relied on by the plaintiffs as a major inducement in completing the transaction."[37]

However, the development of liability for negligent misstatement appeared to be restricted by the decision of the Privy Council in *Mutual Life and Citizens Assurance Co. Ltd.* v. *Evatt.*[38] The respondent was a policy-holder in the appellant insurance company. He sought information and advice from the appellants concerning the financial stability of a company (Palmer) and the safety of investments in Palmer. Palmer was, like the appellants, a subsidiary company of M.L.C. Ltd. The appellants gratuitously gave the respondent information and advice concerning Palmer, stating that the company was financially stable and would continue to be so. Also, they stated that it would be safe to make further investments in Palmer. Mr. Evatt invested in Palmer as a consequence of this advice, and suffered financial loss. He sued Mutual Life under *Hedley Byrne*.

---

[37] Michael Dean (1968) 31 M.L.R. 322 at 324.
[38] [1971] A.C. 793. See now *Shaddock & Associations Pty.* v. *Parramatta City Council (No. 1)* (1980–81) 150 C.L.R. 225.

The case went on appeal from the High Court of Australia to the Judicial Committee of the Privy Council, where the Board was split three to two. The difference of opinion focused on the ambit of the decision in *Hedley Byrne*. The majority was of the view that, in the words of Lord Diplock, who delivered the judgment of the majority[39]:

> "[the absence of an] averment that the company to the knowlege of Mr Evatt carried on the business of giving advice upon investments or in some way had let it be known to him that they claimed to possess the necessary skill and competence to do so and were prepared to exercise the necessary diligence to give reliable advice to him upon the subject matter of his inquiry".

was fatal to Mr. Evatt's claim.

This view of the ambit of *Hedley Byrne* derived from the ancient maxim that those persons following a calling requiring skill and competence are obliged to exercise in their calling such reasonable skill and competence as is appropriate to the calling. The duty arises from the fact that in holding himself out as following such a calling, the person (lawyer, doctor, banker, etc.) has let it be known that he claims to have the skill of the reasonably competent practitioner of that particular calling. The majority did not consider:

> "that the duty to comply with that objective standard should be extended to an adviser who, at the time at which the advice is sought, has not let it be known to the advisee that he claims to possess the standard of skill and competence and is prepared to exercise diligence which is generally shown by persons who carry on the business of giving advice of the kind sought."[40]

The only duty incumbent upon Mutual Life in the circumstances was a duty to be honest. The decision in *Low* v. *Bouverie*[41] was regarded as significant. In that case a trustee was held not to be liable to a person inquiring about incumbrances upon the life interest of the beneficiary under the trust. The trustee mentioned certain incumbrances, but did not mention six prior mortgages, whose existence he had forgotten.

Three members of the House of Lords who had sat in the *Hedley Byrne* appeal also sat in *Mutual Life*. Only one of these, Lord

---

[39] [1971] A.C. 793 at 809.
[40] [1971] A.C. 793 at 804.
[41] [1891] 3 Ch. 82. See Chap. 6, pp. 131–134 *infra*.

Hodson, was a member of the majority. Lord Reid and Lord Morris, in the minority in *Mutual Life*, found themselves in the unusual position of effectively having their own judgments in *Hedley Byrne* explained to them. They were "unable to construe the passages from our speeches cited in the judgment of the majority in the way in which they are there construed."[42] They raised relevant questions about the nature of the skill or competence that, according to the majority, the maker of a statement must have in order to be liable.

> "But then how much skill or competence must he have? Even a man with a professional qualification is seldom an expert on all matters dealt with by members of his profession. Must the adviser be an expert or specialist in the matter on which his advice is sought?"[43]

They did not agree that a duty to take care is the same as a duty to conform to a particular standard or skill. *Low* v. *Bouverie* concerned a person acting in his private capacity as a trustee, and the minority considered that in general a duty of care would only be imposed upon a adviser acting in the course of his business or professional activities. Also, the statements made by the trustee apparently went no further than stating the position to the extent of the trustee's recollection rather than operating as assertions of the truth of the statements.

> "In our judgment when an inquirer consults a business man in the course of his business and makes it plain to him that he is seeking considered advice and intends to act on it in a particular way, any reasonable business man would realise that if he chooses to give advice without any warning or qualification, he is putting himself under a moral obligation to take some care. It appears to us to be well within the principles established by the *Hedley Byrne* case to regard his action in giving such advice as creating a special relationship between him and the inquirer and to translate his moral obligation into a legal obligation to take such care as is reasonable in the whole circumstances."[44]

Essentially, therefore, the majority in *Mutual Life* regarded the *Hedley Byrne* principle as applying to cases where the statement was made in the ordinary course of a business or profession involving the giving of advice of a kind calling for special skill or

[42] [1971] A.C. 793 at 813.
[43] *Ibid.* at 812.
[44] *Ibid.*

competence; or where the adviser, although not carrying on the particular skilled business or profession nevertheless makes it clear before or at the time when his advice is given that he claims to possess skill or competence comparable to that of the practitioner of the particular business or profession and will exercise comparable skill and competence; or where the adviser has a financial interest in the transaction.[45]

The decision caused a degree of concern that the general principle of liability for negligent misstatements expounded in *Hedley Byrne* was being unduly restricted. Certainly, on the facts of the case, if the court was not prepared to imply a holding out of equivalent skill or competence by reason of the giving of the advice, the decision did limit the ambit of *Hedley Byrne* and in any case where advice not strictly the business of the adviser was given without an express claim to equivalent skill or competence, if liability were held not to exist, this might operate with unfortunate consequences for inquirers. A solicitor who habitually provided advice on investments might escape liability if he made no claim to possessing the equivalent skills of a stockbroker, yet a litigation lawyer who gave tax advice for the first time in his life might be liable.

Although the House of Lords has not had the opportunity since then to pronounce on the merits of the judgment in *Mutual Life*, other courts have considered that case and its impact on *Hedley Byrne*. The treatment of the majority view in *Mutual Life* in those decisions has been critical and the minority view has been preferred. Several of these decisions are of especial interest and importance in the development of liability for negligent misstatement, and fall to be examined in the following paragraphs.

In 1976 the Court of Appeal had the opportunity to state its preference between the majority and minority views in *Mutual Life* in the case of *Esso Petroleum Co. Ltd.* v. *Mardon*.[46] The plaintiffs wished to use a site in Southport as a filling station. An experienced employee estimated a throughput of petrol of 200,000 gallons a year, based upon the fronting of the forecourt and the pumps on to a busy main road. However, the planning requirements subsequently made by the local corporation sited the pumps and forecourt at the back of the site, with access from side streets

---

[45] See *W. B. Anderson & Sons Ltd.* v. *Rhodes (Liverpool) Ltd.* [1967] 2 All E.R. 850, *supra*, pp. 69–70. It is not made clear how immediate the financial interest must be for liability to be imposed. Presumably Mutual Life, who were members of the same group as Palmer, would incur some kind of indirect financial benefit from the investment made by Mr. Evatt.

[46] [1976] 1 Q.B. 801. See also, Chap. 5.

only. Despite this, the figure for the estimated throughput was not altered. The defendant, a prospective tenant, was persuaded by the estimate to enter into a tenancy agreement with the plaintiffs. The actual throughput proved to be under 80,000 gallons, the defendant was unable to pay for petrol supplied and the plaintiffs issued a writ claiming possession, moneys owed and mesne profits. The defendant counterclaimed for damages for breach of warranty and, in the alternative, for negligent misstatement.

At first instance, Lawson J. favoured the minority judgment in *Mutual Life*.[47] He considered that the majority view:

> "that the duty of care relating to statements is limited to people who are carrying on, or holding themselves out as carrying on, the business of giving advice in relation to the subject matter of the statements which they make" was "unduly restrictive of the duty under consideration; I much prefer the minority reasoning of Lord Reid and Lord Morris."[48]

He held that the statement as to the throughput was not a warranty, but that there was liability for negligent misstatement, and the defendant, therefore, succeeded on the counterclaim.

The Court of Appeal allowed Mr. Mardon's appeal against the judge's decision that the statement was not a warranty, and dismissed Esso's appeal against the finding of liability in negligence. We shall examine here the judgment only in so far as it pertains to liability for negligent misstatements.

Ormrod L.J. endorsed Lawson J.'s preference for the minority judgment in *Mutual Life*. Shaw L.J. implicitly did so, it may be argued, when, referring to the trial judge's holding that Esso owed Mr. Mardon a duty of care, he said[49]: "I agree entirely with the reasons and conclusions of the judge on this part of the case." Lord Denning M.R. seemed more inclined to the majority *Mutual Life* view when he said[50]:

> "It seems to me that [*Hedley Byrne*], properly understood, covers this particular proposition: if a man, who has or professes to have special knowledge or skill, makes a representation by virtue thereof to another—be it advice, information or opinion—with the intention of inducing him to

[47] [1975] Q.B. 819. Even if he had accepted the majority view he would have held that there was a special relationship because the plaintiffs had a financial interest in the advice that they gave.
[48] [1975] Q.B. 819 at 830.
[49] *Ibid*. at 832.
[50] *Ibid*. at 820.

enter into a contract with him, he is under a duty to use reasonable care to see that the representation is correct, and that the advice, information or opinion is reliable.... This proposition is in line with what I said in [*Candler*] which was approved by the majority of the Privy Council in [*Mutual Life*]."

The primary function of the Esso Petroleum Co. is not the giving of advice. If the majority view in *Mutual Life* confines potential liability to those whose business is solely the giving of advice, *Esso* departs from this, and it is suggested, rightly so. However, it is surely difficult to deny, particularly in circumstances such as those in *Esso*, that the giving of advice forms a very significant part of the company's business. Given that, the decision is explicable in terms of the majority judgment in *Mutual Life*[51] but the lack of a clear consensus in the Court of Appeal favouring the minority view makes it, at best, a shaky authority for that view.

4. HEDLEY BYRNE AND CONTRACT

A further significance of the *Esso Petroleum* case, which has had considerable consequences over the ensuing decade, stems from the fact that Esso and Mr. Mardon were in a contractual relationship. Was the contract the sole governor of their relationship, such that the question of negligence liability could not arise? The court held, in effect, that there could be concurrent liability. Lord Denning stated[52]:

"...in the case of a professional man, the duty to use reasonable care arises not only in contract, but is also imposed by the law apart from contract, and is therefore actionable in tort." Thus "if he negligently gives unsound advice or misleading information or expresses an erroneous opinion, and thereby induces the other side to enter into a contract with him, he is liable in damages."[53]

Negligence in the course of precontractual negotiations is therefore actionable. In *Midland Bank Trust Co. Ltd.* v. *Hett Stubbs & Kemp*[54] Oliver J. relied on the decision in *Esso Petroleum* v. *Mardon* in finding that a solicitor could be concurrently liable in contract and in tort to his client. The solicitor in

[51] See Gravells (1976) 39 M.L.R. 462 at 465.
[52] [1976] Q.B. 801 at 819.
[53] *Ibid.* at 820. See also, *Box* v. *Midland Bank Ltd.* [1979] 2 Lloyd's Rep. 391.
[54] [1979] Ch. 384. See also, *Batty* v. *Metropolitan Property Realisations Ltd.* [1978] Q.B. 554.

that case negligently failed to register an option as an estate contract under the Land Charges Act 1925 and was sued by the grantee of the option when the grantor conveyed the property elsewhere. In holding the solicitor liable in negligence Oliver J. paved the way for plaintiffs to take advantage of the differences between contractual and tortious actions as regards such matters as the date of accrual of the cause of action, the measure of damages and remoteness of damage in deciding in a case of concurrent liability whether to sue in contract or in tort. Though the Privy Council has recently raised doubts about this development,[55] subsequent cases seem to indicate a preference for the broader approach of *Midland Bank*.[56] Liability under *Hedley Byrne* may, therefore, arise in the context of a contractual relationship.[57]

However, though the duty will extend to pre-contract negotiations it is not the case that every pre-contractual statement will be actionable. Thus, in *Holman Construction Ltd.* v. *Delta Timber Co. Ltd.*[58] the plaintiff building contractor wished to tender for a building contract. The defendant, a timber merchant, responded to his invitation to tender for the supply of timber, and gave a quote. Intending to accept this quote the plaintiff entered into the contract, but a few days later, his offer not having yet been accepted by the plaintiff, the defendant realised that there was an error in his calculations and revoked his offer. The plaintiff had to accept the next best quote at an extra cost of over £3,000 and sued the defendant for this sum. It was held that his claim failed. The defendant's offer was said not to be a representation that a careful or even an honest assessment of the price asked had been made; it was merely an expression of an intention to become bound by

---

[55] *Tai Hing Cotton Mill Ltd.* v. *Liu Chong Hing Bank Ltd.* [1986] A.C. 80. ("Their Lordships do not believe that there is anything to the advantage of the law's development in searching for a liability in tort where the parties are in a contractual relationship.") See also, Weir [1963] C.L.J. 216; Kaye (1984) 100 L.Q.R. 680.

[56] *Thake* v. *Maurice* [1986] Q.B. 644; *Forsikringsaktieselskapet Vesta* v. *Butcher and others* [1986] 2 All E.R. 488; *Banque Keyser Ullman S.A.* v. *Skandia (U.K.) Insurance Co. Ltd.* [1987] 2 All E.R. 923.

[57] It may also arise when the statement induces the person to whom it is made to enter into a contract with a third party: *McInerney* v. *Lloyds Bank Ltd.* [1974] 1 Lloyds Rep. 246 at 253, *per* Lord Denning M.R. It has, however, been held that a special relationship does not exist between a manufacturer and a distributor of his goods who purchases the goods in reliance on statements in the manufacturer's promotional literature: *Lambert* v. *Lewis* [1980] 2 W.L.R. 299 (this issue was not discussed in the appeal in the House of Lords).

[58] [1972] N.Z.L.R. 1081. See also, *Dillingham Construction Pty Ltd.* v. *Downs* [1972] 2 N.S.W.R. 49.

contract if the offer was accepted. "The law of offer and acceptance is not to be qualified by some duty of care, the breach of which will give damages merely because the offeror was negligent in assessing its terms."[59] It may be that the parties' negotiations must lead to a contract in order for liability to attach to statements made in the course of the negotiations. To the extent that *Hedley Byrne* seems to have effected a considerable rapprochement between contract and tort, the court's reasoning in *Holman* appears unsatisfactory, given the reasonable reliance that may be argued to have existed in that case. It has been commented that the plaintiff was seeking to obtain some of the advantages of a contract before he had committed himself to it,[60] but it may be questioned why this should not be so. A more satisfactory rationale for the decision would be that no *mis*statement is made in such a case, but merely a promise which is not supported by consideration.

5. THE DEVELOPING EMPHASIS ON REASONABLE RELIANCE

In very many cases the reasonableness of the reliance stems from the fact that the maker of the statement is giving advice on matters concerning which it is his business to give advice. Where this is so, we have the state of affairs envisaged by the majority in *Mutual Life*. Beyond this, if the fact of giving business advice in a business context can be seen as inducing a reasonable reliance, we have the state of affairs envisaged by the minority and, though most *Hedley Byrne* cases will, on their facts, be explicable on the former basis, fact situations, as in *Mutual Life* itself, will arise where the broader statement of the principle appears more desirable. Such a shift in emphasis from the nature of special skill to reasonable reliance may be seen in two subsequent decisions: *Argy Trading Development Co. Ltd.* v. *Lapid Developments Ltd.*[61] and *Howard Marine and Dredging Co. Ltd.* v. *A. Ogden & Sons (Excavations) Ltd.*[62] In both cases, especially the latter, a preference can be seen for the minority view in *Mutual Life*. As a consequence, potential liability extends beyond those such as accountants, lawyers, stockbrokers and others whose profession consists of the giving of skilled advice or information, to encompass persons who give information or

[59] [1972] N.Z.L.R. 1081 at 1083, *per* Henry J.
[60] *Winfield and Jolowicz on Tort* (12th ed., 1984) p. 281, n. 46. *Cf.* Cheshire, Fifoot and Furmston's *Law of Contract* (11th ed., 1986), p. 270.
[61] [1977] 1 W.L.R. 444. See also, *Morash* v. *Lockhart & Richie Ltd.* (1978) 95 D.L.R. (3d) 647.
[62] [1978] Q.B. 574. See also, Chap. 3, pp. 46–47.

advice in a business or professional context where it is reasonable
for the plaintiff to rely on them.

In the former case Croom-Johnson J. held that there was a
special relationship between the parties but there had been no
breach of the duty of care. The defendants leased premises to the
plaintiffs. The plaintiffs covenanted to keep the premises insured
against fire damage during the period of the lease. The premises
were already insured by the defendants under a block policy, and
it was agreed that the plaintiffs would not take out separate
insurance, but simply pay an appropriate portion of the block
policy. The block policy was renewed for a further year, but during
that year the defendants were taken over by a bank, which decided
not to renew the policy. The plaintiffs were not informed of this
decision. Later the premises were gutted by fire. The plaintiffs
were uninsured and claimed damages under *Hedley Byrne, inter
alia*,[63] for the failure of the defendants to inform them of the non-
renewal of the insurance policy.

Croom-Johnson J., in holding ("with some hesitation")[64] that
there was a special relationship, appeared to favour the minority
view in *Mutual Life*. He quoted Lord Diplock in that case on the
need to treat the *Hedley Byrne* principle as a developing and
flexible one, and referred to the judgment of Ormrod L.J. in *Esso*,
noting his preference for the minority view, and stating, without
comment: "The minority had said that it was enough if the advice
was sought and given in a business or professional context."[65] The
fact that there was a business relationship between the parties
seems to have been important in persuading the learned judge to
hold, on balance, that there was a special relationship. However,
the fact that he was only just prepared to hold that there was a
special relationship appears to have caused Croom-Johnson J. to
take a restricted view of the content of the duty owed. He said:

> "What duty was thereby created? At best it was a duty not
> then and there to give negligent information. . . . If special
> relationships in the *Hedley Byrne* sense are to be created in
> circumstances such as these, then the duty which is to be
> imposed must be circumscribed closely and ought to be
> limited to a duty to exercise care only at the time when the
> duty is purported to be discharged in the first place."[66]

---

[63] A claim for breach of contract was dismissed on the grounds of absence of
consideration.
[64] [1977] 3 All E.R. 785 at 800.
[65] *Ibid.* at 799.
[66] *Ibid.* at 800.

The *Howard Marine* case again concerned a business relationship yet denied liability for negligent misstatement. Leaving aside the Misrepresentation Act claim[67] we shall concentrate on the alleged misstatement liability. Here an incorrect response was given by the marine manager of the plaintiffs,[68] contractors, to a question concerning the capacity of sea-going barges which the defendants wished to hire to dump soil, to be excavated in the course of construction of a sewage works, out at sea. The answer was honest, based on the manager's recollection of the figure given in the Lloyds Register. That figure was incorrect; the manager had seen the correct figure in shipping documents, but had not remembered it.

Lord Denning M.R. and Shaw L.J. expressly followed the minority view in *Mutual Life*. However, the former considered that the oral nature of the marine manager's response, and the failure of the defendants to verify the figure were important factors. He said: " ... the duty is one of honesty and no more whenever the opinion, information or advice is given in circumstances in which it appears that it is unconsidered and it would not be reasonable for the recipient to act on it without taking further steps to check it."[69] Bridge L.J. did not express a concluded view on common law liability, as he considered the plaintiffs to be liable under the Misrepresentation Act, but he doubted whether there was a duty: if there were, he doubted whether the evidence established a breach.

Shaw L.J. took a different view.

> "The information which had been asked for more than once cannot be regarded as other than important whatever the circumstances in which it was sought and given ... What was asked for was a specific fact. Ogdens had not themselves any direct means of ascertaining what the fact was ... All [the marine manager] had to do was to look at documents in Howards' possession and to read them accurately ... That he chose to answer an important question from mere recollection 'off the cuff' does not in my view diminish, if I may adopt the language of Lord Pearce, the 'gravity of the inquiry or the importance and influence attached to the answer.' "[70]

It is suggested that Shaw L.J.'s is the preferable view. As his judgment makes clear, this is not the equivalent of the casual

[67] See Chap. 3, pp. 46–47.
[68] The defendants claimed damages under the Misrepresentation Act and at common law by way of counterclaim.
[69] [1978] Q.B. 574 at 592.   [70] *Ibid.* at 600–601.

inquiry to the solicitor in the golf club bar, but, by virtue of its repetition and the fact that it concerned information readily accessible to the marine manager, was of sufficient seriousness and concerned such reasonable reliance, that liability should have been imposed.

At least, in both of these cases, the ghost of *Mutual Life* appears to have been laid. The context of the advice; business or professional, is all-important, the fact that the advice or information is given by a person whose business is not specifically concerned with the furnishing of such information or advice is not a reason to deny liability. The reliance must be reasonable: this essentially is the reason why liability was denied in each of these cases. The court, in accepting a broader range of defendants than the majority in *Mutual Life* found acceptable, perhaps did not wish to risk a massive expansion of liability as a consequence of this more liberal (though, it is suggested, more consistent with *Hedley Byrne*) view, and, therefore, adopted a restrictive approach to the nature of the reliance in each case. Subsequently, a more generous view of reasonable reliance has on occasion been adopted, as the fear of unlimited liability has not materialised.

Thus, in *Yianni* v. *Edwin Evans & Sons*[71] the defendant surveyor, employed by a building society to carry out a valuation on a property which the plaintiff, the would-be mortgagor, hoped to purchase, was held liable to the plaintiff as a consequence of a negligent survey which failed to reveal the existence of serious defects. Park J. in deciding whether or not a duty of care existed, followed the guidelines laid down by Lord Wilberforce in *Anns* v. *Merton London Borough Council*[72]

> "...the position has now been reached that in order to establish that a duty of care arises in a particular situation, it is not necessary to bring the facts of that situation within those of previous situations in which a duty of care has been held to exist. Rather the question has to be approached in two stages. First one has to ask whether, as between the alleged wrongdoer and the person who has suffered damage there is a sufficient relationship of proximity or neighbourhood such that, in the reasonable contemplation of the former, carelessness on his part may be likely to cause damage to the latter, in which case a prima facie duty of care arises. Secondly, if the

---

[71] [1982] Q.B. 438. See also, *Gordon* v. *Moen* [1971] N.Z.L.R. 526. *Cf. Shankie-Williams and others* v. *Heavey* (1986) 279 E.G. 316; *Harris* v. *Wyre Forest District Council and another* [1988] E.G. 57.
[72] [1978] A.C. 728 at 751–752.

first question is answered affirmatively, it is necessary to consider whether there are any considerations which ought to negative, or to reduce or limit the scope of the duty or the class of person to whom it is owed or the damages to which a breach of it may give rise ... Examples of this are *Hedley Byrne & Co. Ltd.* v. *Heller & Partners Ltd.* where the class of potential plaintiffs was reduced to those shown to have relied on the correctness of statements made."

Park J. found the sufficient relationship of proximity in the fact that the defendants knew that the building society would rely upon the correctness of the valuation report in offering a loan to the plaintiff, and the fact that such an offer was made would induce the plaintiff to believe that the property was sufficiently valuable to cause the society to make the advance, which was 80 per cent. of the purchase price. Expert evidence had established that 85–90 per cent. of building society mortgage applicants relied upon the society's valuation rather than commissioning an independent survey, even though, as in the instant case, they were frequently advised to commission such a survey. The plaintiff had not read a paragraph in the society's explanatory booklet which informed him that the valuation report was exclusively for the use of the directors and officers of the society, and recommended the instruction of an independent surveyor.[73] But, because most people did as the plaintiff had done, awareness of such conduct was imputed to the defendants.

The learned judge saw no negativing, reducing or limiting factors to redeem the defendants. A decision against them would not lead to extensive liability of mortgage valuers to third parties. The only person to whom the valuer would be liable was the person named in the survey report. The plaintiff had not been guilty of contributory negligence: his reliance outweighed the failure to read the society's literature and to employ a surveyor.

There are two grounds for criticism of this decision. As has been strongly argued elsewhere,[74] it is questionable whether there was an undertaking of responsibility such as to found liability under *Hedley Byrne* v. *Heller*. It is arguable that the defendants did not undertake responsibility *vis-à-vis* the plaintiff: indeed, the standard practice prior to 1980 was that surveyors made mortgage valuation reports for building societies on the understanding that they

---

[73] However, he had earlier signed an application form which, *inter alia*, recommended consulting a surveyor for the information and protection of the applicant. The plaintiff could not afford to employ a surveyor, however.

[74] See (1981) 45 Conv. 435 at 437–438 (M. Brazier and G. Pople).

undertook no responsibility to the mortgagor and the report would not be disclosed.[75] The emphasis in the judgment is very much on reasonable reliance, following from the fact that the defendants realised that, as most would-be mortgagors would rely upon the valuation as a consequence of being made an offer of a loan by the society, so the plaintiffs would and did rely.

The second criticism relates to the question of whether the reliance was reasonable. The plaintiff had considered whether or not to have a survey, and decided not to: on financial grounds. "Ought surveyors to be responsible when a gamble consciously undertaken fails to pay off?"[76] Is conduct rendered reasonable by the fact that it is engaged in by a large number of people? Does the fact that many others are careless drivers relieve one of the consequences of one's careless driving? The decision certainly takes a generous view of reasonable reliance,[77] though of more general interest is the stress placed on that aspect of *Hedley Byrne* liability. This reflects the emphasis in the remarks of Sir Robert Megarry V.C. in *Ross* v. *Caunters*[78]:

> "[*Hedley Byrne's*] importance is that the House of Lords rejected pure *Donoghue* v. *Stevenson* principles as forming the basis of liability for negligent mis-statements and instead based liability on the plaintiff having trusted the defendant to exercise due care in giving information on a matter in which the defendant had a special skill, and knew or ought to have known of the plaintiff's reliance on his skill and judgment. In this type of case, reliance forms part of the test of liability, as well as part of the chain of causation: and the effect of such a test of liability is to confine the extent of liability far more closely than would an application of pure *Donoghue* v. *Stevenson* principles."

These words were quoted with approval by Woolf J. at first instance in *JEB Fasteners* v. *Marks, Bloom & Co.*[79]

> "The importance of this passage is that if Sir Robert Megarry V-C is right, as with respect I think he is, the fact of reliance on the statement is sufficient limitation on liability to overcome the danger raised by Cardozo C.J."[80]

---

[75] *Ibid.* pp. 437–438 and n. 14.
[76] *Ibid.* at 439.
[77] *Ibid. passim* and see also, Holyoak and Allen, *Civil Liability for Defective Premises* (Butterworths, 1982) pp. 368–369.
[78] [1980] Ch. 297 at 313–314. Discussed in detail *infra* pp. 94–95.
[79] [1981] 3 All E.R. 289 at 296.
[80] *Supra*, n. 34.

This case concerned a claim against a firm of accountants alleging negligence in the preparation of a company's accounts. During a period when the plaintiffs were negotiating to take over a manufacturing company, the defendant, the company's accountants, aware of the negotiations, produced audited accounts for the company's first trading year and, having certified them as accurate, made them available to the plaintiffs. There were substantial inaccuracies in the figures, in particular an inflated value was put on the company's stock. The plaintiffs had reservations about the stock value, being aware of some inaccuracy, but they wished to acquire the services of the company's two directors, and the take-over took place. This proved to be an unfortunate move, the plaintiffs lost money and sued the defendants for negligent misstatement.

Woolf J. made a thorough analysis of the case law, and concluded:

"Without laying down any principle which is intended to be of general application, on the basis of the authorities which I have cited, the appropriate test for establishing whether a duty of care exists appears in this case to be whether the defendants knew or reasonably should have foreseen at the time the accounts were audited that a person might rely on those accounts for the purpose of deciding whether or not to take over the company and therefore could suffer loss if the accounts were inaccurate."[81]

The plaintiff need not, therefore, be foreseeable as an identified individual. Woolf J. held that reliance was foreseeable, that there had been reliance in the sense that the plaintiffs had studied the accounts prior to the take-over and the picture of the company presented thereby had encouraged them to take over the company. However, because the motive behind the take-over was the obtaining of the services of the two directors and the plaintiffs had formed their own views as to the value of the stock, they would have effected the take-over in any event and therefore, the defendants' negligence had not been the cause of the plaintiffs' loss.

The plaintiffs appealed, but the Court of Appeal upheld the decision of the trial judge. The trial judge, it was held, had unnecessarily complicated matters by separating out the question of reliance and the question of whether the reliance caused the

---

[81] [1981] 3 All E.R. 289 at 296. See also, *Haig* v. *Bamford* (1977) 72 D.L.R. (3d) 68; *Scott Group Ltd.* v. *McFarlane* [1978] 1 N.Z.L.R. 553.

loss. Encouragement and reliance, in the sense in which there must be reliance under *Hedley Byrne*, are not necessarily synonymous. There had not been reliance, in the sense of the misstatement playing a real and substantial part, in inducing the plaintiffs to act, for the "primary impulse leading to the take-over"[82] was the obtaining of the services of the two directors.

> "In such a case the cause of action is the same as in all claims for damages for misrepresentation.[83] The representation must be false, and it must induce the plaintiff to act on it to his detriment. If it does, he relies on it; if it does not, he does not."[84]

The operative cause of and inducement for the take-over was the opportunity to acquire the services of the directors: hence, there was no reliance in the required sense upon the accounts.

6. ARE AFFIRMATIVE DUTIES ACTIONABLE UNDER HEDLEY BYRNE?

It may be argued that the limitation of the duty in *Argy* v. *Lapid* to a duty not then and there to give negligent information does not accord with principle. Either there is a special relationship or there is not. Surely Hellers could have been liable if they had subsequently discovered that an initial statement, at the time accurate, concerning Easipower's creditworthiness, was no longer true, and failed to inform Hedley Byrne's bankers of this?[85] Further, in so far as the decision appears to preclude, to a very large extent, the recognition of affirmative duties, it is inconsistent with other cases. In *Midland Bank Trust Co. Ltd.* v. *Hett, Stubbs & Kemp*[86] Oliver J. did not confine liability under *Hedley Byrne* v. *Heller* to misstatements but, as the facts of the case show, extended it to professional nonfeasance. Again, in *Cornish* v. *Midland Bank plc*[87] the plaintiff, who was a customer of the defendant, signed a second mortage in favour of the defendant without realising, and without being informed by the bank, that it was worded in such a way as to secure not only a loan for £2,000 for renovations to a farmhouse jointly owned by the plaintiff and

---

[82] [1983] 1 All E.R. 583 at 586, *per* Sir Sebag Shaw.
[83] See Chap. 2.
[84] *Per* Stephenson L.J.: see [1983] 1 All E.R. 583 at 588.
[85] See Gravells (1978) 94 L.Q.R. 334 at 336–337 for a convincing argument along these lines.
[86] [1979] Ch. 384. *Supra*, pp. 75–76.
[87] [1985] 3 All E.R. 513.

her husband, but also unlimited further advances to the husband. Such advances were in fact made and, when the farmhouse was subsequently sold, the proceeds of sale were barely adequate to cover the first and second mortgages and the sale expenses. The bank accepted that they owed a duty of care on the facts of the case, since they had sought (inadequately) to explain the effect of the second mortgage to the plaintiff. Kerr L.J. said:

> "... if it had been necessary to decide this issue I think that I would have inclined to the view that in the circumstances of this case the bank owed a duty to the plaintiff, as the bank's customer, to proffer to her some adequate explanation of the nature and effect of the document... I think that [expert evidence of the standard banking practice] would have supported the conclusion that bankers themselves recognise that their proper professional standards would not be consistent with mere silence on their part in such situations."[88]

It may be that the courts are not prepared to extend the duty to speak beyond certain cases of professional liability, but to draw such a line would be unnecessarily arbitrary. The duty of care under *Hedley Byrne* v. *Heller* is sufficiently circumscribed that if a special relationship does exist it should normally extend to a failure to speak. Certainly, a duty to reveal that a change in circumstances renders a previously true statement untrue may be imposed. Thus, in *Cherry Ltd.* v. *Allied Insurance Brokers Ltd.*[89] the plaintiffs instructed the defendants, their brokers, with whose services they were dissatisfied, to cancel their insurance policies which covered loss resulting from damage to their premises. The defendants were advised that the insurers (General Accident) would not cancel the policies, and informed the plaintiffs of this. The plaintiffs then cancelled the new insurance policies that they had taken out, assuming that they remained covered under the old policies. Subsequently, General Accident agreed to cancel the old policies, but the defendants failed to inform the plaintiffs of this. Shortly afterwards the plaintiffs' premises were seriously damaged by fire. Cantley J. held that the plaintiffs were entitled to damages under *Hedley Byrne* v. *Heller* as the defendants should have realised that the plaintiffs would act in the way that they did upon the information that General Accident would not cancel. The damages comprised such sum as the plaintiffs would have

---

[88] *Ibid.* at 522–523.
[89] [1978] 1 Lloyds L.R. 274. See also, *J. & J. C. Abrams Ltd.* v. *Ancliffe* [1978] 2 N.Z.L.R. 420 (affirmed) [1981] 1 N.Z.L.R. 244.

recovered under the General Accident policy if that policy had been in force at the date of the fire.

Imposing a duty upon a defendant to inform a plaintiff of a change in circumstances is one thing, but it is quite another to impose upon him a requirement that he fulfill a promise made, in the absence of consideration. However, in *Meates* v. *Attorney-General*[90] the New Zealand Court of Appeal held the New Zealand Government liable for failure to perform certain non-contractual promises of support to a company whose shareholders, the plaintiffs, suffered financial loss after acting on the promises which were not kept. Further, in *The Zephyr*[91] Hobhouse J. held that an insurance broker acting for insurers was liable to make good an undertaking that he gave to re-insurers that he would use reasonable endeavours to ensure that a slip which they had signed would be "signed down" (thereby reducing their initial risk exposure).[92]

Subsequently, in the Court of Appeal in *The Zephyr*,[93] however, Mustill L.J. asserted the traditional approach. He considered that the broker's undertaking "bears to my mind no resemblance to the kind of obligation to avoid doing something, or to avoid doing something badly, which is at present the subject-matter of the English law of negligence."[94] The Court of Appeal considered that it was contrary to fundamental principle to enforce a gratuitous promise in such circumstances. It may also be argued that it is difficult to characterise the undertaking given as a *mis*statement in such a case.

7. The Ambit of Hedley Byrne, and its Relationship to Section 2(1) of the Misrepresentation Act 1967

To sum up the effect of 20 years' case law: liability for negligent misstatements causing pure economic loss will be imposed where, in a professional or business context a person gives professional or

---

[90] [1983] N.Z.L.R. 308. See Vennell (1985) 11 N.Z.U.L.R. 179; Todd (1985) 1 P.N. 2.
[91] [1984] 1 Lloyds L.R. 58.
[92] See Reynolds (1985) 11 N.Z.U.L.R. 215 at 228. For a full analysis of the process of "signing down," see the judgment of Mustill L.J. in the Court of Appeal in *The Zephyr* [1985] 2 Lloyds L.R. 529 at 531–532.
[93] [1985] 2 Lloyds L.R. 529.
[94] *Ibid.* at 531. His learned brethren agreed.

business advice or information[95] such that it is reasonably foreseeable that another will rely upon that advice or information, and that other does so rely, that reliance being reasonable, and suffers economic loss. The floodgates have not opened: the "special relationship" has proved to be a serviceable safety valve.[96]

During most of the same period, the claim for negligent misstatement has co-existed with the action for damages under section 2(1) of the Misrepresentation Act 1967, discussed in Chapter 3. Though there are similarities between the two (for example, the measure of damages and, to a large extent, the nature of the statement made[97]) there are also significant differences. A major distinction lies in the fact that the claim under section 2(1) can only be brought where a contract is induced by the misrepresentation, whereas an ensuing contract is not an essential element of the claim under *Hedley Byrne*. Where a contract does ensue from a misrepresentation it will normally be advisable to claim under section 2(1), given the considerable benefit to the representee of the reversed burden of proof that comes into play under the subsection, as opposed to the need to establish the assumption of responsibility and the reasonable reliance that a *Hedley Byrne* claim requires. Consequently, a representee will, in all probability, elect to sue under section 2(1) where the misrepresentation induced him to contract with the representor, and will claim under *Hedley Byrne* where there is no such ensuing contract. However, the claim under *Hedley Byrne* may still be of significance where a contract ensues, for example, if liability for misrepresentation but not for misstatement is purportedly excluded by the representor.

8. EXCLUSION OF LIABILITY UNDER HEDLEY BYRNE

In considering the possibility of excluding liability for negligent misstatement, it should not be forgotten that in *Hedley Byrne* v. *Heller* itself the respondents were able to avoid liability because

---

[95] "However the question whether the furnishing of information is in any particular case to be treated as equivalent to advice must depend upon the facts of the case, and in particular upon the precise circumstances in which the relevant information has been given," *per* Lord Goff of Chieveley, delivering the advice of the Privy Council in *Royal Bank Trust Co. (Trinidad) Ltd.* v. *Pampellonne* [1987] 1 Lloyds L.R. 218 at 225.

[96] For an analysis of negligent misstatement from an economist's perspective, see Bishop (1980) 96 L.Q.R. 360.

[97] See [1983] 1 All E.R. 583 at 586 quoted *supra*, p. 84.

they had provided the reference "without responsibility." This clearly negatived the assumption of responsibility which is an essential element of liability for negligent misstatement, and hence at common law a disclaimer in such terms, provided it is clearly made to the recipient of the advice or information at the time such advice or information is provided, will suffice to avoid liability.

The position must now, however, be considered in the light of the Unfair Contract Terms Act, 1977. Section 2 of the Act provides as follows:

Negligence liability

2. (1) A person cannot by reference to any contract term or to a notice given to persons generally or to particular persons exclude or restrict his liability for death or personal injury resulting from negligence.

(2) In the case of other loss or damage, a person cannot so exclude or restrict his liability for negligence except in so far as the term or notice satisfies the requirement of reasonableness.

(3) Where a contract term or notice purports to exclude or restrict liability for negligence a person's agreement to or awareness of it is not of itself to be taken as indicating his voluntary acceptance of any risk.

Thus, an attempt to exclude liability for negligent misstatement will be entirely ineffective if the liability (which must be "business liability" as defined below) is for death or personal injury, and subject to the requirement of reasonableness in cases of other loss or damage. The "reasonableness" test is defined in section 11 of the Act.

11.(1) In relation to a contract term, the requirement of reasonableness for the purposes of this Part of the Act, section 3 of the Misrepresentation Act 1967 and section 3 of the Misrepresentation Act (Northern Ireland) 1967 is that the term shall have been a fair and reasonable one to be included having regard to the circumstances which were, or ought reasonably to have been, known to or in the contemplation of the parties when the contract was made.

(2) In determining for the purposes of section 6 or 7 above whether a contract term satisfies the requirement of reason-ableness, regard shall be had in particular to the matters specified in Schedule 2 to this Act; but this subsection does not prevent the court or arbitrator from holding, in accord-ance with any rule of law, that a term which purports to exclude or restrict any relevant liability is not a term of the contract.

(3) In relation to a notice (not being a notice having contractual effect), the requirement of reasonableness under this Act is that it should be fair and reasonable to allow reliance on it, having regard to all the circumstances obtaining when the liability arose or (but for the notice) would have arisen.

(4) Where by reference to a contract term or notice a person seeks to restrict liability to a specified sum of money, and the question arises (under this or any other Act) whether the term or notice satisfies the requirement of reasonableness, regard shall be had in particular (but without prejudice to subsection (2) above in the case of contract terms) to—

(*a*) the resources which he could expect to be available to him for the purpose of meeting the liability should it arise; and

(*b*) how far it was open to him to cover himself by insurance.

(5) It is for those claiming that a contract term or notice satisfies the requirement of reasonableness to show that it does,

This control applies only to business liability of the maker of the statement, as defined in section 1(3) of the Act.

(3) In the case of both contract and tort, sections 2 to 7 apply (except to where the contrary is stated in section 6(4) only to business liability, that is liability for breach of obligations or duties arising—

(*a*) from things done or to be done by a person in the course of a business (whether his own business or another's); or

(*b*) from the occupation of premises used for business purposes of the occupier;

and references to liability are to be read accordingly.

In section 4 of the Act "business" is defined as including a profession and the activities of any government department or local or public authority. Beyond this, it is thought that the courts are likely to take a broad view of what constitutes a business.

As an example of the courts' approach to purported exclusions of liability for misstatements, following Park J.'s decision in *Yianni* v. *Edwin Evans & Sons*[98] the courts have had the opportunity to examine attempts to exclude the liability of mortgagee's surveyors to the mortgagor. Much seems to turn upon the knowledge and

---

[98] [1982] Q.B. 438. For the facts of this case see pp. 80–81 *supra*.

experience of the mortgagor. In *Stevenson* v. *Nationwide Building Society*[99] the plaintiff was an estate agent who sought a mortgage from the defendant so as to enable him to purchase premises for new offices. The survey was carried out by the society's own valuer. The mortgage application form contained the following clause:

> "I/We understand that the report and valuation on the property made by the Society's valuer is confidential and is intended solely for the consideration of the Society in determining what advance (if any) may be made on the security, and that no responsibility is implied or accepted by the Society or its valuer for either the value or condition of the property by reason of such inspection and report."

The valuer failed to discover the existence of serious defects in the property, and the plaintiff claimed damages when the existence of the defects was subsequently manifested. His counsel accepted that the above clause constituted a valid disclaimer, subject to the Unfair Contract Terms Act, but argued that it failed to satisfy the requirement of reasonableness. The judge did not agree. The disclaimer followed an accepted standard practice, and in a separate clause the mortgage application form gave a full warning of the possibility that a valuation inspection might not reveal defects which a structural survey would reveal, and offered the opportunity to the applicant of a structural survey which could be made (at extra cost) at the same time as the valuation inspection. Further, the fact that the plaintiff was well familiar with such disclaimers and with the possibility of obtaining a survey, and with the difference between a valuation inspection and a structural survey, was held to render the disclaimer reasonable.

Subsequently, however, in *Smith* v. *Eric S. Bush*[1] a disclaimer in similar circumstances was held to be unreasonable. The plaintiff in this case, however, was a private householder, who had agreed to purchase a property for £17,500 and was seeking a mortgage of £3,500. The salient words of the disclaimer on the mortage application form were as follows:

> "I/We understand that neither the Society nor the Surveyor or the firm of Surveyors will warrant, represent or give any assurance to me/us that the statements, conclusions and opinions expressed or implied in the report and mortgage valuation will be accurate or valid and the Surveyor(s) report

[99] (1984) 272 E.G. 663.
[1] [1987] 3 All E.R. 179. Leave to appeal to the House of Lords has been given.

will be supplied without any acceptance of responsibility on their part to me/us."

On her copy of the report it was stated that the report was not, and should not be taken as a structural survey, and the denial of acceptance of responsibility was repeated.

The surveyor failed to detect the absence of support of the brickwork of the chimneys, though this could have been easily discovered. The trial judge's finding that the surveyor had breached his duty of care to the plaintiff was not appealed; the only contested issue concerned the effectiveness of the disclaimers. The Court of Appeal held that they failed to satisfy the requirement of reasonableness, despite the fact that the plaintiff realised that it was not part of the surveyor's duty to carry out a full structural survey and that she was, therefore, in effect gambling on there being no hidden defects in the house which a reasonably careful usual inspection might not reveal.

Dillon L.J. stated:

"But where he is dealing with a property at the lower end of the market and he knows that the purchaser is likely to rely on his report, and not instruct his or her own surveyor, I find it very difficult to see why it should be fair and reasonable to allow him to rely on an automatic blanket exclusion of all liability for negligence if his visual inspection of a property turns out not to have been reasonably careful."[2]

Later in his judgment he appeared to take the view that though it might be different where the plaintiff was a surveyor or lawyer who understood such matters, most purchasers would not see the need to incur the extra cost of a structural survey.

It is difficult to generalise from these rather specific instances, for the circumstances of the particular case are all important under the requirement of reasonableness. However, on the basis that the characterisation of the plaintiff appears to be a significant factor, it may be that if *Hedley Byrne* v. *Heller's* facts were repeated today, a court would take the view that the "without responsibility" clause satisfied the requirement of reasonableness, since "if the alternative is that such information is withheld, it does not seem unreasonable that it is only given on the limited liability basis."[3]

However, it may be argued that the Unfair Contract Terms Act does not apply to a disclaimer of tortious liability designed to prevent a liability from ever arising, as opposed to a purported

---

[2] *Ibid.* at 184.
[3] Yates and Hawkins *op. cit.* p. 57 *supra*; p. 149.

exclusion of an existing liability, on the basis that a person cannot be said to be assuming a liability at the very moment when he declares that he does not.[4] Against this it may be argued[5] that a proper interpretation of section 13 of the Unfair Contract Terms Act allows the requirement of reasonableness to govern a *Hedley Byrne* disclaimer. Section 13 provides:

Varieties of exemption clause

13. (1) To the extent that this Part of this Act prevents the exclusion or restriction of any liability it also prevents—

(*a*) making the liability or its enforcement subject to restrictive or onerous conditions;
(*b*) excluding or restricting any right or remedy in respect of the liability, or subjecting a person to any prejudice in consequence of his pursuing any such right or remedy;
(*c*) excluding or restricting rules of evidence or procedure;

and (to that extent) sections 2 and 5 to 7 also prevent excluding or restricting liability by reference to terms and notices which exclude or restrict the relevant obligation or duty.

(2) But an agreement in writing to submit present or future differences to arbitration is not to be treated under this Part of this Act as excluding or restricting any liability.

The use of the words "liability," "obligation" and "duty" in section 13 suggests that a liability must exist already for the statutory controls to operate, though it may be argued that if "liability" can be read to mean "potential liability," the difficulties vanish. It might seem curious to impose statutory controls over a contract term that seeks to exclude liability for misrepresentation, as section 3 of the Misrepresentation Act (as substituted by section 8 of the Unfair Contract Terms Act) does, and not over a disclaimer of *Hedley Byrne* liability, though it may be argued that this is a consequence of the different nature of the duties owed. Liability under *Hedley Byrne* arises as a consequence of, *inter alia*, an assumption of responsibility by the giver of the advice or information, whereas liability under section 2(1) of the Misrepresentation Act does not contain this element. Further, it is clear that in other respects the Unfair Contract Terms Act does not

---

[4] See *Hedley Byrne & Co. Ltd.* v. *Heller & Partners Ltd.* [1964] A.C. 465 at 533 (*per* Lord Devlin); 540 (*per* Lord Pearce); Coote (1978) 41 M.L.R. 312 at 316.
[5] See Stanton (1985) 1 P.N. 132. Cf. Holyoak (1985) 1 P.N. 49.

treat misrepresentations and misstatements in the same way. If the 1977 Act does control *Hedley Byrne* disclaimers, it does so only in cases of business liability, whereas all misrepresentations which induce contracts have to satisfy the requirement of reasonableness. In a recent negligent valuation case,[6] the Court of Appeal held that the disclaimer on the mortgage application form had the effect of precluding the defendants (the mortgagees and the surveyor, who was their employee) from coming under a duty of care to the plaintiff mortgagors. Section 2(2) of the Unfair Contract Terms Act was held to be inapplicable to such a case where a disclaimer prevented a duty of care from coming into existence in the first place.

9. CONCLUSION: HEDLEY BYRNE AND ECONOMIC LOSS GENERALLY

It is worth briefly considering to what extent the future of *Hedley Byrne* liability is related to the future of liability for pure economic loss generally. In 1982 in *Junior Books Ltd. v. Veitchi Co. Ltd.*[7] the House of Lords imposed liability for pure economic loss created by a negligent act. In the years between *Hedley Byrne* and *Junior Books* the courts were faced with a number of cases in which plaintiffs claimed that such loss should be compensated, and a variety of responses resulted. It is the nature of the loss rather than the question whether the loss resulted from words or acts that has increasingly been seen as being the dominant concern. Certainly words are more volatile than acts, but, as we have seen, personal injury or property damage resulting from a negligent misstatement is usually actionable under ordinary *Donoghue v. Stevenson* principles, and more than anything else it is fear of the pure economic losses that may result from a negligent misstatement that has led to the need for a limited duty of care.

This was achieved in *Hedley Byrne*. Could a similar restraint be devised for delimiting the duty of care where it was a negligent act that caused pure economic loss? After all, the line dividing an "act" from a "misstatement" may be a very narrow one. Consider two cases. *In Ministry of Housing and Local Government v. Sharp*[8] there was, in the words of Sir Robert Megarry V-C,[9]

"the claim by the plaintiff ministry against the local authority whose clerk had negligently failed to mention in the certificate

---

[6] *Harris v. Wyre Forest District Council and another* [1988] E.G. 57. Leave to appeal to the House of Lords has been given.

[7] [1983] A.C. 320.

[8] [1970] 2 Q.B. 223. See also, *Lawton v. B.O.C. Transhield Ltd.* [1987] 2 All E.R. 608.

[9] In *Ross v. Caunters* [1980] Ch. 297 at 316–317.

given in response to a local land charge search made by an intending purchaser that the ministry had a charge on the land in question. The purchaser had accordingly taken the land free from the charge, and the ministry then sued the local authority for the value of the charge that had been lost."

Lord Denning M.R. considered that the case came four square within the principles of his dissent in *Candler* v. *Crane Christmas*, approved in *Hedley Byrne*. The local authority was vicariously liable for the clerk, who owed a duty of care to anyone who he knew or ought to have known might be injured if he made a mistake. Salmon L.J., however, seemed to prefer to base his judgment on *Donoghue* v. *Stevenson*. He recognised that

> "the present case does not precisely fit into any category of negligence yet considered by the courts. The plaintiff has not been misled by any careless statement made to him by the defendant or made by the defendant to someone else who the defendant knew would be likely to pass it on to a third party such as the plaintiff, in circumstances in which the third party might reasonably be expected to rely upon it."[10]

Hedley Byrne had opened the door to the possibility of an award of damages for pure economic loss, and the proximity between the council and the incumbrancer, given that the former must or should have known that unless reasonable care were employed in the making of the search and the preparation of the certificate, loss would be suffered by an incumbrancer or chargee whose charge was carelessly omitted from the certificate, was as close as that between the parties in *Donoghue* v. *Stevenson*. The judgment of Cross L.J. was equivocal.

Clearly in this case there was room for doubt as to whether the basis of liability was a statement or an act, but, given the close proximity between plaintiff and defendant, liability could be imposed without raising alarming implications for future cases. The second case to be considered, *Ross* v. *Caunters*,[11] gave rise to similar problems. A testator's solicitor failed to warn him that attestation of the will by a beneficiary's spouse would invalidate a gift to the beneficiary. The beneficiary sued the solicitor for negligence. In the Canadian case of *Whittingham* v. *Crease & Co.*[12] on similar facts, Aikens J. held the solicitor liable, basing his

---

[10] [1970] 2 Q.B. 223 at 278.
[11] [1980] Ch. 297. *Cf. Clarke* v. *Bruce Lance & Co. and others* [1988] 1 All E.R. 364.
[12] [1978] 5 W.W.R. 5. See also, *Biakanja* v. *Irving* (1958) 320 P. 2d 16 (Supreme Court of California).

judgment on *Hedley Byrne*. The learned judge considered that there had been an implied representation by the solicitor that the will would be effective: the fact that there had been passive rather than active reliance by the plaintiff was no bar to recovery.

Sir Robert Megarry V-C in *Ross* adopted a different approach. He considered that the solicitor owed a duty of care on the basis of *Donoghue* v. *Stevenson* and that the presence of passive reliance or the absence of any reliance was irrelevant to the imposition of liability. He accepted that the reasoning in *Whittingham* v. *Crease* was one way of reaching the right result, but the absence of any reliance, express or implied, precluded the use of similar reasoning in the instant case. The *Sharp* case provided the necessary authority for the imposition of liability for pure economic loss as a consequence of a negligent act. He quoted[13] the words of Salmon L.J.[14]:

> "So far, however, as the law of negligence relating to civil actions is concerned, the existence of a duty to take reasonable care no longer depends upon whether it is physical injury or financial loss which can reasonably be foreseen as a result of a failure to take such care."

Sir Robert Megarry was well aware of the problems of indeterminate liability that might arise if there were no modification of the *Donoghue* v. *Stevenson* test to avoid such problems. He did not seek to lay down a test, as the facts of *Ross* were such that any test based upon *Donoghue* v. *Stevenson* would surely include a claim of the kind brought in *Ross*. There was a high degree of proximity between the negligence and the loss. The defendants clearly knew of the plaintiff individually and knew that their negligence would be likely to cause her financial loss. He left it to the future case-law to evolve the necessary test or tests.

The matter was taken a stage further in *Junior Books Ltd.* v. *Veitchi Co. Ltd.*[15] The House of Lords held liable a sub-contractor, employed by the main contractors, to the respondents, in whose factory the sub-contractor laid a defective floor. The losses were purely economic, covering such matters as the cost of the removal of machinery, loss of profits due to disturbance of business and wages of employees thrown away. The fact that the losses were purely economic was held to be irrelevant. The twofold test in *Anns* applied: was there a sufficient relationship of proximity between the parties: if so, were there any considerations

---

[13] [1980] Ch. 297 at 317–318.
[14] [1970] 2 Q.B. 223 at 278.
[15] [1982] 3 W.L.R. 477.

negativing, reducing or limiting the scope of the duty or the class of persons to whom it was owed or the damages to which a breach of the duty might give rise?

Judges in subsequent cases in which plaintiffs have suffered pure economic loss resulting from a negligent act have emphasised the high degree of proximity and reliance that existed in *Junior Books*. Thus, in *Muirhead* v. *Industrial Tank Specialities Ltd.*[16] Robert Goff L.J. regarded *Junior Books* as being essentially confined to its own facts. In *Governors of the Peabody Donation Fund* v. *Sir Lindsay Parkinson & Co. Ltd.*[17] Lord Keith stated that the temptation to regard the *Anns* twofold test as definitive should be resisted, and in *Leigh & Sillivan Ltd.* v. *Aliakmon Shipping Co. Ltd.*[18] Lord Brandon considered that the test was only applicable to novel factual situations, not to situations in which the existence of a duty had repeatedly been held not to exist.

The variety of contexts in which pure economic loss may result from a negligent act is such that the courts' wariness, since *Junior Books*, to espouse an all-embracing formula is understandable. The *Hedley Byrne* formula will no doubt be of assistance in a number of cases,[19] though in other situations the absence of reliance by the defendant on the plaintiff will not necessarily bar a claim.[20] However, a close degree of proximity and an absence of risk of unlimited liability are likely to be required in such a situation. *Hedley Byrne* opened up the possibility of the recovery of damage for pure economic loss, and illustrates clearly the utility of a restricted but flexible delimitation of the general duty of care by means essentially of the requirement of reasonable reliance. As such, the decision is likely to remain very influential in the development of rules governing liability for pure economic loss caused by a negligent act.

---

[16] [1986] Q.B. 507. See also, *Candlewood Navigation Corporation Ltd.* v. *Mitsui OSK Lines Ltd.* [1986] A.C. 1.

[17] [1985] A.C. 210 at 240.

[18] [1986] A.C. 785 at 815. See also, *Curran* v. *Northern Ireland Housing Association* [1987] 2 All E.R. 13; *Yuen Kun-yeu* v. *A-G of Hong Kong* [1987] 2 All E.R. 705, displaying a similarly restrictive approach to the *Anns* test.

[19] See, *e.g.* the judgment of Robert Goff L.J. in *Muirhead* at p. 715.

[20] See *Ross* v. *Caunters* [1980] Ch. 297.

Chapter 5

CONTRACTUAL LIABILITY

We have briefly traced above[1] the historical development of the
concept of warranty, and noted its translation from tort to contract
and the requirement of an intention to warrant that became one of
its elements. It is now necessary to examine in detail the tests
developed by the courts for determining whether or not a
statement is to be characterised as a term or a representation and
what the consequences of that characterisation are. At the same
time the distinction (frequently blurred by the courts) between a
collateral term and the situation where a pre-contractual statement
amounts to an entire collateral contract[2] will be examined, and the
significance of the distinction between "one contract" and "two
contract" cases explored.

1. REPRESENTATION OR TERM?

(a) Introduction

It is quite possible for a descriptive statement to be written into
a contract, and, if this is so, no difficulty arises as to whether it is a
term or a representation: if untrue the statement will be actionable
as a breach of contract. More frequently, however, the statement
will be made in the course of negotiations leading to the contract,
and it will then be necessary for the court to decide whether it is a
so-called "mere representation" which if untrue will lead to the
remedies discussed in Chapter 3,[3] or whether it is part of the
contract, whose untruth will entitle the innocent party to repudiation of the contract and/or damages. This is a difficult question of
construction, and, it has to be said at the outset, an air of
artificiality hangs over the whole process. In *Esso Petroleum Co.
Ltd.* v. *Mardon*[4] Lord Denning M.R. explained:

"Ever since *Heilbut, Symons & Co.* v. *Buckleton* [[1913] A.C.
30] we have had to contend with the law as laid down by the
House of Lords that an innocent misrepresentation gives no
right to damages. In order to escape from that rule, the

[1] Chap. 1 *supra*, pp. 1–3.
[2] See Wedderburn [1959] C.L.J. 58.
[3] See p. 29 *et seq. supra*.
[4] [1976] Q.B. 801.

pleader used to allege—I often did it myself—that the misrepresentation was fraudulent, or alternatively a collateral warranty. At the trial we nearly always succeeded on collateral warranty."[5]

In searching for the elusive intention to assume a contractual liability that will allow characterisation of the statement as a warranty rather than a representation, the courts, at least up to the enactment of the Misrepresentation Act 1967, have frequently been able to find a remedy in damages or deny a liability in worthy cases, and even since 1967 it may be to a plaintiff's benefit to persuade a court to treat a statement as contractual.[6]

(b) The parol evidence rule

An initial problem confronting any attempt to incorporate an oral statement within a written contract lies in the so-called "parol evidence" rule.[7] Thus, in *Jacobs* v. *Batavia and General Plantations Trust*[8] P.O. Lawrence J. said: "It is firmly established as a rule of law that parol evidence cannot be admitted to add to, vary or contradict a deed or other written instrument."[9] The policy arguments in favour of such a rule are clear, but experience has shown that an excessively rigid application would cause unacceptable hardship, and a number of exceptions to the rule have developed,[10] impinge though this may upon the promotion of certainty which is the main benefit of the rule. Examples of such exceptions (or cases to which the scope of the rule does not extend) include cases where extrinsic evidence is admissible to prove custom[11]; to identify the subject matter of the contract[12] and to prove an invalidating cause, such as *non est factum*[13] or lack of consideration.

For our purposes it is of especial significance to note that the parol evidence rule does not apply if the presumption that the writing was intended to include all the terms of the contract can be

---

[5] *Ibid.* at 817.

[6] See *infra*; pp. 117–118.

[7] The rule does not purport to restrict only oral evidence, but all forms of extrinsic evidence.

[8] [1924] 1 Ch. 287. See also, *Hawrish* v. *Bank of Montreal* (1969) 2 D.L.R. (3d) 600.

[9] [1924] 1 Ch. 287 at 295.

[10] See *Chitty on Contracts* (25th ed., 1983), paras. 804–833; Treitel, *The Law of Contract* (7th ed., 1987), pp. 150–158.

[11] *e.g. Smith* v. *Wilson* (1832) 3 B. & Ad. 728; *Brown* v. *Byrne* (1854) 3 E & B 703.

[12] *e.g. Macdonald* v. *Longbottom* (1859) 1 E. & E. 977; *Scarfe* v. *Adams* [1981] 1 All E.R. 843.

[13] See *Roe* v. *R. A. Naylor Ltd.* (1918) 87 L.J.K.B. 958 at 964–965.

rebutted.[14] If it can be shown that the parties intended to make a partly oral, partly written, contract, there is (subject to contrary statutory provision) no difficulty in introducing parol evidence to prove the oral terms. As Wedderburn notes[15]: "The strength of the presumption against parol evidence will depend upon the exact nature of the written agreement and its surrounding circumstances." In 1986 the Law Commission[16] examined the parol evidence rule and concluded that, in so far as any such rule of law could be said to have an independent existence, it did not have the effect of excluding evidence which ought to be admitted if justice was to be done between the parties. In the Commission's view evidence would only be excluded when its reception would be inconsistent with the parties' intention, and the various exceptions to the rule were in reality situations in which the rule could never apply.

As examples of cases on either side of the line we may contrast *Otto* v. *Bolton and Norris*[17] with *Smith* v. *Jeffryes*.[18] In the former the defendant builder/vendor assured the plaintiff, a would-be purchaser of a house, which was in the course of construction by the defendant, that the house was well built. In reliance on that assurance the plaintiff agreed to buy the house. It later transpired that the house was not well built, especially in that the ceilings of the first floor were defective and unsafe. In awarding the plaintiff damages Atkinson J. stated:

> "I have no doubt here that the statement amounted to a warranty. I am quite satisfied that Mr. Norris intended it to be a contractual promise collateral to the contract of purchase. I am satisfied that he knew that the contract was entered into on the basis of this assurance that he had given."[19]

In the latter case the defendant, by a written contract, agreed to sell to the plaintiff 60 tons of "ware potatoes" at £5 per ton. It appeared that in the area where the contract was made there were three qualities of potatoes: wares, middlings and chats. The defendant tendered potatoes known as "kidney wares" which the

---

[14] See *Gillespie Bros. & Co.* v. *Cheney, Eggar & Co.* [1896] 2 Q.B. 59 at 62, *per* Lord Russell of Killowen C.J.

[15] [1959] C.L.J. 58 at 64.

[16] Law Com. No. 154.

[17] [1936] 2 K.B. 46. See also, *Allen* v. *Pink* (1838) 4 M. & W. 120; *Beckett* v. *Nurse* [1948] 1 K.B. 535.

[18] (1846) 15 M. & W. 561. See also, *Harnor* v. *Groves* (1855) 15 C.B. 667; *Powell* v. *Edmunds* (1810) 12 East 6; *Hutton* v. *Watling* [1948] Ch. 398.

[19] [1936] 2 K.B. 46 at 51.

plaintiff alleged were inferior to "Regent's wares" and sought to adduce parol evidence to the effect that "Regent's wares" were those in fact contracted for. It was held that such evidence, which had been admitted at trial, ought not to have been admitted, as it went to vary and limit the written contract between the parties. A new trial was ordered.

It may be easier to persuade a court that an oral statement should form part of a written contract where such a statement adds to rather than varying or contradicting the written agreement.[20] Ultimately though, it is a matter of construction of the particular document, in order to see whether it looks like a complete contract or whether it appears to leave room for extra oral warranties. Wedderburn[21] detected a weakening of the presumption; perhaps if this is the case, the practice described by Lord Denning above[22] may be responsible; and any or all of these elements may go to explain the different conclusions reached in cases such as *Otto* v. *Bolton and Norris* and *Smith* v. *Jeffryes*.

(c) Ascertainment of the parties' intention

We shall deal later on with the case where the previous oral statement is claimed to operate as a separate contract, collateral to the written contract. Returning for the moment to cases where it is argued that a statement made in the course of negotiations is a term of the contract rather than a mere representation, it can be seen that the courts, in seeking to ascertain whether the maker of the statement had the intention (ascertained from an objective point of view)[23] to warrant the truth of his statement or not, have dealt with the cases before them in such a way that a number of rather loose guiding principles can be seen to have emerged.

Relative knowledge of the parties. Of especial importance is the relative knowledge or means of knowledge of the parties with regard to the statements made. Thus in *Oscar Chess Ltd.* v.

---

[20] Note *Hutton* v. *Watling* (*supra*, n. 18) and *Leggott* v. *Barrett* (1880) 15 Ch.D. 306.

[21] *Supra*, n. 2 at 63.

[22] *Supra*, n. 5.

[23] "The intention of the parties can only be deduced from the totality of the evidence," *per* Lord Moulton in *Heilbut, Symons & Co.* v. *Buckleton* [1913] A.C. 30 at 51. See also, *Lambert* v. *Lewis* [1982] A.C. 225 at 267, *per* Stephenson L.J. (in the Court of Appeal).

Williams[24] the defendant, a private person, wished to buy a Hillman Minx from the plaintiffs, car dealers, and to offer a secondhand Morris in part exchange. The logbook of the Morris described it as being a 1948 model, the defendant confirmed this in good faith, and the plaintiffs believed him. The transaction took place, but some months later the plaintiffs discovered that the car was in fact a 1939 model, worth £115 less than it would have been if it had been made in 1948. They sued the defendant for the £115. The Court of Appeal reversed the decision of the county court judge that the statement as to the car's age was a term of the contract.

Lord Denning M.R. noted that "it must have been obvious to both that the seller had himself no personal knowledge of the year when the car was made."[25] He also commented that the plaintiffs could have checked the year of the car by taking the engine number and chassis number and writing to the manufacturers. He said "they are experts, and, not having made that check at the time, I do not think they should now be allowed to recover against the innocent seller who produced to them all the evidence he had, namely the registration book."[26] Hodson L.J. agreed. He said: "The defendant was stating an opinion on a matter of which he had no special knowledge or on which the buyer might be expected also to have an opinion and to exercise his judgment."[27] He also stressed that, as was stated by Lord Moulton in *Heilbut, Symons & Co.* v. *Buckleton*,[28] this was not a decisive test, but a feature which might assist in deciding whether or not a warranty was intended.

In *Dick Bentley Productions Ltd.* v. *Harold Smith (Motors) Ltd.*[29] the plaintiff wished to purchase a "well-vetted" Bentley car. He went to the defendant dealers, who looked out for a car for him, and eventually found one, which, they told him, had done only 20,000 miles since being fitted with a replacement engine and gearbox. The plaintiff purchased the car, which proved to be a considerable disappointment to him, as it needed regular repairs,

---

[24] [1957] 1 W.L.R. 370. See also, *Routledge* v. *McKay* [1954] 1 W.L.R. 615. As is noted in Beale, Bishop & Furmston, *Contract Cases and Materials* (1985) p. 215, there is a clear economic rationale behind the principle of making the party best able to discover the truth the person upon whom the risk falls, as he is the "least cost avoider," (See Posner and Rosenfield (1977) J.L.S. 83 at 87–92) in that he may be in a better position to prevent the risk from materialising, and he also may be the superior insurer.

[25] [1957] 1 W.L.R. 370 at 376.

[26] *Ibid.* at 377.

[27] *Ibid.* at 378.

[28] [1913] A.C. 30.

[29] [1965] 1 W.L.R. 623.

and it was also discovered that the mileage done was in fact nearer
100,000 miles. In agreeing with the county court judge that the
statement as to mileage was a warranty, Lord Denning M.R.
distinguished the instant case from the *Oscar Chess* decision in that
the defendant in that case was innocent of any fault, whereas:

> "Here we have a dealer, Smith, who was in a position to
> know, or at least to find out, the history of the car. He would
> get it by writing to the makers. He did not do so. Indeed it was
> done later. When the history of this car was examined, his
> statement turned out to be quite wrong. He ought to have
> known better. There was no reasonable foundation for it."[30]

Salmon L.J. preferred simply to find that the statement was a
warranty as it had been intended by Smith to operate as such.

It is not altogether clear what relevance the element of
negligence should have to such a case.[31] Fault is not historically a
relevant element in determining contractual liability. It would be
preferable, in a case such as *Dick Bentley* where the existence of
special knowledge is regarded as a significant factor, to determine
the character of the statement made on that basis alone, though no
doubt it will frequently be the case that carelessness by a person
who possessed or had ready access to special knowledge is the
reason why the statement he made was untrue, or is the cause of
his failure to check the statement made by the other party who is
not a person with special knowledge.

Importance of the statement. A further guiding principle that in
some cases will be of assistance to the court in characterising the
statement made is whether the statement is of such importance
that had it not been made the representee would not have entered
into the contract at all. If so, it is likely to be a term of the contract.
In *Couchman* v. *Hill*,[32] for example, the plaintiff purchased a
heifer from the defendant at an auction. The heifer was described
in the sale catalogue as "unserved." The catalogue stated that the
sale would be subject to the auctioneers' usual conditions and that
all lots must be taken subject to all faults or errors of description.
The conditions of sale, which were exhibited at the auction, stated
that the lots were sold "with all faults, imperfections and errors of

---

[30] *Ibid.* at 628.
[31] See Cheshire, Fifoot and Furmston's *Law of Contract* (11th ed., 1986) p. 124;
Treitel, *The Law of Contract* (7th ed., 1987) p. 272 and *Redgrave* v. *Hurd* (1881)
20 Ch.D. 1, where the carelessness of the representor did not cause his
representation to be treated as a warranty.
[32] [1947] K.B. 554.

description." The plaintiff, prior to the sale, asked both the auctioneer and the defendant whether they could confirm that the heifer was unserved and received confirmation from both of them. The plaintiff accordingly purchased the heifer. She was later discovered to be in calf and died some 10 weeks after the sale as a result of the strain of carrying a calf at too young an age. The plaintiff claimed damages for breach of warranty. Scott L.J. held that the assurances that had been given amounted to an unqualified oral condition, the breach of which the plaintiff was entitled to treat as a breach of warranty and recover the damages claimed. The learned judge was of the view that the purpose for which the plaintiff asked about the condition of the heifer was to obtain a clear warranty, and that this was the only condition on which he would bid. Also, both the defendant and the auctioneer, though they denied giving the assurances alleged, admitted that if they had given the assurances they would have been bound by them.

Again, in *Bannerman* v. *White and others*[33] the defendant, intending to buy hops, asked the plaintiff seller if sulphur had been used in their treatment, adding that if it had been used he would not even trouble to ask the price. The plaintiff assured him that sulphur had not been used and subsequently the defendant agreed to purchase the hops. It later transpired that sulphur had in fact been used in the cultivation of a portion of the hops, and the buyer was held to be justified in his refusal to pay the price as the assurance was found by the Court of Common Pleas to be a term of the contract.

Verification. If during the course of negotiations a party makes a statement, but advises the other party to verify its accuracy, a court is unlikely to hold that the statement is a term.[34] Indeed, such a statement may not even be regarded as a representation if the representee contracts subsequently as a result of the exercise of his own judgment rather than under the influence of the original statement.[35] However, if the plaintiff is persuaded to contract by a statement from the defendant whose object is to prevent him from discovering the truth, such a statement is likely to be treated as a term. Thus, in *Schawel* v. *Read*[36] the plaintiff who wished to purchase a stallion for stud purposes, discontinued his examination of the stallion on the assurance by the vendor that: "You need not look for anything; the horse is perfectly sound. If there was

[33] (1861) 10 C.B.(N.S.) 844.
[34] See *Ecay* v. *Godfrey* (1974) 80 Ll.L.R. 286.
[35] See Chap. 2, pp. 16–17 *supra*.
[36] [1913] 2 I.R. 64.

anything the matter with the horse I should tell you." The plaintiff subsequently purchased the stallion without further examination. The stallion was in fact unfit for stud purposes. The House of Lords agreed with the jury's view that the statement of the seller amounted to a warranty.

The case of *Hopkins* v. *Tanqueray*[37] appears to go against this. A would-be purchaser of a horse refrained from examining it on the seller's assurance that the horse was perfectly sound. He purchased the horse the following day at an auction at Tattersall's, without further examining it. The horse was subsequently found to be unsound. The seller's statement was held not to be a warranty but was a mere representation. It was well known to both parties that horses sold at Tattersall's were sold without warranty, and it was largely for this reason that no intention to warrant was found. Thus, Crowder J. stated:

> "I think it abundantly clear upon the evidence that the matter here relied on was not understood or intended as forming part of the contract which might be made at the auction on the following day, which it was well known to both parties would be without a warranty."[38]

Both parties' knowledge of the terms of sales at Tattersall's is the factor that differentiates this case from *Schawel* v. *Reade*.

No decisive test. It must be stressed, however, that none of these principles provides a decisive test for the resolution of any dispute. In *Heilbut, Symons & Co.* v. *Buckleton*[39] Lord Moulton stated:

> "It is, therefore, evident that the use of the phrase 'decisive test' cannot be defended ... it may well be that the features thus referred to in the judgment of the Court of Appeal in [*De Lassalle* v. *Guildford*[40]] may be criteria of value in guiding a jury in coming to a decision whether or not a warranty was intended; but they cannot be said to furnish decisive tests, because it cannot be said as a matter of law that the presence or absence of those features is conclusive of the intention of the parties. The intention of the parties can only be deduced

---

[37] (1854) 15 C.B. 130.
[38] *Ibid.* at 142.
[39] [1913] A.C. 30.
[40] [1901] 2 K.B. 215 at 221. The Court of Appeal in that case stated that it was a decisive test whether the vendor assumed to assert a fact of which the buyer was ignorant or merely stated an opinion on a matter concerning which he had no special knowledge and on which the buyer could also be expected to have an opinion and to exercise his judgment.

from the totality of the evidence, and no secondary principles of such a kind can be universally true."[41]

This inevitably makes the business of prediction a somewhat chancy affair, though since the enactment of the Misrepresentation Act 1967 with the provision, in section 2(1) of a remedy in damages for a negligent misrepresentation, the need from a representee's point of view, to persuade a court that the representor's statement was a term, is diminished, though not necessarily removed entirely, given the difference between the measure of damages in contract and in tort.[42]

2. COLLATERAL CONTRACTS

In certain circumstances the court may be prepared to find that a statement made during the course of negotiations operates as a separate collateral contract.[43] Early cases indicate that the use of this device was argued by parties who wished to circumvent the requirements of the Statute of Frauds.[44] Thus, in *Lindley* v. *Lacey*[45] the plaintiff and the defendant were negotiating for the sale of the fixtures, furniture and goodwill of a business. The plaintiff was induced to sign a written contract for the sale by an oral promise made by the defendant to settle an action pending at the time against the plaintiff at the suit of Chase, a third party. The plaintiff sued for breach of this oral agreement and the court enforced the promise as a collateral agreement which was entirely separate from the written contract. Erle C.J. said:

"I think it is clear from the evidence that there was a distinct collateral agreement that Chase's action should be settled by the defendant, and that evidence of that agreement, which was perfectly consistent with the written agreement, was admissible."[46]

---

[41] [1913] A.C. 30 at 50–51.
[42] See *infra*, pp. 117–118.
[43] Wedderburn [1959] C.L.J. 58.
[44] The Statute of Frauds 1677 had the purpose of requiring formality in contracts, because of concern that oral promises were too readily accepted by the courts. *Inter alia* the Statute required agreements to transfer interests in land and contracts for the sale of goods worth more than 10 pounds to be in writing under signature.
[45] (1864) 17 C.B.(N.S.) 578.
[46] *Ibid*. at 587.

This went beyond the authorities cited in the judgment, for example *Harris* v. *Pickett*[47] and *Wallis* v. *Littell*,[48] which were cases of collateral terms rather than collateral contract: *i.e.* one-contract rather than two-contract cases.

Greig[49] has argued that the use of the device of the collateral contract was originally restricted to cases where the representation in question did not concern the subject matter of the main contract. This is certainly true of *Lindley* v. *Lacey*[50] and also of *Morgan* v. *Griffith*,[51] where the respondent refused to sign a lease of grass land until the appellant would agree to destroy the rabbits which overran the land. The appellant refused to put a term in the lease to that effect, but orally agreed to destroy the rabbits. The respondent thereupon signed the lease, but the appellant failed to destroy the rabbits. It was held that the oral statement was a binding collateral agreement. Pigott B. said:

> "The verbal agreement in this case, although it does affect the mode of enjoyment of the land demised is, I think, purely collateral to the lease. It was on the basis of its being performed that the lease was signed by plaintiff and it does not appear to me to contain any terms which conflict with the written document."[52]

In *Kennard* v. *Ashman*[53] Wills J. expressed the view that the cases as to collateral agreements had gone quite far enough. He held that an assurance that a house to be leased was well built did not operate as an agreement collateral to the lease. Wills J. saw no evidence that either party looked upon this assurance as a warranty, but added that if there had been such a promise it would have been so closely connected with the very subject of the contract of tenancy that it ought to have formed part of the lease. In *Jones* v. *Lavington*[54] Collins M.R. did not accept that there could be a collateral agreement as to quiet enjoyment where the main contract was a lease. He said: "Such an agreement, if there was one, was in reference to the subject-matter itself of the

---

[47] (1859) 4 Hurlst. & N. 1.
[48] (1861) 11 C.B.(N.S.) 369.
[49] (1971) 87 L.Q.R. 179 at 184–5.
[50] *Supra*, p. 105.
[51] (1871) L.R. 6 Ex. 70. See also, *Erskine* v. *Adeane* (1873) L.R. 8 Ch. 756; *Angell* v. *Duke* (1875) L.R. 10 Q.B. 174.
[52] (1871) L.R. 6 Ex. 70 at 73.
[53] (1894) 10 T.L.R. 213.
[54] [1903] 1 K.B. 253. See also, *Gale* v. *Harvey* (1893) 95 L.T.J. 82.

contract, and must be found in it."[55] As we shall see, however, a more flexible approach was adopted in subsequent cases.

At the same time, while the courts began to come to terms with this new device of the collateral contract, the case law shows, perhaps inevitably, a certain amount of confusion between the collateral term, sometimes referred to as a warranty (*e.g.* in *Schawel* v. *Reade* and *Hopkins* v. *Tanqueray*), and the collateral contract. This confusion stemmed largely from the somewhat ambiguous nature of the word "warranty." As Wedderburn has explained,[56] a warranty is always collateral in the sense that, though it is part of the contract, it is collateral to its express object. Such an undertaking may or may not be collateral in the sense that it comprises the obligation of a second contract, which is separate from the written agreement. In *De Lassalle* v. *Guildford*[57] the plaintiff was induced to enter into a lease by an assurance given by the defendant that the drains were in good order. The lease was silent as regards the drains. The plaintiff claimed damages for breach of warranty. A. L. Smith M.R. stated:

> "To create a warranty no special form of words is necessary. It must be a collateral undertaking forming part of the contract by agreement of the parties express or implied, and must be given during the course of the dealing which leads to the bargain, and should then enter into the bargain as part of it."[58]

He then went on to state that the lease did not cover the whole ground and did not contain the whole of the contract between the parties. Yet the cases cited by the Master of the Rolls in support of a finding that a warranty existed and had been breached were *Morgan* v. *Griffith*,[59] *Erskine* v. *Adeane*[60] and *Angell* v. *Duke*,[61] all cases of collateral contracts, *i.e.* two-contract rather than one-contract cases. A. L. Smith M.R. said:

> "If in the rabbit cases the agreements were collateral and outside the leases, the leases not containing the whole terms and the collateral agreements not contradicting the leases, I

---

[55] [1903] 1 K.B. 253 at 256.
[56] [1959] C.L.J. 58 at 66. See *Chanter* v. *Hopkins* (1838) 4 M. & W. 399 at 404 (Lord Abinger). See also, Stoljar (1952) 15 M.L.R. 425.
[57] [1901] 2 K.B. 215.
[58] *Ibid.* at 221.
[59] (1871) L.R. 6 Ex. 70 *supra*, p. 106.
[60] (1873) L.R. 8 Ch. 756 *supra*, n. 51.
[61] (1875) L.R. 10 Q.B. 174 *supra*, n. 51.

cannot see why the warranty in this case is not collateral also."[62]

The decision in *De Lassalle* v. *Guildford*, despite the degree of confusion between one-contract and two-contract analysis manifested in the judgment, appears essentially to be a collateral contract, *i.e.* two-contract, case. As such, it illustrates a considerable advantage of collateral contracts: the avoidance of the parol evidence rule. If a statement such as that of the landlord in *De Lassalle* was regarded as a separate contract, then the written contract was not added to, varied or contradicted.

The House of Lords had an opportunity to provide a measure of clarity to the developing law of collateral contracts in *Heilbut, Symons & Co.* v. *Buckleton*.[63] The defendants (the appellants before the House of Lords), a firm of rubber merchants, had underwritten a large number of shares in a rubber and produce company which was in the course of formation. The defendants instructed their Liverpool manager to ask his friends to take shares in the company. The plaintiff learned of the availability of the shares and telephoned the manager to make enquiries. In the course of the conversation the plaintiff said: "I understand you are bringing out a rubber company" to which the manager replied: "We are." The plaintiff was subsequently allotted a large number of shares. At the time there was a rubber boom, but later it was discovered that there was a large deficiency in rubber trees which were said in the prospectus to exist on the company's estate, and the shares fell in value.

The plaintiff claimed damages for fraudulent misrepresentation and alternatively damages for breach of warranty that the company was a rubber company whose main object was to produce rubber. At trial the jury found that there was no fraudulent misrepresentation, but found that the company could not properly be described as a rubber company and that the defendants had warranted that the company was a rubber company. The Court of Appeal dismissed the defendants' appeal, but this decision was reversed by the House of Lords.

Their Lordships emphasised the exceptional nature, as they saw it, of the collateral contract. Thus, Viscount Haldane L.C. said:

---

[62] [1901] 2 K.B. 215 at 223. See also, *Lloyd (Edward) Ltd.* v. *Sturgeon Falls Pulp Co. Ltd.* (1901) 85 L.T. 162. As Wedderburn indicates, Bruce J. who was the judge in the *Lloyd* case and also the trial judge in *De Lassalle*, favoured a strict adherence to the parol evidence rule, and appears to have experienced especial difficulty in adapting his views to take account of the development of the collateral contract.

[63] [1913] A.C. 30.

"It is contrary to the general policy of the law of England to presume the making of such a collateral contract in the absence of language expressing or implying it"[64] and Lord Moulton said: "it is evident, both on principle and on authority, that there may be a contract the consideration for which is the making of some other contract... But such collateral contracts must from their very nature be rare."[65] They also stressed the need to show an intention to make a collateral contract. In the words of Lord Moulton:

> "Such collateral contracts, the sole effect of which is to vary or add to the terms of the principal contract, are therefore viewed with suspicion by the law. They must be proved strictly. Not only the terms of such contracts but the existence of an *animus contrahendi* on the part of all the parties to them must be clearly shewn. Any laxity on these points would enable parties to escape from the full performance of the obligations of contracts unquestionably entered into by them and more especially would have the effect of lessening the authority of written contracts by making it possible to vary them by suggesting the existence of verbal collateral agreements relating to the same subject matter."[66]

The court saw no indication of any intention to make such a contract on the facts of the case, and considered that to treat a statement of the kind made by the manager as a collateral contract would be tantamount to saying that the making of any representation prior to a contract relating to the subject matter of that contract amounted to a collateral contract. In the court's view the plaintiff was largely persuaded to purchase the shares because of his belief that a firm of the standing of the defendants would not be bringing the company out if they did not believe that it was all right and the issue should not have been submitted to the jury.

Again, a certain confusion can be detected concerning collateral warranties and collateral contracts. Thus, in speaking of what must be established by the plaintiff in order to succeed, Lord Moulton stated: "He must shew a warranty, *i.e.* a contract collateral to the main contract to take the shares"[67] and Viscount Haldane saw no indication of evidence of "words either expressing or, in my opinion, implying a special contract of warranty collateral to the main contract."[68] This use of the word "warranty" to mean, in

[64] *Ibid.* at 37.
[65] *Ibid.* at 47.
[66] *Ibid.* See also, *I.B.A.* v. *E.M.I. & B.I.C.C.* (1980) 14 Build. L.R. 1.
[67] [1913] A.C. 30 at 47.
[68] *Ibid.* at 37.

effect, a binding guarantee, risks blurring the distinction between the notion of a warranty as a statement of fact, forming part of the contract but collateral to its main purpose, and a separate collateral contract. This might have had serious consequences if the one-contract cases had been assimilated to the two-contract cases, with the need in the latter category to rebut a presumption against their existence. By and large, however, the courts have paid lip-service to the limitations of the *Heilbut Symons* approach, though the absence of a clear distinction between the one-contract and the two-contract analysis has persisted.[69]

As was noted above,[70] the early cases on collateral contracts restricted the applicability of the doctrine to cases where the representation in question did not concern the subject matter of the main contract.[71] Certainly, the court would not permit an oral statement to prevail over a contradictory written document.[72] The passing of time saw signs of a more flexible approach. Thus, in *Webster* v. *Higgin*,[73] the defendant wished to purchase a car from the plaintiff, on hire purchase. During negotiations the plaintiff's agent told the defendant that if he bought the car, the plaintiff would guarantee that it was in good condition and that the defendant would have no trouble with it. The defendant subsequently signed a hire purchase agreement which stated, *inter alia*:

> "The hirer is deemed to have examined (or caused to be examined) the vehicle prior to this agreement and satisfied himself as to its condition, and no warranty, condition, description or representation on the part of the owner as to the state or quality of the vehicle is given or implied . . . any statutory or other warranty, condition, description or representation whether express or implied as to the state, quality, fitness or roadworthiness being hereby expressly excluded."

The car turned out to be, in the words of Lord Greene, M.R., "a mass of second-hand and dilapidated ironmongery."[74]

---

[69] See, *e.g. Miller* v. *Cannon Hill Estates* [1931] 2 K.B. 113; *Mahon* v *Ainscough* 1 All E.R. 337; *Oscar Chess Ltd.* v. *Williams* [1957] 1 W.L.R. 370.
[70] *Supra*, p. 106.
[71] Though, as Wedderburn implies ([1959] C.L.J. 58 at 81) it may be more satisfactory to say that the oral contracts in cases such as *Erskine* v. *Adeane* and *De Lassalle* v. *Guildford* survived because they were not contradicted by the writing.
[72] See *Angell* v. *Duke* (1875) L.R. 10 Q.B. 174; *Henderson* v. *Arthur* [1907] 1 K.B. 10.
[73] [1948] 2 All E.R. 127.
[74] *Ibid.* at 128.

At first sight any attempt to characterise the agent's assurance as a collateral contract appeared to be doomed to failure, as it directly contradicted the terms of the hire purchase agreement. However, the Court of Appeal managed to interpret the clause quoted above as not excluding the "collateral guarantee" which was given. The clause stated: "no warranty . . . is given" and not "no warranty . . . has been given," and this difference in tense was crucial, as very clear words were needed for the clause to be interpreted to apply to warranties that had been given; since "the result would, as I have said, been farcical because the guarantee would then be offered in consideration of the purchaser signing a document by which he agreed that the guarantee should be of no value whatsoever."[75]

This approach displays a commendable willingness to make use of the *contra proferentem* principle to avoid a harsh result. At the same time, however, it accepts the validity of the rule prohibiting contradiction, and therefore accords perfectly with the accepted principle. The decision of Harman J. in *City and Westminster Properties (1934) Ltd.* v. *Mudd*[76] is a very different matter, however. The defendant was the tenant of premises which comprised a ground floor shop and basement. The plaintiffs were his landlords. The parties were in the process of negotiating a new lease, a draft of which contained a clause which specified, *inter alia*, that the premises were to be used for business purposes only, and that the lessee was not permitted to lodge, dwell or sleep on the premises. The defendant, who had previously been permitted by the plaintiffs to sleep on the premises, objected to the clause. He was assured by the plaintiffs' agent that if he signed the lease the plaintiffs would not object to his continuing to reside on the premises. The defendant subsequently executed the lease (which retained the clause stating that he might not reside on the premises) and continued to live there. Several years later, when he asked for a new lease, the plaintiffs' managing director, having visited the premises and learned that the defendant was residing there, gave him notice to quit. The plaintiffs brought an action for forfeiture of the lease. Harman J. held that, though the defendant had indeed breached the terms of the lease, the words of the plaintiffs' agent amounted to a contract, acted upon by the plaintiff to his detriment and from which the plaintiffs could not be allowed to resile.

---

[75] *Ibid.* at 129, *per* Lord Greene M.R.
[76] [1959] Ch. 129.

Clearly, this was a case where the previous oral statement conflicted with the subsequent written documents, and therefore the decision itself conflicted with longstanding authority.[77] It has been cogently argued, however, that the reasoning behind *City and Westminster* v. *Mudd* is perfectly acceptable.[78] If the promise had been made to the defendant after the execution of the lease, the doctrine of equitable estoppel[79] would have operated so as to allow the defendant at least a short-term period during which to remain in occupation and indeed, if the effect of the promise were to suspend the covenant restricting the use of the premises to business purposes only for the period of the defendant's personal use, the equity would have remained during that period. There seems little logic and still less justice in the defendant's position being radically different depending upon whether the promise was made to him before or after the execution of the lease. The decision in *City and Westminster* v. *Mudd* survives today, and may be defended on the basis that the intention to make a collateral contract in such a case must be proved, and separate consideration must be shown.[80] Since, however, there now exists a remedy in damages under the Misrepresentation Act[81] it may be thought preferable, in the interests of the sanctity of written contracts, for a claim under the Act to be made in such cases. However, if the contractual measure of damages is desired by a plaintiff[82] or if the assurance given is as to the future (in which case the Act would not apply)[83] resort to the collateral contract will be necessary.

An interesting recent case is *Brikom Investments Ltd.* v. *Carr*[84] where the plaintiffs, the landlords of four blocks of flats, offered to sell 99-year leases to their sitting tenants. The plaintiffs made oral representations that they would repair the roofs (which were in a bad condition) at their own expense. The leases which were later signed by the tenants required the tenants to contribute to the cost of, *inter alia*, roof maintenance. Subsequently, the plaintiffs had the roofs repaired and claimed contributions from the tenants,

---

[77] See, *e.g. Erskine* v. *Adeane* (1873) L.R. 8 Ch. 756 at 766, *per* Mellish L.J.; *Carter* v. *Salmon* (1880) 43 L.T. 490; especially *per* Cotton L.J. at 492–493; *Horncastle* v. *Equitable Society* (1906) 22 T.L.R. 735; *Henderson* v. *Arthur* [1907] 1 K.B. 10.

[78] Wedderburn [1959] C.L.J. 58 at 83–84.

[79] See *infra*, Chap. 6, p. 137 *et seq.*

[80] See Treitel *The Law of Contract* (7th ed., 1987) p. 274.

[81] See *supra*, Chap. 3, p. 45 *et seq.*

[82] *Sed quaere* whether Harman J. would have been as happy to find a collateral contract if Mr. Mudd had been claiming damages rather than defending an action for forfeiture.

[83] See *supra*, Chap. 2, p. 12.

[84] [1979] Q.B. 467.

who refused to pay. The first defendant, who was an original lessee (the other two defendants were respectively an assignee and an assignee of an assignee of original purchasers of leases) was held to have a collateral contract with the landlords. In the words of Cumming-Bruce L.J. "consideration moved from Mrs. Carr because she entered into the agreement for a lease, and then made the deed in reliance upon the assurance."[85] Roskill L.J., citing *De Lassalle* v. *Guildford* with approval, said:

> "Where two parties are about to enter an agreement for a lease—a lease which imposes on the lessee a very burdensome obligation in respect to repairs—I can see no reason why one party cannot say to the other: 'In relation to those outstanding matters, whatever may be our legal position under the terms of the lease, we will not as landlords enforce that obligation against you.' I see no reason why effect should not be given to such a position."[86]

It does not appear to have troubled the Court of Appeal that the oral statement contradicted the terms of the lease.[87]

Although in many cases it will not matter whether the court engages in a one-contract or two-contract analysis, *i.e.* whether the inducing statement is treated as a collateral term or a separate collateral contract,[88] in a number of situations there are clear advantages to the representee in establishing the existence of a collateral contract. For example, as we have noted above, collateral contracts were used from the earliest days of the device to avoid the restrictions imposed by the Statute of Frauds. Though the Law Reform (Enforcement of Contracts) Act 1954 has considerably reduced the number of contracts required to be evidenced in writing, the part of section 4 of the Statute of Frauds that was not repealed in 1954[89] and, more importantly, section 40 of the Law of Property Act 1925, remain as cases where the requirement that the contract shall be in or evidenced in writing continues. As a simple example of the continuing value of the collateral contract in such a context, in *Jameson* v. *Kinmell Bay*

---

[85] *Ibid.* at 490.

[86] *Ibid.* at 488.

[87] In their report on the parol evidence rule (Law Com. No. 154) in 1986, the Law Commission considered that the courts today would follow this approach and give effect to an oral contract which was inconsistent to a written contract to which it was collateral, if it was established that the parties intended to make such a collateral contract (para. 2.36).

[88] See, *e.g. Quickmaid Rental Services Ltd.* v. *Reece* (1970) 114 S.J. 372.

[89] *i.e.* "any special promise to answer for the debt, default or miscarriage of another person."

Land Co. Ltd.[90] the defendants were developers from whom the plaintiff was interested in purchasing a house. The defendants' agent orally represented to the plaintiff that a suitable access road would be built by the defendants, close to the plot which the plaintiff contemplated buying. In reliance on this promise the plaintiff entered into a contract to purchase the plot. Two years later, the access road not having been built, the plaintiff claimed damages. The Court of Appeal agreed with the trial judge that he was entitled to succeed. Lord Hanworth M.R. could not see that there was in section 40 of the Law of Property Act anything which applied to the contract to construct the road, viewed as a separate contract, and Lawrence L.J. agreed that section 40 had nothing to do with the case. Clearly, it would not have been possible to sue on the agent's representation if the court had not been prepared to find two contracts rather than one, since, in the absence of a sufficient act of part performance the memorandum would not have contained all the material terms.[91]

An especial advantage of the collateral contract is that it enables the innocent party to sue on it even where the main contract is illegal, to the extent that the innocent party would not be allowed to sue on the main contract. For example, in *Strongman (1945) Ltd.* v. *Sincock*[92] the plaintiffs, a firm of builders, agreed with the defendant, an architect, to supply materials and carry out certain work at premises owned by him. The defendant undertook orally to obtain all the licences required by regulation 56A of the Defence (General) Regulations 1939. He obtained licences for £2,150 worth of work, but work to the value of £6,359 was carried out. The builders claimed the balance of the price over the licensed amount, or alternatively damages for a similar amount for breach of the warranty that the architect would obtain the licences.

The Court of Appeal held that, though the builders could not recover the price under the contract as the contract was illegal, as being totally prohibited by the regulations, they were entitled to damages for breach of the collateral contract contained in the assurance given by the architect that he would obtain all the necessary licences. In order to succeed in such a case, a plaintiff must not have been morally to blame or culpably negligent (as the builders here had not been). The fact that the architect was not in a position to obtain a licence as of right did not mean that he could not give a warranty. "A man can give a warranty although he

---

[90] (1931) 47 T.L.R. 593.
[91] Wedderburn [1959] C.L.J. 58 at 72.
[92] [1955] 2 Q.B. 525. See also, *Mouat* v. *Betts Motors Ltd.* [1959] A.C. 71.

cannot carry it into effect."[93] Though the Court of Appeal did not consider the matter, it would appear that the consideration for the collateral contract in such a case is to be found in the formation of an illegal main contract. This seems surprising, though if, as has been suggested,[94] the basis for the rule that in general a contract cannot be enforced if the promise of one (or both) of the parties is illegal is the demands of public policy, the extremely dim view that the Court of Appeal took of the merits of the defendant in *Strongman*[95] may indicate that, at least in this instance, public policy militated in favour of the plaintiffs. In other such cases it may be safer for a plaintiff to claim in deceit[96] or perhaps negligent misrepresentation, though it will usually be necessary for him to show that he was unaware of the illegality. Awareness of the illegality may mean that he is *in pari delicto* with the defendant and he is likely, therefore, to be refused the assistance of the court.[97]

The collateral contract analysis is not limited to cases involving two parties only. It may be invoked in situations where X gives an assurance or promise to Y which induces him to make a contract with Z. An early example of this can be seen in cases on breach of warranty of authority by an agent. The classic case is *Collen* v. *Wright*,[98] in which the defendant, who was the agent of a third party, negotiated with the plaintiff, who wanted to lease a farm belonging to the third party. The plaintiff entered into possession, but the third party denied that the defendant had the authority to make the agreement, and repudiated it. The plaintiff subsequently claimed damages from the defendant[99] on the basis that his representation that he had the authority of the third party to enter into the agreement was a warranty which had been breached. Willes J. said:

> "The obligation arising in such a case is well expressed by saying that a person, professing to contract as agent for another, impliedly, if not expressly, undertakes to or prom-

---

[93] [1955] 2 Q.B. 525 at 540, *per* Romer L.J.

[94] See *Chitty on Contracts* (25th ed., 1983) para. 1031.

[95] *e.g.* "My Lord has spoken of the acknowledgment of Mr. Dingle Foot [counsel for the defendant] that he came here without merits. It was quite clear as the argument proceeded that he was not merely without merits but had a considerable quantity of demerits." [1955] 2 Q.B. 525 at 538, *per* Birkett L.J.

[96] See *Shelley* v. *Paddock* [1980] Q.B. 348. See also, *Saunders* v. *Edwards* [1987] 2 All E.R. 651.

[97] See, however, *Saunders* v. *Edwards* [1987] 2 All E.R. 651.

[98] (1857) 8 E. & B. 647.

[99] An action for specific performance against the third party having failed because of the agent's lack of authority. The costs of this action were ultimately recovered by the plaintiff in his claim against the defendant.

ises the person who enters into such contract, upon the faith of the professed agent being duly authorised, that the authority which he professes to have does in point of fact exist. The fact of entering into the transaction with the professed agent, as such, is good consideration for the promise."[1]

The question whether it was justifiable for the plaintiff to rely upon the defendant's representation of authority was raised, but the court[2] took the view that the defendant, of all people, should have known the extent of his authority and, therefore, the reliance was justifiable.

A more recent illustration of this approach can be seen in *Wells (Merstham) Ltd.* v. *Buckland Sand and Silica Ltd.*.[3] The plaintiffs were chrysanthemum growers and the defendants were sand merchants. The plaintiffs told the defendants that they wanted a fine sand for propagating chrysanthemum plants. The defendants assured the plaintiffs that B.W. sand supplied by them had a low iron oxide content and would be suitable for the plaintiffs' purposes. The plaintiffs ordered a load of the sand direct from the defendants and two other loads through another company which frequently bought sand from the defendants. In fact the sand supplied had a high iron oxide content, which proved deleterious to the plants, to the extent of £2,500 worth of damage. This sum the plaintiffs claimed in an action for breach of warranty. It was held that they were entitled to succeed. It was irrelevant that the purchases after the first were made by the plaintiffs from a third party. Edmund Davies J. said:

> "As between A (a potential seller of goods) and B (a potential buyer) two ingredients, and two only, are in my judgment required in order to bring about a collateral contract containing a warranty: (1) a promise or assertion by A as to the nature, quality or quantity of the goods which B may reasonably regard as being made *animo contrahendi*, and (2) acquisition by B of the goods in reliance on that promise or assertion."[4]

The consideration, for the collateral contract was, of course, the act of entering into the main contract.

---

[1] (1857) 8 E. & B. 647 at 657–658.
[2] With the exception of Cockburn L.J., who dissented.
[3] [1965] 2 Q.B. 170. See also, *Shanklin Pier Ltd.* v. *Detel Products Ltd.* [1951] 2 K.B. 854; *Andrews* v. *Hopkinson* [1957] 1 Q.B. 229 (the "good little bus" case); *Yeoman Credit Ltd.* v. *Odgers* [1962] 1 All E.R. 789.
[4] [1965] 2 Q.B. 170 at 180.

The use of the collateral contract in three-party situations proved to be of especial value in those cases in which, since 1964, a remedy has been available in negligence,[5] but, since there was no contract between the representor and representee, it was irrelevant in such cases that prior to 1967 no damages were available for negligent misrepresentation. Of course the need to prove contractual intention remains significant in those cases in which it is sought to argue contractual liability.[6]

3. BENEFITS OF A CONTRACTUAL CLAIM

The existence of a remedy in damages under section 2(1) of the Misrepresentation Act 1967 has, no doubt, removed the need in some cases to establish that the defendant's statement was a term or a collateral contract. Detailed analysis of the relationship between the various types of claim for "misrepresentation" in the broadest sense is provided in Chapter 7; for now it is worth noting that if damages are sought and fraud or negligence cannot be proved, or the defendant is able to prove that he was not negligent,[7] it will be necessary to argue that the defendant's statement was contractual. In addition, the contractual measure of damages may be preferable to the plaintiff, since in contract the plaintiff may be compensated to the extent of being put in the position he would have been in if the statement had been true, whereas the tortious measure of damages will simply put him in the position he would have been in if the statement had not been made. Thus, a plaintiff representee who has suffered expectation losses will seek to frame his cause of action accordingly. In a case such as *Schawel* v. *Reade*,[8] where the defendant assured the plaintiff that the horse which the latter was interested in purchasing for stud purposes was perfectly sound, it may be possible in a breach of contract claim to obtain damages for the loss of stud value which is likely to exceed the purchase price of the horse, though the difference between that latter figure and the

---

[5] *Hedley Byrne & Co. Ltd.* v. *Heller & Partners Ltd.* [1964] A.C. 465.
[6] For a modern example of the continuing importance of this requirement, see *I.B.A.* v. *E.M.I. & B.I.C.C.* (1980) 14 Build. L.R. 1. E.M.I. had agreed to construct a television mast for the plaintiffs. They did so on the basis that the actual work would be done by B.I.C.C. as subcontractors. The latter were not a party to the main contract. B.I.C.C. wrote to I.B.A. expressing their satisfaction with the mast, which however later collapsed. B.I.C.C.'s letter was held not to have contractual effect, as there was no intention to contract. However, they were liable in negligence.
[7] See Misrepresentation Act 1967, s.2(1) and discussion at p. 45 *et seq.*
[8] [1913] 2 I.R. 881, *supra*, pp. 103–104.

actual value is all that would be available in a claim in negligence.[9] The fact that contractual liability is strict, by contrast with negligence liability, which is fault-based, may also be a relevant factor, as also may be the fact that an assurance as to the future will not usually be actionable as a misrepresentation.[10]

4. Exclusion[11] Clauses

It may be sought to exclude liability for a collateral warranty or a collateral contract by means of a term inserted in the main contract. This may either be done within an all-purpose clause seeking to exclude liability for all pre-contractual statements, or by specific reference to collateral warranties and collateral contracts. Since exclusion clauses are, as noted below, interpreted *contra proferentem*, the latter course would appear to be the wiser.

At common law, the courts' concern that exclusion clauses were open to abuse by a dominant party manifested itself by means of such devices as the interpretation of ambiguous words in an exclusion clause against the party seeking to rely on them.[12] This is an aspect of the general *contra proferentem* rule whereby such clauses are strictly construed against parties who invoke them. However, where such a clause seeks to limit rather than exclude liability, the courts may be more generously inclined towards it.[13]

Webster v. *Higgin*[14] illustrates well the operation of the *contra proferentem* principle in the context of a collateral contract (or collateral guarantee, as it was described in the judgment). To state in the clause that "no warranty, condition, description or representation . . . is given" could not exclude liability for breach of the collateral guarantee that had already been given. Very clear

---

[9] Though if fraud can be established the plaintiff may benefit from the fact that the test for remoteness of damage may be more extensive in deceit than in negligence. See p. 44 *supra*.

[10] *Supra*, Chap. 2, p. 12. But note *Edgington* v. *Fitzmaurice* (1885) 29 Ch.D. 459, discussed *supra*, pp. 12–13. That is not to say that such an assurance will necessarily be actionable as a warranty; see *Esso Petroleum Co. Ltd.* v. *Mardon* [1976] Q.B. 801 at 826, *per* Ormrod L.J.

[11] Unless otherwise indicated, in this section references to "exclusion" should be read as being equally applicable to limitations on liability. For good general discussion of the law concerning exclusion of liability, see Yates, *Exclusion Clauses in Contracts* (2nd ed., 1982); Yates and Hawkins, *Standard Business Contracts: Exclusions and Related Devices* (1986).

[12] See *White* v. *John Warwick & Co. Ltd.* [1953] 2 All E.R. 1021; *Houghton* v. *Trafalgar Insurance* [1954] 1 Q.B. 247.

[13] See *Ailsa Craig Fishing Ltd.* v. *Malvern Fishing Co. Ltd.* [1983] 1 All E.R. 101.

[14] [1948] 2 All E.R. 127. For the facts, see *supra*, p. 110.

wording was needed, as the consequence of interpreting the clause in favour of the plaintiff would have been, in Lord Greene M.R.'s word, "farcical."

Quite apart from the common law rules, statutory control of exclusion clauses is of considerable importance. Section 3 of the Unfair Contract Terms Act 1977 provides as follows:

Liability arising in Contract

3.(1) This section applies as between contracting parties where one of them deals as consumer or on the other's written standard terms of business.

(2) As against that party, the other cannot by reference to any contract term—

(a) when himself in breach of contract, exclude or restrict any liability of his in respect of the breach; or

(b) claim to be entitled—

(i) to render a contractual performance substantially different from that which was reasonably expected of him, or

(ii) in respect of the whole or any part of his contractual obligation, to render no performance at all,

except in so far as (in any of the cases mentioned above in this subsection) the contract term satisfies the requirement of reasonableness.

"Dealing as consumer" is defined in section 12 of the Act.

12.(1) a party to a contract "deals as consumer" in relation to another party if—

(a) he neither makes the contract in the course of a business nor holds himself out as doing so; and

(b) the other party does make the contract in the course of a business; and

(c) in the case of a contract governed by the law of sale of goods or hire-purchase, or by section 7 of this Act, the goods passing under or in pursuance of the contract are of a type ordinarily supplied for private use or consumption.

(2) But on a sale by auction or by competitive tender the buyer is not in any circumstances to be regarded as dealing as consumer.

(3) Subject to this, it is for those claiming that a party does not deal as consumer to show that he does not.

The "reasonableness" test is defined in section 11 of the Act.

11.(1) In relation to a contract term, the requirement of reasonableness for the purpose of this Part of this Act, section 3 of the Misrepresentation Act 1967 and section 3 of the Misrepresentation Act (Northern Ireland) 1967 is that the term shall have been a fair and reasonable one to be included having regard to the circumstances which were, or ought reasonably to have been, known to or in the contemplation of the parties when the contract was made.

(2) In determining for the purposes of section 6 or 7 above whether a contract term satisfies the requirement of reasonableness, regard shall be had in particular to the matters specified in Schedule 2 to this Act; but this subsection does not prevent the court or arbitrator from holding, in accordance with any rule of law, that a term which purports to exclude or restrict any relevant liability is not a term of the contract.

(3) In relation to a notice (not being a notice having contractual effect), the requirement of reasonableness under this Act is that it should be fair and reasonable to allow reliance on it, having regard to all the circumstances obtaining when the liability arose or (but for the notice) would have arisen.

(4) Where by reference to a contract term or notice a person seeks to restrict liability to a specified sum of money, and the question arises (under this or any other Act) whether the term or notice satisfies the requirement of reasonableness, regard shall be had in particular (but without prejudice to subsection (2) above in the case of contract terms) to—

(a) the resources which he could expect to be available to him for the purpose of meeting the liability should it arise; and

(b) how far it was open to him to cover himself by insurance.

(5) It is for those claiming that a contract term or notice satisfies the requirement of reasonableness to show that it does.

Thus, if a party seeks to exclude or limit his liability for a collateral warranty or a collateral contract, his attempt to do so will be subject first of all to the common law tests of interpretation, and further to the requirements of the Unfair Contract Terms Act. It should be noted further that section 4 of the Act subjects unreasonable indemnity clauses to the requirement of reasonableness, and section 5 renders entirely ineffective any attempt in a "guarantee"[15] of consumer goods to exclude or restrict liability for loss or damage.

These controls only operate, however, in the case of "business liability," which is defined in section 1(3) of the Act as follows:

> (3) In the case of both contract and tort, sections 2 to 7 apply
> (except to where the contrary is stated in section 6(4) only to business liability, that is liability for breach of obligations or duties arising—
>
>   (a) from things done or to be done by a person in the course of a business (whether his own business or another's); or
>   (b) from the occupation of premises used for business purposes of the occupier;
>
> and references to liability are to be read accordingly.

"Business" is defined in section 14 of the Act as including "a profession and the activities of any government department or local or public authority." It is thought that "business liability" is likely to be interpreted broadly. Thus it has been suggested[16]: "that a 'business' need not be carried on with a view to a profit, and that 'business liability' is intended to cover any liability not incurred in a purely private capacity."

Suppose that in *Webster* v. *Higgin* the court had been prepared to accept that the exclusion clause did in fact operate to exclude the plaintiff's liability at common law. Under the Unfair Contract Terms Act this clause would, by section 3, be subjected to the requirement of reasonableness, since it is clear that the defendant was dealing as a consumer, and the plaintiff was acting in the course of a business. Though the Act provides limited guidance only on the meaning of reasonableness, it is thought unlikely that a blanket exclusion of the type employed in *Webster* would be regarded as reasonable in such a case, given the expertise of the plaintiff and the fact that the defendant's acquaintance with motor cars was limited to an ability to drive them.

---

[15] Defined in s.5(2)(b) as "anything in writing [which] contains or purports to contain some promise or assurance (however worded or presented) that defects will be made good by complete or partial replacement, or by repair, monetary compensation or otherwise."

[16] *Chitty on Contracts* (25th ed., 1983) para. 914.

5. Conclusion

As has been lucidly demonstrated[17] the transfer of the remedy to a representee from deceit to *assumpsit* imported a number of problems that have had a profound effect upon the development of the law in this area. The need to find consideration to support contractual liability led to the requirement that the parties must have intended that the representor's statement form part of the contract.

To establish this intention was a difficult task, as the statement in reality was very frequently an inducement to contract rather than forming part of the contract, and an onerous burden was placed upon the representee in requiring him to prove that intention, especially since, as the need to prove fraud developed as the essence of the action in deceit, he had no alternative cause of action save the possibility of rescission of the contract in equity. The absence of a claim for negligent misrepresentation for so long was no doubt, as the quotation from Lord Denning M.R. in *Esso Petroleum Co. Ltd.* v. *Mardon*[18] indicates, a factor in the courts' frequent willingness to find an intention to warrant, and this willingness no doubt reduced the burden on the representee. Together with the courts' concern to protect the doctrine of consideration[19] and the effect of the decision of the House of Lords in *Derry* v. *Peek*,[20] this flexible use of the warranty device held back the development of a claim in damages for negligent misrepresentation to the extent that it was not until more than 30 years had elapsed since the decision in *Donoghue* v. *Stevenson* that the possibility of such a claim was admitted.

Is there any need for statements of the kind we have described in this chapter to continue to be treated as contractual? It might be argued that the development of the claim at common law for negligent misstatement and the availability of damages under section 2(1) of the Misrepresentation Act provide perfectly adequate remedies for the representee, and allow the concept of warranty in effect to return to tort. Such statements are, it may be argued, essentially inducements to contract rather than terms of the contract or separate contracts in their own right, and as such should not entitle the representee to contractual remedies for their breach. Such an approach has a pleasing tidiness to it. The need

[17] Greig (1971) 87 L.Q.R. 179.
[18] [1976] Q.B. 801 at 817. See pp. 97–98 *supra*.
[19] See *Winterbottom* v. *Wright* (1842) 10 M. & W. 109; Greig (1971) 87 L.Q.R. 179 at 191.
[20] (1889) 14 App.Cas. 337.

for the difficult and uncertain task of distinguishing between representations and terms would be removed. The parol evidence rule (such as it is) does not apply to misrepresentations, and other advantages of the collateral contract, as exemplified by *Jameson* v. *Kinmell Bay Land Co. Ltd.*[21] and *Strongman (1945) Ltd.* v. *Sincock*[22] could be matched by the availability of damages for the misrepresentations made in those cases. Since misrepresentation also operates outside the contract, the requirement of writing on the one hand and the illegality of the subsequent contract on the other would pose no more of a problem to misrepresentation than they do to the collateral contract.

We have noted above[23] the benefits to a plaintiff of the collateral contract or collateral warranty over a claim under section 2(1) or a claim under *Hedley Byrne* v. *Heller*. As the reports demonstrate, the advantages of the contractual measure of damages and strict liability continue to influence the choice of cause of action. But if such statements do not really form part of the contract, should a plaintiff be entitled to make such a choice?

Against this it may be said that if the parties "intended that the representation was to form part of the basis of the contractual relations between them"[24] then that is their choice and all the court can do is to search for manifestations of that intention. Surely it would be excessively arbitrary to exclude all statements "made during the course of negotiations" from the contract, for who, other than the parties, is to say when negotiation ends and agreement begins? It may be that the absence of any other remedy in damages for a large number of misrepresentations led the court in the past to be too ready to find contractual intention manifested whenever they felt that to do so would do justice between the parties, but it might be excessive to go to the other extreme and treat all statements "made in the course of negotiations" as representations. In conclusion, it is suggested that there has to be room for the law of contract in this area, though the courts should be alive to the existence of other remedies and bear in mind the context in which most of the precedents cited to them were decided.

[21] [1931] 47 T.L.R. 593.
[22] [1955] 2 Q.B. 525.
[23] pp. 117–118 *supra*.
[24] *Per* Ormrod L.J. in *Esso Petroleum Co. Ltd.* v. *Mardon* [1976] Q.B. 801 at 826.

Chapter 6

ESTOPPEL

An account of the law of misrepresentation would not be complete without some indication of the *rôle* played by estoppel in this area of the law. The history of estoppel and actionable misrepresentation shows close links between the two concepts, and a number of recent case law developments suggest that estoppel's *rôle* is still capable of further growth and expansion.

1. Estoppel by Representation

An early line of cases suggests that the origins of estoppel by representation may lie in the Court of Chancery. In *Hunt* v. *Carew*[1] a father was seised of an estate for life, with remainder in tail to his son. The plaintiff thought that the father had the inheritance, and asked the son to help him to obtain a lease from the father, determinable upon lives, offering a £400 fine and a small yearly rent. The son told the plaintiff that his father had the power to make such a lease, the father purportedly granted it and the son received £300 of the fine. The plaintiff later discovered the true facts and, upon the son's refusal to confirm the lease, brought a bill in Chancery. The Court ordered:

> "That since the plaintiff was not acquainted that the father had exceeded his power, and he relying on the affirmation of the son (who had most of the money), that the lease would be good without his joining, by which he was deceived: that therefore both should join at their own costs to make an assurance, and confirm the lease to the plaintiff during the estate thereby granted."[2]

Though the term "estoppel" is not used in these early cases, the effect of the court's order appears to be that of estoppel, in that the defendant is prevented from defending himself by denying the truth of his statement.

---

[1] (1649) Nels. 46. See also, *Dyer* v. *Dyer* (1682) 2 Ch.Cas. 108 (held that estoppel would not arise out of an innocent misrepresentation).

[2] (1649) Nels. 48.

Such early cases[3] founded the liability of the representor to make his representation good upon fraud. But it became increasingly established that a finding of fraud was not always necessary. Thus, in *Hunsden* v. *Cheyney*[4] a mother, who was entitled to a term of years in land limited to her in tail, stood by while her son negotiated a marriage on the basis that the term was to come to him on his mother's death, and undertook to settle the reversion upon the issue of the marriage after his mother's decease. On the suit of a child of the marriage, the mother was compelled to make the settlement good, although it was insisted that she was not guilty of any fraud, but was ignorant of her title and did not realise that as tenant in tail she could dispose of the term. This appears to be a case of gross negligence[5] rather than fraud. Certainly by the early nineteenth century it was clear that a finding of fraud was not necessary against a representor in order for him to be required to make his representation good. Thus in *Burrowes* v. *Lock*[6] the plaintiff took an assignment of the interest of one Cartwright in a fund of which the defendant was trustee. The defendant was aware that 10 years earlier Cartwright had made a prior assignment to his (*i.e.* Cartwright's) brother, but he had forgotten this, and represented to the plaintiff that Cartwright's interest was unencumbered. Sir William Grant M.R. held that the defendant was in conscience bound to make the representation good, (in effect by paying the full amount of the interest to the plaintiff without deducting the incumbrance), on the basis that he had at least been guilty of gross negligence.

(a) The position at common law

At common law the development of estoppel by representation occurred later than in equity, but in 1837 we find the classic statement of the ambit of this category of estoppel in the judgment of Lord Denman C.J. in *Pickard* v. *Sears*.[7] He said:

---

[3] See also, *Draper* v. *Borlace* (1699) 2 Vern. 369; *Arnot* v. *Biscoe* (1743) 1 Ves.Sen. 95; *Evans* v. *Bicknell* (1801) 6 Ves. 174 "It is a very old head of equity, that if a representation is made to another person, going to deal in a matter of interest upon the faith of that representation, the former shall make that representation good, if he knows it to be false," *per* Lord Eldon L.C. at 183.

[4] (1690) 2 Vern. 150. See also, *Teasdale* v. *Teasdale* (1726) Sel.Cas. *temp* King 59.

[5] See Sheridan (1952) 15 M.L.R. 325 at 329.

[6] (1805) 10 Ves. 470.

[7] (1837) 6 Ad. & El. 469. See also, *Montefiori* v. *Montefiori* (1762) 1 Wm.Bl. 363.

"But the rule of law is clear, that, where one by his words or conduct wilfully[8] causes another to believe the existence of a certain state of things, and induces him to act on that belief, so as to alter his own previous position, the former is concluded from averring against the latter a different state of things as existing at the same time ... "[9]

In consequence, the defendant was held to be entitled to resist the plaintiff's action in trover. The plaintiff was the legal owner of the goods, though they were in the possession of another. The goods were seized under an execution against the person in possession, and sold to the defendant. The plaintiff knew that this sale was contemplated but, though prior to the sale he came to the premises where the goods were stored, he gave no notice of his claim. This conduct was held to amount to an authorisation of the sale of the goods, and he was estopped from denying the defendant's title. This, as has been pointed out,[10] is different from the equitable development, whereby a representor could be required to make his representation good. At common law the rule in *Pickard* v. *Sears* simply prevented the plaintiff from denying the truth of what he had (by implication) said. There appears to be no indication in the common law cases that a representor could be required to make his representation good, *i.e.* that the estoppel could amount to a cause of action.

(b) Equitable developments

In *Pulsford* v. *Richards*[11] Sir John Romilly M.R., in the course of a general discussion of the available equitable remedies for

---

[8] "Wilfully" was explained by Parke B. in *Freeman* v. *Cooke* (1848) 2 Exch. 654 at 663 as requiring that the representor meant his representation to be acted upon and that it was acted upon. It would suffice that the representor so conducted himself that a reasonable man would take the representation to be true, believe that it was meant that he should act upon it, and so act upon it.

[9] (1837) 6 Ad. & El. 469 at 474.

[10] See Jackson (1965) 81 L.Q.R. 84 at 97. As was pointed out by Lord Cranworth V-C in *West* v. *Jones* (1851) 1 Sim(N.S.) 205 at 207–208, it was "a principle perfectly familiar, not only to Courts of Equity but also to Courts of law; namely that where a party has, by words or by conduct, made a representation to another leading him to believe in the existence of a particular fact of [sic] state of facts, and that other person has acted on the faith of such a representation, then the party who made the representation shall not afterwards be heard to say that the facts were not as he represented them to be." This would appear to have been the limit of the common law jurisdiction, however, whereas the action to make a representation good in equity permitted a plaintiff to sue on the misrepresentation as, for example, in *Burrowes* v. *Lock*.

[11] (1853) 17 Beav. 87. See Chap. 1, pp. 4–5.

misrepresentation, underlined the extent to which the appropriate remedy was at large and in the discretion of the Court. Of especial significance are the following remarks:

> "...if the representation be one which can be made good, the party to the contract shall be compelled or may be at liberty to do so; but if the representation made be one which cannot be made good, the person deceived shall be at liberty, if he please, to avoid the contract."[12]

The Master of the Rolls went on to furnish examples which tend to suggest that where it was practically possible to do so, the Court would require the representor to make his representation good. It is also clear[13] that these principles applied equally to fraudulent and to negligent statements.

Perhaps the highwater mark of this line of cases can be seen in *Slim* v. *Croucher*.[14] A person sought a loan upon the security of a lease, which he represented he was entitled to have granted to him for a period of $98^{1}/_{2}$ years. The lender required a written intimation from the alleged lessor of his intention to grant the lease. The lessor, aware of its purpose, signed the required intimation. The loan was thereafter made on the faith of the intimation, and subsequently the lessor granted a lease which was then mortgaged by the borrower to the lender. It later transpired that the lessor had some time previously demised the same premises for the same term to the borrower, who had since assigned it for value. The lender, therefore, had no interest in the land. It was held that the court had jurisdiction to direct repayment by the lessor to the lender of the sum he had advanced with interest, although there was no evidence of fraud. The lessor had simply forgotten the previous lease when he granted the second.

(c) Jorden v. Money

It does not appear to have troubled the court in *Slim* v. *Croucher* that the representation in question looked very like an assertion as to the future, *i.e.* that a valid lease would be granted in the future. It may be that the other members of the Court of Appeal shared the view of Lord Campbell L.C. that it was the misrepresentation of a fact rather than a promise.[15] In any event,

---

[12] (1853) 17 Beav. 87 at 95.
[13] *Ibid.* at 94.
[14] (1860) 1 De G.F. & J. 518.
[15] *Ibid.* at 524. *Cf.* Kay L.J. in *Low* v. *Bouverie* [1891] 3 Ch. 82 at 109.

six years previously in the important case of *Jorden* v. *Money*[16] the House of Lords had held that estoppel could not arise from a representation of future intention; a statement of fact was necessary. The facts of *Jorden* v. *Money* were as follows. Money was indebted to Marnell in the sum of £1200. Marnell had judgment entered against Money for this sum, and also took a bond from Money for £1200. Marnell subsequently died, leaving his sister, Mrs. Jorden, entitled to the benefit of the judgment and the bond. Money wished to get married, and Mrs. Jorden stated orally to him and to others that she would not enforce the debt. However, she refused to give up the bond. On the strength of these assurances, Money duly married, but a few years later, Mrs. Jorden served Money with a writ of *scire facias* to revive the earlier judgment. Money sought, *inter alia*, an injunction to restrain her from enforcing execution of the judgment. He succeeded before the trial judge and a majority of the Court of Appeal, but failed before the House of Lords (containing the erstwhile dissenter in the Court of Appeal, Lord Cranworth, who had become Lord Chancellor) by a majority.[17]

Upon questionable, if any, authority[18] Lord Cranworth stated:

"I think that doctrine [*i.e.* the rule in *Pickard* v. *Sears*] does not apply to a case where the representation is not a representation of a fact, but a statement of something which the party intends or does not intend to do."[19]

Lord Brougham agreed.[20] Lord St.Leonards, however, considered that:

"it is utterly immaterial whether it is a misrepresentation of fact, as it actually existed, or a misrepresentation of an intention to do, or to abstain from doing, an act which would lead to the damage of the party whom you thereby induced to

---

[16] (1854) 5 H.L.C. 185; 23 L.J.Ch. 865.
[17] Meagher, Gummow & Lehane, *Equity—Doctrines and Remedies* (2nd ed., 1984) comment as follows: "Yet while the plaintiff had both the numbers and quality in support, he lost in the final analysis because of Lord Cranworth's encore in the House of Lords. Such a decision can have little to recommend it as a precedent" (at para. 1703).
[18] Jackson (1965) 81 L.Q.R. 84 at 90 finds none at all. The best that can be said for Lords Cranworth and Brougham is that cases such as *Neville* v. *Wilkinson* (1782) 1 Bro.C.C. 543, upon which they relied, provide negative support for the proposition that a representation must be of fact in order to found an estoppel since that was the type of representation that had been made in those cases.
[19] (1854) 5 H.L.C. 185 at 214–215.
[20] *Ibid.* at 226.

deal, in marriage or in purchase, or anything of that sort, upon the faith of that representation."[21]

The decision in *Jorden* v. *Money* has not gone uncriticised[22] but it has received constant judicial support.[23] Henceforth a representation had to be a statement of fact rather than of intention in order to found an estoppel. Subject to that limitation the line of cases represented by *Burrowes* v. *Lock* could and did continue. Thus, in *Stephens* v. *Venables (No. 2)*[24] Sir John Romilly M.R. regarded *Burrowes* v. *Lock* as surviving *Jorden* v. *Money*. However, it should be noted that a possible way of circumventing *Jorden* v. *Money* is to construe a statement of intention as a representation of the fact that this intention exists. If there is in fact no such intention there may be said to have been a misrepresentation of an existing fact.[25] Thus, in *Salisbury (Marquess)* v. *Gilmore*[26] a tenant failed to leave premises in good repair at the expiration of his lease, contrary to the terms of the lease, since he had been told that the landlords intended to pull down the premises at the expiration of the lease. In an action by the landlord for breach of covenant the tenant relied upon a statutory defence which disallowed the recovery of damages for failure to repair where the premises were to be pulled down. It was argued that estoppel did not apply, on the basis of *Jorden* v. *Money*, since the landlord's statement had been one of intention. MacKinnon L.J. said[27]:

"But the question must be what is the substance of the intimation by the man concerned, not what is the form or language of it. A statement using the words 'intend' or 'intention' in the form, may be, in substance, a representation of fact . . . In substance the communication . . . stated facts. 'This house is so old and out of date that any sensible landlord

---

[21] *Ibid.* at 248.
[22] See, *e.g.* Jackson (1965) 81 L.Q.R. 84.
[23] *Citizens Bank of Louisiana* v. *First National Bank of New Orleans* (1873) L.R. 6 H.L. 352 at 360; *Maddison* v. *Alderson* (1883) 8 App.Cas. 467 at 473; *Chadwick* v. *Manning* [1896] A.C. 231 at 238; *Bank of Baroda Ltd.* v. *Punjab National Bank Ltd.* [1944] A.C. 176 at 192. *Loffus* v. *Maw* (1862) 3 Giff. 592, in which the Vice-Chancellor (Sir John Stuart) regarded *Jorden* v. *Money* as irreconcilable with *Hammersley* v. *De Biel* (1845) 12 Cl. & Fin. 45, was itself disapproved of in *Maddison* v. *Alderson* on the basis that *Hammersley* was a case of contract and hence the statement of intention in that case was properly actionable. But see Jackson *supra*, n. 22 at 93–95 and Dawson (1982) 1 Canta L.R. 329 at 334–342.
[24] (1862) 31 Beav. 124. See also, *Simmons* v. *Rose; In re Ward* (1862) 31 Beav. 1.
[25] See *Edgington* v. *Fitzmaurice* (1885) 29 Ch.D. 459 *supra*, pp. 12–13.
[26] [1942] 2 K.B. 38.
[27] *Ibid.* at 51–52.

would rebuild it at the end of the term'... That being the substance of the statement to the defendant, I do not think the rule in *Jorden* v. *Money* avails to prevent him relying on the principle stated by Bowen L.J. [in *Birmingham & District Land Co.* v. *London & North West Railway Co.*[28]] merely because the words of the letter happen to use the word 'intention.' "[29]

(d) The decline of the doctrine of making representations good

At common law, as we have noted above,[30] estoppel operated so as to prevent the plaintiff from denying the truth of his earlier statement, but did not extend to permitting a representee to sue on the representation to have it made good. If, however, he could establish fraud, *Pasley* v. *Freeman*[31] had established that an action on the case lay for deceit. The essence of the common law action can be seen in *Taylor* v. *Ashton*[32] where the defendants, directors of a bank, were alleged to have made false and fraudulent representations concerning the state of their bank in a report, which was designed to induce people to buy shares. Parke B. said: "... we are of opinion that, independently of any contract between the parties, no one can be made responsible for a representation of this kind, unless it be fraudulently made. That is the doctrine laid down in *Pasley* v. *Freeman* ... "[33]

Subsequently, in *Derry* v. *Peek*[34] the House of Lords held that a person was not liable in deceit for a false representation, carelessly made, provided that he had an honest belief in its truth. A plaintiff had to be able to show that the representation was made knowingly, or without belief in its truth, or recklessly, without caring whether it was true or false.

This was regarded by the Court of Appeal in *Low* v. *Bouverie*[35] as casting doubts over the line of cases in equity, such as *Burrowes*

---

[28] (1888) 40 Ch.D. 268 *infra*, p. 139.

[29] Ultimately the case was decided on the footing that the statutory defence was available. It should be noted that in *Jorden* v. *Money* Lord Brougham expressly stated that there had been no misrepresentation of intention by Mrs. Jorden since at the time when she said she would not enforce the debt this was her actual intention. See also, Spencer, Bower and Turner, *Estoppel by Representation* (3rd ed., 1977) pp. 33–34.

[30] *Supra*, p. 127.

[31] (1789) 3 T.R. 51 *supra*, p. 39.

[32] (1843) 11 M. & W. 401.

[33] *Ibid.* at 415.

[34] (1889) 14 App.Cas. 337. *Supra*, pp. 40–41. *Cf. Cann* v. *Willson* (1888) 39 Ch.D. 39.

[35] [1891] 3 Ch. 82.

v. *Lock* and *Slim* v. *Croucher*, which had decided in effect that
liability was incurred by the person who made a careless but
honest false representation to another about to deal in a matter of
business upon the faith of the representation. The Court of Appeal
held that *Slim* v. *Croucher* was inconsistent with, and consequently
overruled by *Derry* v. *Peek*. *Burrowes* v. *Lock* was held to be
supportable on the ground of estoppel, "but estoppel is not a cause
of action—it is a rule of evidence which precludes a person from
denying the truth of some previous statement made by himself."[36]
In *Burrowes* the assignee plaintiff had an independent cause of
action against the trustee founded on the assignment, and the
trustee, because of his misrepresentation, was prevented from
raising the defence that he was already bound to pay part of the
fund to Cartwright's brother, to whom it had earlier been
assigned. No such independent cause of action existed in *Slim*; the
whole basis of the plaintiff's claim was the misrepresentation of the
lessor.

In *Low* v. *Bouverie*, Vice-Admiral Bouverie, who was entitled
under a settlement to a life interest in a trust fund, applied to the
plaintiff for a loan on the security of the life interest. He referred
the plaintiff to the defendant, who was one of the trustees of the
settlement, for information as to his means and position. In
response to an inquiry from the plaintiff asking what the trust fund
consisted of, and whether Admiral Bouverie's life interest was
subject to any incumbrances, the defendant replied that the life
interest was subject to certain incumbrances which were mentioned, but did not state that there were no other incumbrances.
The plaintiff had not stated in his request for information that the
Admiral had applied for a loan. The plaintiff thereafter made a
loan to Admiral Bouverie on the security of a mortgage by him of
his life interest. Later the plaintiff discovered that the life interest
was subject to several incumbrances other than those mentioned
by the defendant, but whose existence the defendant had forgotten
when he replied to the plaintiff's inquiries. As his security was
insufficient, he brought an action against the defendant, claiming a
declaration that he was liable to pay to him the total amount due
under his mortgage, and payment accordingly. The Court of
Appeal held that the defendant was not liable. He had not been
dishonest, so an action in deceit did not lie. He was not liable in
warranty, as there was no intention to contract, nor was there any
consideration. He would have been estopped from denying the
truth of his words, and hence would have been required, as trustee

---

[36] *Ibid.* at 101, *per* Lindley L.J. See also, 105, *per* Bowen L.J.

for the plaintiff, to pay to him the Admiral's life interest in the fund, subject to the incumbrances whose existence he had disclosed,[37] save that his reply to the plaintiff was ambiguous. "But in order to create an estoppel, the statement by which the Defendant is held bound must be clear and unambiguous"[38] and the defendant's reply was held to have been quite consistent with the view that the incumbrances which he mentioned were all that he knew of or remembered.

In so far as *Burrowes* v. *Lock* was a decision on the ground of estoppel, the Court of Appeal was content to support it, but not if it purported to be founded on a principle of equity that the maker of a false but honest representation was liable to the representee who acted upon it. It has been argued[39] that this subjection of the equitable principle of making representations good to the more limited common law rule, as exemplified by cases such as *Pickard* v. *Sears*, whereby a cause of action could not be founded on an estoppel, is to ignore the basis of the equitable rule. Essentially the Court of Appeal in *Low* took the view that damages for misrepresentation were only available in deceit or on a warranty: in the absence of fraud or an intention to warrant the only relief could come by way of estoppel (or, of course, rescission where appropriate). Part of the difficulty, no doubt, is that the courts in early cases such as *Burrowes* did not clearly state whether their judgments were founded on estoppel or on a wider principle of making representations good, in circumstances where an estoppel would not arise. Cases such as *Hunsden* v. *Cheyney*[40] might also be explained in the alternative as decided on the basis of estoppel or as founded on some broader principle. In *Low* itself, the Court held that on the facts the defendant had not made the clear and unambiguous representation which is necessary for there to be an estoppel. Lindley L.J. stated that the case would otherwise have been indistinguishable from *Burrowes* v. *Lock*: the plaintiff would have been entitled, not to damages for misrepresentation, but to an order, as noted above, to the defendant, as the plaintiff's trustee, to pay to him the Admiral's life interest, subject to the disclosed incumbrances. It may be noted that if a claim in misrepresentation had been allowed, the result would not have been dissimilar.

---

[37] *Ibid.* at 103, *per* Lindley L.J.
[38] *Ibid.* at 113, *per* Kay L.J.
[39] Jackson (1965) 81 L.Q.R. 84 at 97–98.
[40] (1690) 2 Vern. 150. *Supra*, n. 4.

Rightly or wrongly, the effect of *Derry* v. *Peek* and *Low* v. *Bouverie* was for the time being to bring to an end any possible claim outside contract for an honest misrepresentation. Subsequently, as we have noted elsewhere,[41] statutory and common law developments have filled that gap. But no attempt was made to revive the equitable jurisdiction of making representations good, and *Slim* v. *Croucher* remains overruled.

(e) The ambit of estoppel by representation today

The metes and bounds of estoppel by representation have remained largely unchanged since the end of the nineteenth century. The classic definition of estoppel by representation is that of Spencer Bower and Turner[42]:

> "where one person ('the representor') has made a representation to another person ('the representee') in words or by acts or conduct, or (being under a duty to the representee to speak or act) by silence or inaction, with the intention (actual or presumptive), and with the result, of inducing the representee on the faith of such representation to alter his position to his detriment, the representor, in any litigation which may afterwards take place between him and the representee, is estopped, as against the representee, from making or attempting to establish by evidence any averment substantially at variance with his former representation, if the representee at the proper time and in the proper manner objects thereto."

The essential characteristics of an estoppel by representation parallel closely the elements of an actionable misrepresentation. Thus, as we have seen, the representation must be one of fact, not of intention.[43] A representation of law will not ground an estoppel.[44] The representation must be material,[45] and it must be precise and unambiguous.[46] The representee must have relied on

---

[41] *Supra*, p. 45 *et seq*; Chap. 4.

[42] *Supra*, n. 29 at p. 4. The definition was adopted by Sir Raymond Evershed M.R. in *Hopgood* v. *Brown* [1955] 1 All E.R. 550 at 559.

[43] *Supra*, p. 129.

[44] *Territorial and Auxiliary Forces Association of the County of London* v. *Nichols* [1949] 1 K.B. 35.

[45] *Freeman* v. *Cooke* (1848) 2 Exch. 654.

[46] *Low* v. *Bouverie* [1891] 3 Ch. 82.

the representation[47] and must, by his reliance have been induced[48] to alter his position to his detriment.[49] "Detriment" has been defined by Spencer Bower and Turner as "some prejudicial effect upon his temporal interests."[50] Examples of this include becoming contractually liable to deliver property to a third person at a future date,[51] supplying goods on credit which would otherwise not have been given,[52] failing to take action for his protection or security[53] and buying back goods already sold.[54]

If a legal duty is owed by the representor to the representee to make a disclosure, his failure to speak may amount to a representation. The classes of case in which a duty has been held to exist include[55] cases where a person who has a title, right or claim to property is aware that another person, unaware of the title etc., is acting with regard to the property in a manner inconsistent with the title etc.; he must be undeceived by the former immediately, otherwise the former will be estopped from asserting his title, right or claim.[56] Failure by a principal to notify the other party to a transaction of limitations on the apparent general authority of his agent[57] or partner[58] will similarly raise an estoppel, as will failure by one party to a transaction or negotiation to undeceive the other party where he is aware that the latter is

---

[47] *United Overseas Bank* v. *Jiwani* [1977] 1 All E.R. 733. It should also be noted that, in the words of Brett J. in *Carr* v. *London and North Western Railway Co.* (1875) L.R.C.P. 307 at 317: "... if a man, whatever his real meaning may be, so conducts himself that a reasonable man would take his conduct to mean a certain representation of facts, and that it was a true representation, and that the latter was intended to act upon it in a particular way, and he with such belief does act in that way to his damage, the first is estopped from denying that the facts were as represented."

[48] *Nippon Menkwa Kabushiki Kaisha* v. *Dawsons Bank Ltd.* (1935) 51 Lloyds L.R. 147.

[49] *McKenzie* v. *British Linen Co.* (1881) 6 App.Cas. 82. See generally, Spencer Bower and Turner *op. cit.* n. 29 *supra*, pp. 104–112.

[50] *Op. cit.* n. 29 *supra*, p. 110.

[51] *Balkis Consolidated Co.* v. *Tomkinson* [1893] A.C. 396 at 405.

[52] *Cornish* v. *Abington* (1859) 4 H. & N. 549.

[53] *Dixon* v. *Kennaway & Co. Ltd.* [1900] 1 Ch. 833; *Greenwood* v. *Martin's Bank Ltd.* [1933] A.C. 51.

[54] *Seton, Laing & Co.* v. *Lafone* (1887) 19 Q.B.D. 68 at 71, 72.

[55] See Spencer, Bower and Turner *op. cit.* n. 29 *supra*, pp. 48–79.

[56] See, *e.g. Savage* v. *Foster* (1723) 9 Mod.Rep. 35 (land); *Pickard* v. *Sears* (1837) 6 Ad. & El. 469 (chattels). An insured person who remains silent though aware that insurance moneys have been paid out by her insurers to an unauthorised person without her knowledge will be estopped from later arguing that the receipts were forged: *Australian Temperance and General Mutual Life Assurance Society Ltd.* v. *Johnson* [1933] N.Z.L.R. 408.

[57] See, *e.g. Weiner* v. *Harris* [1910] 1 K.B. 285.

[58] *Re Rowland & Crankshaw* (1886) 1 Ch.App. 421.

mistaken about some matter vital to the transaction, in circumstances where the failure to speak must inevitably perpetuate the error.[59] If circumstances change to the knowledge of the representor, subsequent to the making of a representation, he is under a duty to disclose this change of circumstances to the representee, for as Spencer Bower and Turner note[60]: "silence as to supervening facts is a representation that no such facts have occurred, on which, therefore, not only proceedings for non-disclosure or misrepresentation,[61] but also an estoppel, may be founded." A duty of disclosure is also owed by a customer to his banker, for example in cases where a customer, though aware of forgeries of cheques, fails to notify his banker promptly of this.[62] On the other hand, there has been held to be no legal duty to speak, and hence no estoppel, in a wide variety of cases; for example a lessor who failed to mention to his lessee that failure to paint premises in the final year of the lease would amount to a breach of covenant was not estopped from setting up the breach of covenant against the lessee, thereby preventing him from exercising his option to renew,[63] and failure by an executor to inform a legatee of a condition attaching to his legacy which, if breached would entitle the executor to take, does not amount to an admission of the legatee's title.[64]

In his influential judgment in *Grundt* v. *Great Boulder Pty. Gold Mines Ltd.*[65] Dixon J. spelled out the governing principles of estoppel by representation:

" . . . the real detriment or harm from which the law seeks to give protection is that which would flow from the change of position if the assumption were deserted that led to it. So long as the assumption is adhered to, the party who altered his situation upon the faith of it cannot complain. His complaint is that when afterwards the other party makes a different state of affairs the basis of an assertion of rights against him then, if it is allowed, his own original change of position will operate as a detriment. His action or inaction must be such that, if the assumption upon which he proceeded were shown to be

[59] See *Marsden* v. *Marsden* [1973] 2 All E.R. 851. *Cf. Leslie & Co.* v. *Commissioners of Works* (1914) 78 J.P. 462.
[60] *Op. cit.* n. 29 *supra*, p. 54.
[61] See Chap. 2, p. 21 *et seq. supra*.
[62] See *Greenwood* v. *Martins Bank Ltd.* [1932] 1 K.B. 371 and Chap. 7 *infra*, p. 161. See also, *London Joint Stock Bank* v. *Macmillan* [1918] A.C. 777.
[63] *West Country Cleaners (Falmouth) Ltd.* v. *Saly* [1966] 1 W.L.R. 1485.
[64] *Re Lewis, Lewis* v. *Lewis* [1904] 2 Ch. 656 at 661, 662.
[65] (1938) 59 C.L.R. 641 at 674–675.

wrong, and an inconsistent state of affairs were accepted as the foundation of the rights and duties of himself and the opposite party, the consequence would be to make his original act or failure to act a source of prejudice."

2. EQUITABLE ESTOPPEL

We have seen in previous chapters that representations as to the future, or promises, are not actionable as misrepresentations[66] or as misstatements[67] and, as *Jorden* v. *Money*, however controversially, makes clear, such representations cannot found an estoppel by representation. The law has traditionally taken the view that a promise which is not kept is only actionable if supported by consideration in an action for breach of contract. However, two important developments in equity, promissory estoppel and proprietary estoppel, have enabled promisees to obtain relief despite the absence of consideration. It is proposed to examine these developments below since, although they do not concern untrue representations in the sense in which the law examined previously in this book does, in that an untrue representation has not been made,[68] nevertheless it is thought that it would be artificial to omit a discussion of the law's treatment of non-contractual representations as to the future. This is especially so, given on the one hand the development of promissory estoppel as a specific device to evade the restrictions of *Jorden* v. *Money* and on the other hand the increasingly close relationship that proprietary estoppel bears to the doctrine, discussed above, of making representations good.

(a) Promissory estoppel

In *Central London Property Trust Ltd.* v. *High Trees House Ltd.*[69] Denning J. managed to evade the restriction imposed by the decision of the House of Lords in *Jorden* v. *Money*[70] that an estoppel can only arise from a statement of fact. He based his reasoning upon the decision of the House of Lords in

---

[66] See *Maddison* v. *Alderson* (1883) 8 App.Cas. 467, Chap. 2, p. 12 *supra*.

[67] See *The Zephyr* [1985] 2 Lloyds L.R. 529, Chap. 4, p. 86, *supra*.

[68] If, of course, it can be shown that the representor did not in fact intend to fulfil his undertaking then he may be liable for misrepresentation (see *Edgington* v. *Fitzmaurice* (1885) 29 Ch.D. 459, Chapter 2 *supra*; or an estoppel may be raised (see *Salisbury (Marquess)* v. *Gilmore* [1942] 2 K.B. 38, *supra*, p. 130) for there will have been a misrepresentation of an existing fact in such cases.

[69] [1947] K.B. 130.

[70] (1854) 5 H.L.C. 185. *Supra*, p. 129.

Hughes v. *Metropolitan Railway Co.*[71] In that case the appellant landlord gave the respondents notice in October to repair within six months property which they leased from him. The parties then entered into negotiations for the sale of the lease to the appellant, and the repairs were not carried out during that time. The negotiations broke down at the end of December, and in April, the six month period having expired, an action of ejectment was commenced. The House of Lords held that the respondents were entitled to be relieved against the forfeiture, since the period of negotiations had the effect of suspending the notice. Lord Cairns L.C. said[72]:

> "... it is the first principle upon which all Courts of Equity proceed, that if parties who have entered into definite and distinct terms involving certain legal results—certain penalties or legal forfeiture—afterwards by their own act or with their own consent enter upon a course of negotiation which had the effect of leading one of the parties to suppose that the strict rights arising under the contract will not be enforced, or will be kept in suspense, or held in abeyance, the person who otherwise might have enforced those rights will not be allowed to enforce them where it would be inequitable having regard to the dealings which have thus taken place between the parties."

In the *High Trees* case a landlord agreed in 1940 to reduce the ground rent payable by the defendant because the latter was unable to find sub-tenants owing to war conditions then prevailing. By the beginning of 1945 all the flats were let and the landlord claimed the full rent as from the middle of that year. This claim succeeded. It was clear that the landlord's undertaking to reduce the rent was not a representation of existing fact such as to found an estoppel under *Jorden* v. *Money*. It was a representation as to the future. However, Denning J. held that a promise which is intended to be binding, intended to be acted upon and in fact acted upon, could bind the promisor, not to the extent of giving a cause of action in damages for breach of the promise, but in that the court would refuse to allow the promisor to act inconsistently with the promise. Thus it would not have been possible for the landlord to claim the full rent for the period between 1940 and 1945. However, the claim for the full rent from mid-1945 onwards could succeed since it had been understood by the parties that the

[71] (1877) 2 App.Cas. 439.
[72] *Ibid.* at 448.

promise only applied under the conditions prevailing at the time when it was made.

It may be that *Hughes* v. *Metropolitan Railway Co.* is not the soundest of foundations for a broad principle such as that expounded by Denning J, since *Hughes* may be said to be based upon a narrower equitable jurisdiction to relieve against forfeiture where the default has been caused or induced by the party seeking the forfeiture.[73] The decision of the Court of Appeal in *Birmingham and District Land Co.* v. *London & North West Railway Co.*,[74] upon which Denning J. also relied, provides closer support, especially in the judgment of Bowen L.J.,[75] who expressly stated that the principle in *Hughes* went beyond forfeiture and was of general application to cases where a party to a contract led his co-contractor to believe that rights under the contract would not be enforced or would be suspended. In such cases equity would intervene to protect the promisee. Whether this (and, therefore *High Trees* also) can stand with *Jorden* v. *Money* must almost certainly be regarded as academic now, for *High Trees* has survived for 40 years, and during that time may be said to have become sufficiently well established that it is highly unlikely that the House of Lords would now turn round and refute it.[76]

The circumstances in which a promise may found an estoppel now fall to be examined. There must be existing legal relations between the parties. These will usually be contractual, but need not necessarily be so.[77] There must be a clear, unambiguous[78] promise, intended to affect the legal relationship between the parties, and indicating that the promisor will not enforce his rights, or will suspend them. The promisee must rely upon the promise of the promisor. Lord Denning has doubted whether such

---

[73] See Meagher Gummow & Lehane *op. cit.* n. 17 *supra*, para. 1707.

[74] (1888) 40 Ch.D. 268.

[75] *Ibid.* at 286.

[76] Though in *Woodhouse A.C. Israel Cocoa Ltd. S.A.* v. *Nigerian Produce Marketing Co. Ltd.* [1972] A.C. 741, Lord Hailsham L.C. said (at 758) " . . . the time may soon come when the whole sequence of cases based on promissory estoppel since the war . . . may need to be revised and reduced to a coherent body of doctrine by the courts. I do not mean to say that any are to be regarded with suspicion."

[77] See *Durham Fancy Goods Ltd.* v. *Michael Jackson (Fancy Goods) Ltd.* [1968] 2 Q.B. 839 (statutory obligation). See also, *Pacol* v. *Trade Lines Ltd.* [1982] 1 Lloyds Rep. 456. On liability for post-contractual representations generally, see Dugdale and Yates (1976) 39 M.L.R. 680.

[78] See *Woodhouse A.C. Israel Cocoa Ltd. S.A.* v. *Nigerian Produce Marketing Co. Ltd.* [1972] A.C. 741; *John Burrows Ltd.* v. *Subsurface Surveys Ltd.* (1968) 68 D.L.R. (2d) 354.

reliance must be detrimental,[79] though other judges have taken a different view.[80] In *Ajayi* v. *R. T. Briscoe (Nigeria) Ltd.*[81] the Privy Council stated that the doctrine of promissory estoppel was subject to a number of qualifications, including: "that the other party has altered his position,"[82] and it may be that no "detriment" in the sense in which a detriment is required in cases of estoppel by representation is necessary,[83] and it will suffice that the promisee will be disadvantaged by a return to the *status quo ante*. It is also said to be a requirement that it must be "inequitable" for the promisor to go back on his promise.[84] This will very frequently overlap the "detrimental" reliance of the promisee outlined above. Thus in *The Post Chaser*[85] it was not inequitable for the promisor to re-assert his strict legal rights two days after making his promise, since it was impossible to say that the promisee had acted to his detriment during that time.

It is generally believed that the effect of the doctrine is to suspend rather than to extinguish the rights of the promisor. Thus, in *Hughes* v. *Metropolitan Railway Co.* the landlord did not lose the right to have the premises repaired; the covenant could be enforced upon giving reasonable notice to the tenant. In *Tool Metal Manufacturing Co. Ltd.* v. *Tungsten Electric Co. Ltd.*[86] the appellants granted the respondents a licence for the use of a patent. This provided that the respondents should pay a sum called "compensation" if in any one month during the continuance of the licence they sold or used more than a stipulated quota. After the outbreak of war in 1939 the payment of compensation was suspended, the appellants voluntarily forgoing the payment, as the parties contemplated the making of a new agreement. Negotiations for a new contract were begun, but broke down, and in 1945 the respondents sued the appellants for, *inter alia*, breach of contract. The appellants counterclaimed for payment of compen-

---

[79] See, *e.g.* W. J. *Alan & Co. Ltd.* v. *El Nasr Export and Import Co.* [1972] 2 Q.B. 189 at 213; *Brikom Investments Ltd.* v. *Carr* [1979] Q.B. 467 at 482.

[80] See *Morrow* v. *Carty* [1957] NI 174; *Fontana N.V.* v. *Mautner* (1979) 254 E.G. 199.

[81] [1964] 1 W.L.R. 1326.

[82] *Ibid.* at 559.

[83] *Supra,* p. 135. However, under the broad definition provided by Dixon J. in the *Grundt* case (*supra,* pp. 136–137) the ambit of "detriment" in cases of estoppel by representation and promissory estoppel may be similar.

[84] See, *e.g. D & C Builders Ltd.* v. *Rees* [1966] 2 Q.B. 617 at 625, *per* Lord Denning M.R.

[85] [1981] 2 Lloyds Rep. 695.

[86] [1955] 1 W.L.R. 761.

sation as from June 1 of that year. It was held by the House of Lords that the counterclaim constituted reasonable notice of the appellants' intention to resume their strict legal rights. In *Ajayi* v. *R. T. Briscoe (Nigeria) Ltd.*[87] Lord Hodson, who delivered the advice of the Privy Council, stated that one of the qualifications to which the doctrine of promissory estoppel was subject was "that the promisor can resile from his promise on giving reasonable notice, which need not be a formal notice, giving the promisee a reasonable opportunity of resuming his position."[88] However, he went on to note a further qualification: "the promise only becomes final and irrevocable if the promisee cannot resume his position."[89] In addition, the circumstances may be such that to require performance even after reasonable notice would be inequitable.[90]

Promissory estoppel cannot operate so as to create new rights. Thus, in *Combe* v. *Combe*[91] a wife obtained a decree *nisi* in divorce proceedings against her husband. The husband then promised to pay her £100 per annum by way of maintenance. The wife, in reliance on this promise, forbore from applying to the court for maintenance. The decree was later made absolute, but the husband failed to pay the promised maintenance. The wife sued him on his promise, but the Court of Appeal held that she could not succeed, as there was no consideration for the husband's promise. Denning L.J. stated:

> "that [the High Trees] principle does not create new causes of action where none existed before. It only prevents a party from insisting upon his strict legal rights, when it would be unjust to allow him to enforce them, having regard to the dealings which have taken place between the parties."[92]

However, the statement in *Combe* v. *Combe* that the doctrine operates as a shield and not as a sword[93] is potentially misleading, in that it may be possible for a plaintiff to rely upon it, provided

---

[87] [1964] 1 W.L.R. 1326. *Supra*, p. 140.
[88] [1964] 3 All E.R. 556 at 559.
[89] *Ibid.*
[90] See *Ogilvy* v. *Hope-Davies* [1976] 1 All E.R. 683 at 689. See generally, Thompson [1983] C.L.J. 257 at 260–263.
[91] [1951] 2 K.B. 215. *Cf. Re Wyvern Developments Ltd.* [1974] 1 W.L.R. 1097.
[92] 1951] 2 K.B. 215 at 219. See also, *Argy Trading Development Co. Ltd.* v. *Lapid Developments Ltd.* [1977] 1 W.L.R. 444 at 457; *The Proodos C* [1980] 2 Lloyds Rep. 390 at 392.
[93] [1951] 2 K.B. 215 at 224, *per* Birkett L.J.

that he is able to show that he has an independent cause of action. For example[94] if the landlord in *Hughes* v. *Metropolian Railway Co.* had gone into possession of the property, it would have been perfectly possible for the tenant to seek an injunction against him, basing his claim on the lease. The doctrine of promissory estoppel would operate so as to prevent the landlord from raising a defence that he was entitled to forfeit.

(b) Proprietary estoppel

Further, the so-called doctrine of proprietary estoppel also provides for the possibility of relief in equity following a promise in certain cases whose ambit, as will be seen, is far from clear. What is clear is that in such cases estoppel can operate as a cause of action. Thus, in the early case of *Huning* v. *Ferrers*[95] the plaintiff was the lessee of certain mills. The lessor made a settlement of the mills but subsequently granted a new 30 year lease to the plaintiff, who expended a large sum of money on buildings and improvements. The defendant, who was entitled in remainder, informed the lessor (his father) that he did not have the power to grant the lease. However, he did not inform the plaintiff of this, but indeed encouraged the plaintiff's expenditure. Upon the death of the father the defendant recovered the land from the plaintiff in an action in ejectment, and the plaintiff brought an action in Chancery to be allowed to remain in possession for the duration of his lease. He was held to be entitled to this relief, as it would be fraudulent for the defendant to be permitted to insist on his legal rights since he had stood by while the plaintiff had effected the repairs and encouraged his expenditure. Such a decision has the effect of creating an equity in favour of a party who acts to his detriment in reliance upon another's assurance.

Broadly speaking the cases on proprietary estoppel may be said to be divided into two categories. In the first category, a person acquiesces in the mistaken belief of another that that other has rights over the first person's land. The mistake does not have to have been induced by the landowner, but his acquiescence, causing the other party to act in reliance upon the mistaken belief, gives rise to the equity.[96] In the second category the equity arises

---

[94] See Cheshire, Fifoot & Furmston, *Law of Contract* (11th ed., 1986) p. 96.
[95] (1711) Gilb Rep. 85. See also, *East India Co.* v. *Vincent* (1740) 2 Atk. 83; *Jackson* v. *Cator* (1800) 5 Ver. 688.
[96] See, *e.g. Willmott* v. *Barber* (1880) 15 Ch.D. 96 at 105.

as a result of encouragement by the landowner.[97] The other party acts in reliance on the encouragement of the landlord to believe that he has, or will have, an interest in the land. It is not necessary that the claimant should spend money on the land, as is illustrated by the decision of the Court of Appeal in *Greasley* v. *Cooke*.[98] In that case Lord Denning M.R. considered that it was not necessary to show a detriment to the claimant in order for the equity to arise; it was enough that that party acted on the faith of the assurance given and it would be inequitable for the party making the assurance to go back on it. Dunn L.J. however considered that expenditure or some other detriment to the claimant was a necessary element of proprietary estoppel.

Fraud of the defendant has been said to be of the essence in this line of cases,[99] but it is frequently fraud in the equitable sense of unconscionability.[1] Thus, in the leading case of *Dillwyn* v. *Llewellyn*[2] a father placed one of his sons in possession of land belonging to the father and signed a memorandum, which was not sealed, and was therefore ineffective, purporting to convey the land to the son. The son built a house on the land at a cost of £14,000, with the assent and approbation of the father. Subsequently the father died, leaving his real estate upon trust to others. The son obtained a declaration that he was the equitable owner of the land and it was ordered to be conveyed to him accordingly. It is not clear from the judgment of Lord Westbury L.C. whether he was founding his decision on contract or on the basis that, though an incomplete gift will not be completed in favour of a volunteer, the subsequent acts of the donor may bind the donor to make good the state of affairs that his conduct led the donee to believe existed. It is difficult to sustain the contract argument, despite Lord Westbury's belief: "that the subsequent expenditure by the son, with the approbation of the father, implied a valuable consideration originally wanting,"[3] since, as has been cogently pointed out, detrimental reliance does not yet amount to consideration under English law.[4]

It is true that the word "estoppel" appears nowhere in the judgment in *Dillwyn* v. *Llewellyn* and there is much disagreement

[97] See, *e.g. Ramsden* v. *Dyson* (1866) L.R. 1 H.L. 129 at 170.
[98] [1980] 3 All E.R. 710.
[99] Meagher, Gummow & Lehane, *Equity, Doctrines and Remedies* (2nd ed., 1984) para. 1711.
[1] See generally, Sheridan, *Fraud in Equity* (1957).
[2] (1862) 4 De G.F. & J. 517.
[3] *Ibid.* at 522.
[4] Hanbury and Maudsley, *Modern Equity* (12th ed., 1985) p. 857. See however, Atiyah, *Essays in Contract* (1986) pp. 211–212 and discussion *infra*, pp. 163–164.

concerning the case's juridical basis. The effect of the equity held to exist in *Dillwyn*, whereby acquiescence or encouragement by a donor, in the case of a gift, may require the donor to act as though he were contractually bound to the donee, bears at least a strong resemblance to estoppel, save that estoppel will not, of course, usually found a cause of action. Certainly, in *Inwards* v. *Baker*[5] where a father encouraged his son to build a bungalow upon the father's land, the expectation thereby engendered in the son that he would be allowed to remain there during his lifetime was given effect by the Court of Appeal, the case being regarded by Danckwerts L.J.[6] as

> "one of the cases on equity created by estoppel or equitable estoppel, as it is sometimes called, by which the person who has made the expenditure is induced by the expectation of obtaining protection, and equity protects him so that an injustice may not be perpetrated."

However, it is really only in the cases decided in the last 20 years that the terminology of estoppel has been employed.

Leading cases subsequent to *Dillwyn* v. *Llewellyn*, such as *Ramsden* v. *Dyson*[7] and *Plimmer* v. *Wellington Corporation*[8] again speak in general terms about the circumstances in which equity will effect substantial justice between parties in one of whom expectations have been generated by the encouragement or acquiescence of the other. More specific guidelines were furnished by Fry J. in *Willmott* v. *Barber*.[9] He said:

> "What, then, are the elements or requisites necessary to constitute fraud of that description? In the first place the plaintiff must have made a mistake as to his legal rights. Secondly, the plaintiff must have expended some money or must have done some act (not necessarily upon the defendant's land) on the faith of his mistaken belief. Thirdly, the defendant, the possessor the legal right, must know of the existence of his own right which is inconsistent with the right claimed by the plaintiff. If he does not know of it he is in the same position as the plaintiff, and the doctrine of acquiescence is founded upon conduct with a knowledge of legal rights. Fourthly, the defendant, the possessor the legal right,

---

[5] [1965] 2 Q.B. 29.
[6] *Ibid.* at 38.
[7] (1866) L.R. 1 H.L. 129.
[8] (1884) 9 App.Cas. 699.
[9] (1880) 15 Ch.D. 96 at 105–106.

must know of the plaintiff's mistaken belief of his rights. If he does not, there is nothing which calls upon him to assert his own rights. Lastly, the defendant, the possessor of the legal right, must have encouraged the plaintiff in his expenditure of money or in the other acts which he has done, either directly or by abstaining from asserting his legal right. Where all these elements exist, there is fraud of such a nature as will entitle the Court to restrain the possessor of the legal right from exercising it, but, in my judgment, nothing short of this will do."

These five "probanda" have been considered in a number of cases, perhaps most illuminatingly by Oliver J. in *Taylor Fashions* v. *Liverpool Victoria Trustees Co. Ltd.*[10] Oliver J. pointed out that *Willmott* v. *Barber* was a case of waiver by acquiescence, and that, though the five probanda were no doubt necessary elements of a case falling within that category, it did not necessarily follow that they must be found to be present in all cases of estoppel by encouragement or acquiescence, though there certainly existed dicta that supported such general applicability.[11] A number of early cases had not required that the party estopped be aware that the other party's belief was mistaken.[12] Oliver J. was of the view that, since acquiescence or encouragement might take a variety of forms it was neither desirable nor possible to lay down hard and fast rules seeking to dictate universally applicable considerations to guide the court. He said:

"Furthermore the more recent cases indicate, in my judgment, that the application of the *Ramsden* v. *Dyson* L.R.I. H.L. 129 principle—whether you call it proprietary estoppel, estoppel by acquiescence or estoppel by encouragement is really immaterial—requires a very much broader approach which is directed rather at ascertaining whether, in particular individual circumstances, it would be unconscionable for a party to be permitted to deny that which, knowingly or unknowingly, he has allowed or encouraged another to assume to his detriment than to inquiring whether the circumstances can be fitted within the confines of some

---

[10] [1982] Q.B. 133n. See also, *Pacol* v. *Trade Lines Ltd.* [1982] 1 Lloyds Rep. 456.

[11] See, *e.g. Kammins Ballrooms Co. Ltd.* v. *Zenith Investments (Torquay) Ltd.* [1971] A.C. 850 at 884 *per* Lord Diplock.

[12] *e.g. Stiles* v. *Cowper* (1748) 3 Atk. 692; *Gregory* v. *Mighell* (1811) 18 Ves.Jun. 328.

preconceived formula serving as a universal yardstick for every form of unconscionable behaviour."[13]

Subsequently, in *Amalgamated Investment & Property Co. Ltd.* v. *Texas Commerce International Bank Ltd.*[14] Robert Goff J. agreed with Oliver J's approach and stated:

> "It is no doubt helpful to establish, in broad terms, the criteria which, in certain situations, must be fulfilled before an equitable estoppel can be established; but it cannot be right to restrict equitable estoppel to certain defined categories . . ."[15]

In the same case Lord Denning M.R. spoke in even more general terms:

> "When the parties to a transaction proceed on the basis of an underlying assumption—either of fact or of law—whether due to misrepresentation or mistake makes no difference—on which they have conducted the dealings between them— neither of them will be allowed to go back on that assumption when it would be unfair or unjust to allow him to do so. If one of them does seek to go back on it, the courts will give the other such remedy as the equity of the case demands."[16]

This case is also of interest in that it extended the principle of proprietary estoppel beyond land to other forms of property—the case concerned the question whether the defendant could be estopped from denying that it was party to a contract of guarantee.[17]

In complying with the stipulation of the Privy Council that "the Court must look at the circumstances in each case to decide in what way the equity can be satisfied"[18] the courts have sometimes gone to extraordinary lengths. Thus, in *Pascoe* v. *Turner*[19] the plaintiff and the defendant cohabited in the plaintiff's home. The plaintiff told the defendant that the house and everything in it was hers. In reliance upon this assurance she spent money over a three year period on redecorations, improvements and repairs, to the knowledge of the plaintiff. He later wrote to her giving her two

---

[13] [1981] 1 All E.R. 897 at 915–916; [1982] Q.B. 133n at 151–152.

[14] [1982] Q.B. 84.

[15] *Ibid.* at 103.

[16] *Ibid.* at 122. See the criticism of this by Meagher, Gummow, Lehane *op. cit.* n. 99 *supra* at para. 1722. Eveleigh and Brandon L.JJ. were of the view that the case was one of estoppel by convention.

[17] See also, *Habib Bank Ltd.* v. *Habib Bank A.G. Zurich* [1981] 1 W.L.R. 1265.

[18] *Plimmer* v. *Wellington Corporation* (1884) 9 App.Cas. 699 at 714.

[19] [1979] 1 W.L.R. 431.

months' notice "to determine her licence to occupy." The Court of Appeal held that the defendant occupied the house under a licence revocable at will. The circumstances in which the plaintiff encouraged or acquiesced in the improvement of the house effected by the defendant in the belief that it belonged to her gave rise to an estoppel. In the circumstances (which included the ruthlessness of the plaintiff) it was held that a licence to occupy for her lifetime would not provide her with sufficient security (since such a licence was not registrable as a land charge and thus she could be ousted by a purchaser for value without notice) and hence the equity could only be satisfied by a conveyance of the fee simple to the defendant.

This provides a remarkable windfall for the defendant, though it has been argued that it may be explained on the footing that the object of proprietary estoppel is to provide for the informal creation of interests in land wherever a person has acted detrimentally in reliance upon an oral assurance that he has such an interest.[20] Support for this view can be gleaned from the closing words of Cumming-Bruce L.J.'s judgment in *Pascoe* v. *Turner* ("He has so acted that he must now perfect the gift"),[21] though the fact that the learned Lord Justice was prepared to contemplate the grant of a licence suggests that the remedy would not necessarily have amounted to perfecting the imperfect gift, and it may be that the court will prefer to preserve a general discretion as to remedy.[22] Thus, in *Dodsworth* v. *Dodsworth*[23] the plaintiff invited her brother and his wife, who had just returned to England from Australia, to join her in her bungalow. The brother and wife spent over £700 in improvements to the bungalow, in the expectation, which was induced and encouraged by the plaintiff, that they could remain in the property for as long as they wished. The plaintiff later changed her mind, and started proceedings for possession. The Court of Appeal held that the plaintiff's conduct raised an equity in favour of the defendants. However, to give immediate and direct effect to their expectations would, by virtue of the provisions of the Settled Land Act,[24] give them a greater interest

---

[20] See Moriarty (1984) 100 L.Q.R. 376 at 381–382.

[21] [1979] 1 W.L.R. 431 at 439.

[22] See *Griffiths* v. *Williams* (1978) 248 E.G. 947; Thompson [1986] Conv. 406.

[23] (1973) 228 E.G. 1115.

[24] This would make the defendants joint tenants for life. As such they could sell the property, or quit and let it. In the former case they would be entitled to the income of the invested proceeds for life, and the life of the survivor; in the latter they would be entitled to the net rents. On the question whether there was a settlement within the meaning of s.1 of the Settled Land Act, see *Griffiths* v. *Williams supra*, n. 22 at 949–950.

than the parties had ever contemplated. Consequently it was held that the appropriate remedy was to repay them their outlay on the improvements that they had carried out.[25]

The traditional view is that promissory and proprietary estoppel are separate concepts, despite the similarities between them that exist. Both may arise from promises, or representations as to the future. However, it is said that for a promissory estoppel to arise there must have been such a promise,[26] but a proprietary estoppel may result from acquiescence. Also, there must be pre-existing legal relations between the parties in cases of promissory estoppel, but this is not a necessary element of proprietary estoppel. Both forms of estoppel require reliance. As we have seen,[27] Lord Denning has doubted whether detrimental reliance is necessary in either case, but the more traditional view is that whereas detrimental reliance is a necessary element of proprietary estoppel[28] it is not necessary in cases of promissory estoppel.

It may be argued that promissory and proprietary estoppel are both illustrations of a general principle whereby if one person induces another to rely upon an expectation it is unconscionable to deny a remedy to the latter, provided that the expectation was created, acquiesced in or reliance upon it was encouraged by the former, with the latter changing his position in reliance.[29] Some support for this approach may be gleaned from the judgment of Scarman L.J. in *Crabb* v. *Arun D.C.*.[30] In that case the plaintiff owned land whose outlet to the road was through a point of access (Point A) to a lane owned by the defendants and by a right of way along the lane in a northerly direction to the road. He decided to

[25] See also, *Crabb* v. *Arun D.C.* [1976] Ch. 179 (*infra*) where the conduct of the defendant local authority was held to have been high-handed, to the extent that whereas otherwise the plaintiff would have had to pay for the easement which the defendant's assurance had led him to believe existed, in the circumstances payment was not required., Moriarty (*supra*, n. 20 at 385) regards the decision in *Dodsworth* as consistent with his views on the object of proprietary estoppel in that the interest envisaged in that case was a co- ownership interest which was satisfied by the compensation for the expenditure on improvement.

[26] See however, *The Scaptrade* [1983] 1 Lloyds Rep. 146 at 150, where Robert Goff L.J. considered that acquiescence by owners of a vessel in late payments by charterers under a charter party could amount to a sufficient representation, for the purposes of promissory estoppel, that they could not exercise their strict right of withdrawal in the event of a subsequent late payment.

[27] *Supra*, pp. 139–140, 143.

[28] See, *e.g. Western Fish Products Ltd.* v. *Penwith D.C.* [1981] 2 All E.R. 204 at 217.

[29] See Thompson [1983] C.L.J. 257.

[30] [1976] 1 Ch. 179.

divide his land into two parts, and to sell the northerly part, which contained Point A. This would necessitate a new access point (Point B) in the southerly part of the land, which he planned to retain. The defendants agreed in principle to allow him access at Point B, and to grant him an easement from Point B along the lane. They fenced off his land from the lane and made a gap at Point B. However the defendants subsequently blocked the plaintiff's access at Point B, effectively leaving him landlocked, since by now he had sold the northerly part of his land, and he claimed that they were estopped by their conduct from denying him right of access at Point B and a right of way along the lane. The Court of Appeal agreed.

Scarman L.J. said[31]:

"I do not find helpful the distinction between promissory and proprietary estoppel. This distinction may indeed be valuable to those who have to teach or expound the law; but I do not think that, in solving the particular problem raised by a particular case, putting the law into categories is of the slightest assistance."

In *Taylor Fashions Ltd.* v. *Liverpool Victoria Trustees Co. Ltd.*[32] Oliver J. regarded *Crabb* v. *Arun* as illustrating "the virtual equation of promissory estoppel and proprietary estoppel or estoppel by acquiescence as mere facets of the same principle."[33] The decision of the Court of Appeal in *Crabb* v. *Arun* certainly goes beyond *Willmott* v. *Barber*, though, as we have seen, that does not make it unique, and accords rather with the philosophy later expressed in *Taylor Fashions* and *Amalgamated Investment*. But that of itself does not justify equating proprietary estoppel with promissory estoppel. The need to do justice in the individual case must be balanced by the need to provide a reasonable degree of certainty in the law, and it may be argued that reasons of policy (let alone principle) militate against this kind of assimilation.[34]

3. ESTOPPEL AS A CAUSE OF ACTION

As regards estoppel by representation, Spencer Bower's classic remark: "estoppel must always be either a mine-layer or a mine-

---

[31] *Ibid.* at 193.
[32] [1982] Q.B. 133n. *Supra*, pp. 145–146.
[33] *Ibid.* at 153.
[34] See, *e.g.* Treitel, *The Law of Contract* (7th ed., 1987) p. 114; Meagher, Gummow, Lehane, *Equity—Doctrines and Remedies* (2nd ed., 1984) para. 1722; Spencer, Bower and Turner, *Estoppel by Representation* (3rd ed., 1977) pp. 306–309.

sweeper: it can never be a capital unit"[35] is supported by a number of judicial statements of high authority. In *Nippon Menkwa Kabushiki Kaisha* v. *Dawson's Bank Limited*[36] Lord Russell of Killowen said:

> "Estoppel is not a cause of action. It may (if established) assist a plaintiff in enforcing a cause of action by preventing a defendant from denying the existence of some fact essential to establish the cause of action, or (to put it another way) by preventing a defendant from asserting the existence of some fact the existence of which would destroy the cause of action."

Again, in *Evans* v. *Bartham*[37] Lord Wright stated: "estoppel is a rule of evidence that prevents the person estopped from denying the existence of a fact." Further, though, as Jackson notes,[38] estoppel can be the handle of the sword if not its blade. Lord Wright recognised the peculiar nature of estoppel in his judgment in *Canada and Dominion Sugar Co. Ltd.* v. *Canadian National (West Indies) Steamships Ltd.*[39] when he said:

> "Estoppel is a complex legal notion, involving a combination of several essential elements, the statement to be acted on, action on the faith of it, resulting detriment to the actor. Estoppel is often described as a rule of evidence, as, indeed, it may be so described. But the whole concept is more correctly viewed as a substantive rule of law—the purchaser or other transferee must have acted on it to his detriment. Estoppel is different from contract[40] both in its nature and consequences. But the relationship between the parties must also be such that the imputed truth of the statement is a necessary step in the constitution of the cause of action."[41]

It is difficult to deny that in certain circumstances estoppel may operate as a rule of substantive law. Thus, in cases of promissory

[35] *Op. cit.* n. 34 *supra*, pp. 7–8.
[36] (1935) 51 Lloyds Rep. 147 at 150.
[37] [1937] A.C. 473 at 484. See also, *London Joint Stock Bank Ltd.* v. *Macmillan* [1918] A.C. 777 at 818, *per* Viscount Haldane; *Maritime Electric Company* v. *General Dairies Limited* [1937] A.C. 610 at 620, *per* Lord Maugham. Earlier powerful statements include the words of Lord Esher M.R. in *Seton, Laing Co.* v. *Lafone* (1887) 19 Q.B.D. 68 at 70 and Lindley L.J. and Bowen L.J. in *Low* v. *Bouverie* [1891] 3 Ch. 82 at 101 and 105 respectively. More recently, see the judgment of Slade L.J. in *Avon C.C.* v. *Howlett* [1983] 1 All E.R. 1073 at 1087.
[38] (1965) 81 L.Q.R. 223.
[39] [1947] A.C. 46.
[40] See Atiyah's views on *Crabb* v. *Arun* in (1976) 92 L.Q.R. 174 and the riposte by P. J. Millett *ibid.* at 342.
[41] [1947] A.C. 46 at 56.

estoppel the law does not prevent certain facts from being proved, and the rules of evidence are not an issue in such cases.[42] But to say that estoppel may operate in this way is not the same as asserting that estoppel can operate as a cause of action in itself. Professor Atiyah however has cogently argued that estoppel does so operate—in other words that the representation which founds an estoppel can itself be a cause of action.[43] The essence of his argument is that the "independent cause of action," which it is usually said the plaintiff must have in order to sue, is in fact the damage, and it is the representation that is the cause of action. Thus, in a case such as *Brandt* v. *Liverpool Brazil and River Plate Steam Navigation Co. Ltd.*[44] where shipowners issue a bill of lading which states falsely that goods were shipped in apparent good order and condition, the independent cause of action is said to be the delivery of damaged goods, and the claim succeeds because the shipowner defendants are estopped from denying to the indorsee the truth of their statement in the bill of lading and proving the true fact which had not been correctly stated in the bill. According to Professor Atiyah, however, the delivery of damaged goods is but the damage suffered by the plaintiff; since such delivery is only wrongful because the shipowner has misled the indorsee into believing that the goods were undamaged. The actual cause of action is the misrepresentation.

If this interesting argument is correct, it may well be asked why in fact the courts do not accept an action founded on the estoppel as a cause of action. For, whatever one's view of Professor Atiyah's argument, it must be accepted that it is not possible (proprietary estoppel excepted) to sue on the estoppel. An "independent cause of action" remains a requirement.

Historically, as we have seen, the refusal to allow estoppel to operate as a cause of action is linked to the perceived effect of *Derry* v. *Peek* on claims for non-fraudulent misrepresentation. But, it may be argued, since a claim can now be brought for a non-fraudulent misrepresentation in certain circumstances under section 2(1) of the Misrepresentation Act, and at common law under *Hedley Byrne* v. *Heller*, why should it not be possible today to claim on an estoppel, especially given the existence of the early line of cases on making representations good, with which the developing doctrine of proprietary estoppel appears to have so much in common?

[42] See *Cross on Evidence* (6th ed., 1985) at 96.
[43] *Essays in Contract* (1986) pp. 306–310.
[44] [1924] 1 K.B. 575. See also, *Compania Naviera Vasconzada* v. *Churchill & Sim* [1906] 1 K.B. 237.

Against this, it may be said that, given the existence of the causes of action under section 2(1) and under *Hedley Byrne* v. *Heller*, it is surely appropriate to make use of them rather than reviving an obsolete line of cases of dubious authority. Thus, a repetition of the facts of *Low* v. *Bouverie* or *Burrowes* v. *Lock* today would surely be actionable under *Hedley Byrne* v. *Heller*. The point may also be made that the doctrine of making representations good involves the protection of expectations: in requiring a representor to make good his representation, the effect would be to award a contractual measure of damages to a person who has furnished no consideration. It may be acceptable in such circumstances to compensate the representee to the extent that he has relied to his detriment upon the representation, but to award expectation losses would interfere with accepted notions of the basis of the law of contract.

However, it may be argued that the law is already effectively protecting the expectation interest in proprietary estoppel cases[45] despite the absence of consideration. In such cases the representor is in effect being required to make his representation good. Promissory estoppel also undermines notions of contract in making a promise to forgo existing contractual rights binding without there being any consideration for the promise. Certainly in such cases it is said that promissory estoppel can only be used defensively rather than as a cause of action, though the courts have on occasion evinced a willingness to depart from this,[46] and in any event, even used defensively promissory estoppel represents a powerful challenge to traditional ideas of contract, especially if, as has been argued, it (together with proprietary estoppel) forms part of a general principle whereby it is unconscionable to deny a remedy to one in whom expectations have been generated by another.[47]

On the other hand, it may be pointed out that promissory and proprietary estoppel must be kept clearly separate from estoppel by representation and the rest of the law of misrepresentation since they do not involve misrepresentations of fact but promises which are not kept but which the court will require to be fulfilled if the equity of the situation demands it. The implications of the recent developments in equitable estoppel are such that, as has been perceptively remarked, "what we need now is another

---

[45] And in some cases of estoppel by representation also. See Chap. 7 *infra*, pp. 156–157.
[46] See *Re Wyvern Developments* [1974] 1 W.L.R. 1097.
[47] See Thompson [1983] C.L.J. 257.

Jorden v. *Money* to canvass the whole question of the interrelationship between estoppel and contract,"[48] and the House of Lords is clearly the appropriate forum for such a canvassing. Whether, therefore, in the somewhat anguished words of Meagher Gummow and Lehane, "there is to be revived a general jurisdiction in equity . . . whereby representations are to be made good"[49] remains to be seen.

---

[48] Dawson (1982) 1 Canta. L.R. 329 at 361.
[49] *Equity Doctrines & Remedies* (2nd ed., 1984), para. 1722.

Chapter 7

CONCLUSION

As can be seen from previous chapters, liability for misrepresentation may arise in a number of different contexts: tortious, contractual, equitable and statutory, and misrepresentation may also give rise to an estoppel. The ad hoc nature of the development of the general law of misrepresentation, furthered as recently as the 1960s with the establishing of the common law action for negligent misstatement and the creation of the claim under section 2(1) of the Misrepresentation Act has resulted in a complex variety of possible causes of action (or defences) which is potentially confusing to the victim of an untrue representation who has relied upon it to his detriment. Clearly estoppel, misrepresentation, misstatement and warranty have a number of common characteristics, but equally clearly there are significant differences between them, as regards either their ambit or the circumstances in which relief will be available. It is proposed to examine below certain of these differences and similarities and, in the light of this examination, to consider whether there is any scope for simplification of this complex branch of the law.

1. THE INTEREST PROTECTED

By and large, as we have seen, the general law of misrepresentation protects the reliance interest.[1] Thus, damages under *Hedley Byrne* v. *Heller*, under section 2(1) and in deceit are designed to put the representee in the position he would have been in if no statement had been made and similarly, where rescission is available its intention is similar. It should, however, be recalled that rescission can take no account of consequential losses, except to the extent that the indemnity permits this, and also that, though the claims under section 2(1) and *Hedley Byrne* v. *Heller* will allow recovery of reasonably foreseeable consequential losses, it is necessary to prove deceit in order for the possibility of recovery of all losses flowing directly from the defendant's misrepresentation to arise.

---

[1] Defined by Fuller and Purdue (1936–37) 46 Yale L.J. 52, 373 as being concerned "to put the plaintiff in as good a position as he was in before the promise was made" (at 53–54). See also, Burrows (1983) 99 L.Q.R. 217 at 219–222.

If expectation losses have occurred, these will be irrecoverable, except where a warranty can be proved or an estoppel raised. It is clear that if the statement is characterised as a warranty, or as a collateral contract, it will be possible to recover damages with reference to the position the representee would have been in if the statement had been true.[2] This is uncontroversial. More difficult however, is the situation where the representee is able to employ the representation to raise an estoppel. Since the effect of this is to prevent the representor from averring facts contrary to his representation, the effect may be to protect the representee's expectation interest. This will certainly be true of most of the cases on proprietary estoppel,[3] but it will be true also of some cases of estoppel by representation. Where this is so, it raises the question whether the law should protect an unbargained-for expectation or simply compensate the representee to the extent of his reliance upon the representation. The traditional rationale behind protecting the expectation interest is that it arises as a result of a bargained-for promise, whereas a representation, a statement made gratuitously, will, if untrue, be compensated only to the extent of the representee's reliance on it.[4]

A case of considerable interest in this context is *Avon C.C.* v. *Howlett*.[5] The plaintiffs overpaid the defendant by mistake and, though they had represented to him that he was entitled to treat all the overpayment as his own money, sought to recover the money. At trial the defendant's plea of estoppel succeeded as regards £546.61, which he pleaded as having been spent in detrimental reliance on the misrepresentation, but the plaintiffs were held to be entitled to the balance of £460.39. (In fact the defendant was found by the trial judge to have spent the whole £1,007 in detrimental reliance, but he, and subsequently the Court of Appeal, acceded to the parties' wish to try the case on the basis of the facts as pleaded, as it was a test case on partial estoppel.)

The Court of Appeal held that estoppel barred the whole of the plaintiffs' claim. Slade L.J. asserted the principle that estoppel is a rule of evidence, from which:

> "It follows that a party who, as a result of being able to rely on an estoppel, succeeds on a cause of action on which, without

---

[2] See, *e.g.* Sale of Goods Act 1979, s.53(3).

[3] *e.g. Dillwyn* v. *Llewellyn* (1862) 4 De G.F. & J. 517; *Willmott* v. *Barber* (1880) 15 Ch.D. 96; *Inwards* v. *Baker* [1965] 2 Q.B. 29; *Greasley* v. *Cooke* [1980] 1 W.L.R. 1306, but note also, *Dodsworth* v. *Dodsworth* (1973) 228 E.G. 1115.

[4] Chap. 1 *supra*, p. 9.

[5] [1983] 1 W.L.R. 605.

being able to rely on it, he would necessarily have failed may be able to recover more than the actual damage suffered by him as a result of the representation which gave rise to it."[6]

The Court of Appeal recognised that injustice might result in a case where estoppel denied an action for money had and received where the sum involved bore no relation to any detriment suffered by the recipient, and left open the question whether the application of an estoppel could be made conditional on the giving of an undertaking by the defendant to repay any profit to the plaintiff.[7] Such a course of action was not felt to be required on the facts of the instant case.

This is not an entirely satisfactory method of ensuring that a representee who can raise an estoppel is not compensated to a greater extent than his detrimental reliance on the representation, since it is by no means clear that the court has the power to make the giving of such an undertaking a condition of giving effect to the estoppel. Since estoppel has consistently been regarded by the courts as operating as a complete defence, there exists no control device to make it operate as a *pro tanto* defence only, in appropriate cases. The argument that estoppel does not necessarily operate as a total defence, on the basis that the plaintiff is barred from asserting facts contrary to his representation with regard to only part of the payment,[8] seems contrary to principle, for estoppel has never been held to operate as a partial bar in the way envisaged by this suggestion. As Professor Atiyah implies,[9] there is no question of finding a warranty in a case such as *Avon C.C.* v. *Howlett*, thereby legitimising the protection of the defendant's expectation interest, and the situation must be regarded as an anomaly, though as Burrows notes[10] estoppel by representation only assists in protecting the expectation interest, as it is not a cause of action in itself, and therefore the exception is partial only.

---

[6] *Ibid.* at 1087, *per* Slade L.J. relying on, *inter alia, Greenwood* v. *Martins Bank Ltd.* [1932] K.B. 371, affirmed at [1933] A.C. 51.

[7] This course of action was considered to be appropriate by Viscount Cave L.C. in *R. E. Jones Ltd.* v. *Waring & Gillow Ltd.* [1926] A.C. 670.

[8] See Burrows (1984) 100 L.Q.R. 31 at 34.

[9] *Essays on Contract* (1986) pp. 322–323. See also, Professor Atiyah's argument (*ibid.* at pp. 324–327) that many estoppel cases could in fact just as easily be treated as cases of warranty.

[10] (1983) 99 L.Q.R. 217 at 251 n. 55.

2. NATURE OF LIABILITY: STRICT OR FAULT-BASED

In a number of situations, therefore, it may be possible for a representee to secure the protection of his expectation interest. The closeness between estoppel by representation and warranty in this respect can also be seen to exist, to a certain extent, as regards the question whether fraud, negligence or strict liability must be proved. We have seen that in cases of deceit the representor must be shown to have been fraudulent, in cases of negligent misstatement at common law he must be shown to have been negligent and in cases under section 2(1) of the Misrepresentation Act, in order to be liable he must be unable to discharge the burden of showing reasonable grounds of belief in the truth of his statement. If rescission of the contract for misrepresentation or damages for breach of contract are sought, the liability is strict, though in the former case the remedy is at the discretion of the court. Again the position of estoppel is of interest.[11] The courts have devoted little time to examining whether estoppel by representation operates as a form of strict liability, or whether it is negligence based. In *Freeman* v. *Cooke*,[12] Parke B. emphasised that it must be shown that the representor meant his representation to be acted on, and it was enough that, whatever his real intention was, he conducted himself in such a way that a reasonable man would take the representation to be true. Parke B. went on to say that a person might also be estopped from denying the truth of his representation in a situation where a duty was incumbent upon him to disclose the truth and "by negligence or omission"[13] he failed to do so. As is emphasised by Spencer Bower and Turner,[14] "negligence" in this context connotes the breach of a duty to speak, rather than pertaining to a duty of care with regard to positive misrepresentations. It is not the negligence which estops the representor, but the representation which is implied from it.[15]

However, in *Seton Laing & Co.* v. *Lafone*[16] the defendant warehouseman negligently represented to the owner of goods that

---

[11] Atiyah, *Essays on Contract* (1986) pp. 316–319.

[12] (1848) 2 Ex. 654.

[13] *Ibid.* at 663. See also, *Carr* v. *London & North Western Railway* (1875) L.R. 10 C.P. 307 at 318, *per* Brett J.

[14] *Estoppel by Representation* (3rd ed., 1977) pp. 72–74. See also, Chap. 6, p. 135 *supra*.

[15] See *Saunders* v. *Anglia Building Society* [1971] A.C. 1004 at 1038.

[16] (1887) 19 Q.B.D. 68.

they were in his possession. He was held to be estopped from denying that he had the goods, and was liable in conversion. The negligence here arose from a positive misrepresentation, rather than breach of a duty to speak, yet Lord Esher M.R. regarded the careless making of a false statement which is acted on as comprising an independent, exclusive category of estoppel. Subsequently in *Low* v. *Bouverie*,[17] however, the focus was again upon the effect of the statement rather than whether it was made fraudulently, negligently or innocently, though the Court of Appeal clearly felt that an estoppel could be founded on a fraudulent or an innocent statement. More recently, in *Moorgate Mercantile Co. Ltd.* v. *Twitchings*,[18] the respondent motor dealer, having been informed by a hire purchase central registry that there were no recorded hire purchase agreements in respect of a car which one McLong had offered to sell to him, duly purchased the car and was then sued in conversion by the appellant finance company which owned the car and had in fact let it on hire purchase to McLong. The respondent argued, *inter alia*, that the appellants, in failing to record the agreement with McLong with the registry, were estopped from claiming damages from him in conversion. Lord Edmund-Davies contrasted cases such as *Pickard* v. *Sears*[19] where the estoppel arises on account of the deliberate nature of the representor's statement, with cases where the preclusion arises from a merely negligent act or omission. In the former category of case the owner of goods was *ex hypothesi* unable to deny that he intended others to act as they did. In the latter category the preclusion was based on the existence of a duty of care which must be shown to have been breached by the negligent act or omission under complaint. It may be, therefore, that in cases of estoppel by silence negligence in some form may need to be proved; as Professor Atiyah has commented,[20] the courts appear to have moved unconsciously from the notion of "neglect" to the notion of "negligence." In general, however, it seems that estoppel by representation may arise in the absence of fraud or negligence, thereby providing another ground for comparison with liability on a warranty.

---

[17] [1891] 3 Ch. 82 *supra*, pp. 131–134.
[18] 1977] A.C. 890. The estoppel argument failed, since it was held that the information provided by the registry did not constitute a representation that none of the registry's members had any interests in the car in question.
[19] (1837) 6 Ad & El. 469. *Supra*, pp. 126–127.
[20] *Essays on Contract* (1986), p. 319.

3. LIABILITY FOR SILENCE

As the above quotation from Parke B. in *Freeman* v. *Cooke*[21] suggests, silence or inaction may in certain circumstances comprise a representation for the purposes of estoppel.[22] The representor must owe a legal duty to the representee to speak, and such a duty, as we have seen,[23] arises in quite a wide range of cases. This may be contrasted with the law relating to actionable misrepresentations, where the general rule, as noted above,[24] is that there is no obligation upon a contracting party to disclose material facts known to him, but several exceptions to this exist. This difference may be explained by the fact that estoppel is not a cause of action, and a duty to speak may be imposed more readily upon a person whose failure to do so may deprive him of a cause of action, as in *Pickard* v. *Sears*,[25] than upon one whose failure would rend him liable to damages or rescission of a contract. However, as we have seen, in some cases estoppel may have the effect of depriving a representor of a defence that would otherwise exist. In such a case he will in many ways be in the same position as the defendant in a case of actionable misrepresentation. Thus, in *Algar* v. *Middlesex County Council*[26] the plaintiff, an employee of the defendant, was transferred from one post to another, in which he was to be the "interim registrar" of births and deaths. He wrote to the defendant, including in his letter a request for an assurance that his superannuation rights would be protected. He received no reply to this letter, but the defendant continued to levy him with a contribution to the superannuation fund. It was held that the defendant was estopped from averring that the plaintiff was not entitled to the benefits of the superannuation scheme.

A warranty cannot arise out of silence, for it would be impossible in such a case to find the necessary intention to warrant. But, to complete the picture, liability may arise under *Hedley Byrne* v. *Heller* as a consequence of a failure to speak if the court holds that the representor was under a duty to disclose facts

---

[21] *Supra*, p. 158.

[22] See *Greenwood* v. *Martin's Bank Ltd.* [1933] A.C. 51; Spencer, Bower and Turner (3rd ed., 1977) pp. 48–79.

[23] See Chap. 6, pp. 135–136 *supra*.

[24] Chap. 2, pp. 21–26 *supra*.

[25] (1837) 6 Ad. & El. 469.

[26] [1945] 2 All E.R. 243. The action arose as a consequence of a decision by the defendant that the plaintiff was not superannuable. The plaintiff requested the Minister to state a case for the opinion of the court. Presumably, had the Minister refused to do so, the plaintiff could have sued for breach of contract or sought a declaration.

which he ought to have known.[27] It is clear, therefore, that liability for misrepresentation (in the broadest sense) may arise in a wide variety of situations as a consequence of a failure to speak, though the appropriate remedy will of course depend upon the circumstances in which that liability arises.

To a large extent the available remedies are mutually exclusive, but an overlap may exist in certain situations. Thus, to take the facts of *Greenwood* v. *Martin's Bank Ltd.*,[28] the plaintiff, though aware that his wife was forging his signature on cheques drawn on their joint bank account with the defendants, kept silent. Subsequently, after his wife's death, he disclosed the fact of the forgeries to the defendants and sought to recover from them the sums paid out. It was held that he was estopped by his silence from denying the authenticity of the signatures, as he owed a duty to the defendants to disclose the forgeries when he became aware of them. As has been pointed out,[29] the bank could alternatively have acknowledged the forgery, recredited the plaintiff's account with the amount of the cheques and then sued him for damages. Quite apart from the contract between the banker and customer, upon a breach of which such an action could be founded, it is likely that liability under *Hedley Byrne* v. *Heller* would exist concurrently in such circumstances.

4. RELATIONSHIP BETWEEN REPRESENTOR AND REPRESENTEE

As regards the nature of the relationship that must exist between representor and representee, the different categories of misrepresentation liability have much in common. This is hardly surprising, given the common requirement of reliance that they share. And yet there exist subtle distinctions which themselves reflect differences between the categories. Thus, for liability to be imposed for an actionable misrepresentation, a contract between representor and representee must ensue. If a contract does not ensue, liability must be founded on some other basis; perhaps the existence of a special relationship as defined in *Hedley Byrne* v. *Heller* and subsequent cases.[30] Such a relationship may, in Lord Devlin's words, be "equivalent to contract"[31] in the sense that there is an

---

[27] See *Rust* v. *Abbey Life Assurance Co. Ltd.* [1978] 2 Lloyds L.R. 386, but note *Argy Trading Development Co. Ltd.* v. *Lapid Developments Ltd.* [1977] 1 W.L.R. 444; *supra*, pp. 77–78.

[28] [1933] A.C. 51.

[29] Atiyah, *Essays on Contract* (1986) p. 313.

[30] *Supra*, p. 64 *et seq.*

[31] [1964] A.C. 465 at 530, quoting Lord Shaw in *Nocton* v. *Lord Ashburton* [1914] A.C. 932 at 972. See Goodhart (1964) 74 Yale L.J. 286 at 299.

assumption of responsibility in circumstances in which, but for the absence of consideration, there would be a contract. The fact that a contract does in fact ensue does not prevent liability from arising[32]; the essence of liability is that a duty of care exists, not on the ordinary *Donoghue* v. *Stevenson* basis of reasonable foreseeability, but on a more restrictive basis designed, on policy grounds, to limit the category of cases in which liability for pure economic loss will be imposed. The long-standing belief of the courts that such losses are essentially contractual is in a sense given effect to by means of this delimited duty of care. Though the presence or absence of a contract between representor and representee either at the time when the representation is made or subsequently is irrelevant to *Hedley Byrne* liability, the "special relationship" with its elements of assumption of responsibility and reasonable reliance effects a fairly similar restriction upon the range of persons to whom the duty is owed.[33] The fact that liability under *Hedley Byrne* arises as a result of a voluntary assumption of responsibility provides a further parallel with contract liability, though the traditional distinction between contract and tort liability as being the result of a duty voluntarily accepted by a party in the former case and a duty imposed by the law in the latter has increasingly been seen to be open to question in recent years.[34]

5. Representations as to the Future

As we have noted[35] representations as to the future, or promises, which are not fulfilled are not actionable as misrepresentations or misstatements, nor can they give rise to an estoppel by representation, for (unless it can be shown that the representor had no intention of fulfilling his undertaking, in which case he can be said to have misrepresented his state of mind) there is no *mis*representation in such cases: the complaint is that the representor did not do what he had represented that he would do, rather than that he made an untrue statement.

In such cases the expectations generated by the representation will only be protected at common law if the presence of consideration can be established. If the necessary elements of proprietary estoppel can be established, then again failure to fulfil

---

[32] *Esso Petroleum Co. Ltd.* v. *Mardon* [1976] Q.B. 801.
[33] See, *e.g. Yianni* v. *Edwin Evans & Sons* [1982] Q.B. 438.
[34] See, *e.g. Winfield and Jolowicz on Tort* (12th ed., 1984) p. 5.
[35] Chap. 2 *supra*, p. 12.

a representation as to the future may entail protection of the expectation interest—this time in equity—and with no need to show consideration. Promissory estoppel, however, is mainly concerned with the protection of the reliance interest of the representee; the better view appears to be that the effect of promissory estoppel is suspensory rather than extinctive (unless performance of the original obligation would be impossible or inequitable) and hence, as one commentator has remarked, only the reliance (or status quo) interest of the representee is protected.[36] However, as the same commentator has argued,[37] the reasons for protecting the expectations engendered by a promise are sufficiently powerful to justify extending this protection to cases of promissory estoppel, despite the absence of consideration, and this argument has its attractions, providing as it would for protection of the expectation interest, in all appropriate cases of unkept promises where consideration can be shown or an equitable estoppel raised.

Professor Atiyah has gone so far as to argue that the cases on equitable estoppel are illustrative of his view that an act done in reliance on a promise may be good consideration even though it is not stated or requested by the promisor as an act to be performed by the promisee.[38] This view has its attractions, given the problems that exist in reconciling the traditional definition of consideration to all cases[39] and given also the removal it would entail of what is otherwise a major exception to the general rule that expectations are protected only within a contractual context. It would also provide a solution to the anomalous state of affairs whereby detrimental reliance on an untrue statement may be more likely to be compensated than detrimental reliance on an unkept promise. The degree of reliance in the latter situation may be equal to, if not greater than, that in the former, yet, unless there is consideration for the promise, the likelihood of relief in the latter situation is dependent purely upon equitable remedies, whereas in the former situation the whole range of remedies provided by the law of misrepresentation may be available.

Difficulties remain with Professor Atiyah's view, however. Other than *Dillwyn* v. *Llewellyn* itself, the proprietary estoppel cases do not speak the language of contract. The available remedies, in particular, argue a framework other than the

---

[36] (1983) 99 L.Q.R. 217 at 242 (A. S. Burrows).

[37] *Ibid.* at 262.

[38] *Essays on Contract* (1986) pp. 211–212; 232–233. The whole of Essay 8 is of especial interest in this context.

[39] *Ibid.* See also, Treitel, *The Law of Contract* (7th ed., 1987) pp. 53–55.

contractual. As we have seen,[40] the court appears to prefer in such cases to make an order which is appropriate to the equity of the case, thereby employing a flexibility denied to a purely contractual framework, and the essence of the estoppel claim is prejudice in circumstances of unconscionability rather than breach of an agreement which is supported by consideration.[41] It may, however, be questioned whether, even if the cases, as they appear to do, demonstrate a distinction between estoppel and contract, this distinction should be maintained. To a large extent, it may be argued, the courts' adherence to the doctrine of consideration is counterbalanced by the extent to which relief is available in equity for an unkept promise. The increasing breadth and flexibility of promissory estoppel[42] and proprietary estoppel,[43] the equitable doctrine of part performance[44] and the constructive trust[45] come close to establishing, in the words of one commentator,

> "a general principle that a person who has relied on an otherwise unenforceable promise, which was calculated to induce reliance, is entitled to redress if the non-enforcement of the promise would leave him worse off than if he had not relied on it."[46]

It may be, therefore, that equitable relief is now sufficiently extensive as to provide appropriate relief in deserving cases of detrimental reliance upon an unkept promise.

---

[40] Chap. 6 *supra*, p. 147.

[41] See *Chitty on Contracts* (25th ed., 1983) paras. 230 and 238; Millett (1976) 92 L.Q.R. 342.

[42] As witnessed, for example, by its extention in *The "Henrik Sif"* (*Pacol* v. *Trade Lines Ltd.*) [1982] 1 Lloyds Rep. 456 of the "legal relationship" that must exist between the parties to include a putative contract.

[43] See the quotations from Oliver J. in *Taylor Fashions* v. *Liverpool Victoria Trustees Co. Ltd.* [1981] 1 All E.R. 897 at 915–916, [1982] Q.B. 133n at 151–152 and Robert Goff J. in *Amalgamated Investment & Property Co. Ltd.* v. *Texas Commerce International Bank Ltd.* [1982] Q.B. 84 at 103 cited *supra*, pp. 145, 146, and note the extension, in the latter case, of proprietary estoppel into forms of property other than land, and, in cases such as *Crabb* v. *Arun D.C.* [1976] 1 Ch. 179, beyond the context of family relationships.

[44] See *Steadman* v. *Steadman* [1976] A.C. 536.

[45] See *Re Basham* [1987] 1 All E.R. 405, where Edward Nugee Q.C., sitting as a Deputy Judge of the High Court, described proprietary estoppel as comprising a form of constructive trust, in cases where the representee is led to believe that he will have a right in the future. He also drew parallels between proprietary estoppel and cases of secret trusts and mutual wills.

[46] J. H. Baker [1979] *Current Legal Problems* 17 at 29.

6. POSSIBLE REFORM

To what extent, though, are the differences between the various strands of misrepresentation liability examined above of so fundamental a nature as to require the retention of all these heads of claim? Would it not be possible to subsume all these strands within a general principle of compensation for reliance losses caused by an untrue statement, or at least to find some way of simplying the law?

An initial point is that, since they are not concerned with untrue statements, promissory and proprietary estoppel could not be brought within a general principle along the lines mentioned above. As we have seen in Chapter 6, however, it has been argued that they are illustrations of a general principle whereby, one party having induced another to rely on an expectation, it is unconscionable to deny a remedy to him. Beyond that, the links between the various heads of claim for misrepresentation merit a brief examination, to see if there is any room for simplification.

As we have seen, liability for breach of warranty may take account of expectation losses, as also may estoppel by representation. Can it be argued that all cases of estoppel by representation could be founded in the alternative on breach of warranty?[47] In each case, quite apart from the similarity as regards the measure of damages, there must be a statement of fact, which need not be made fraudulently or negligently, and which is acted on by the representee. However, significant distinctions between the two exist, especially the fact that warranty liability requires an intention to warrant and the fact that estoppel by representation, though in some cases it comes close to it, is not a cause of action in itself. As Professor Atiyah has remarked, "every case of warranty could be treated as a case of estoppel whereas the converse is clearly not true."[48] It may be that some of the estoppel cases could have been treated as cases of warranty, though if the plea of estoppel succeeds there is no reason why the representee would wish to claim a warranty. The type of case where the representee might benefit from claiming a warranty would be where the estoppel argument fails, but, given the similarity between the type of statement required in cases of warranty and cases of estoppel, it

---

[47] This issue is illuminatingly examined by Atiyah, *Essays in Contract* (1986) pp. 319–328.
[48] *Ibid*. at 323.

is likely that if the statement does not raise an estoppel, it would not amount to a warranty either.[49]

Would it be possible for estoppels to be actionable in negligence under *Hedley Byrne* v. *Heller*? One benefit of so channelling cases of estoppel by representation would be to avoid the problem highlighted by *Avon C.C.* v. *Howlett* of awarding expectation losses in a non-bargain situation. Though, as we have seen, estoppel may arise even in the absence of fraud or negligence, it would seem sensible to treat cases such as *Low* v. *Bouverie*,[50] where there appears to have been breach of a duty of care, firmly within the camp of reliance losses. However, where a party envisages the possibility of greater financial benefit in raising an estoppel, it is difficult to see how he could be prevented from preferring that option to suing in negligence. The task of drafting legislation to preclude raising an estoppel in circumstances where there is an arguable claim in negligence would be unlikely to receive an enthusiastic welcome from Parliamentary Counsel.

There is clearly an overlap between the claim under *Hedley Byrne* v. *Heller* and the action under section 2(1) of the Misrepresentation Act. In each case liability in damages is imposed upon a careless representor. As we have seen,[51] there are significant differences between these two causes of action, the main one being those concerning the burden of proof and the nature of the representee's detrimental reliance. Clearly, all *Hedley Byrne* cases could not be subsumed within section 2(1), as a contract between representor and representee is not a necessary consequence of the untrue statement in such cases. Thus, the facts of *Hedley Byrne* itself, should they recur, would not give rise to a section 2(1) claim. It may be that a substantial number of section 2(1) claims could in the alternative be brought at common law, but, as the *Howard Marine* case shows,[52] this is not necessarily the case. The fact that a representation is made which induces the representee to contract with the representor is not *ipso facto* indicative of the existence of a duty of care. In practice the two causes of action are likely to be delineated by the presence or absence of an ensuing contract: if a contract ensues the represen-

---

[49] See, *e.g. Low* v. *Bouverie* [1891] 3 Ch. 82. The lack of clarity and the ambiguity of the representor's statement were such that the plea of estoppel failed, and these factors would surely have denied the possibility of characterising the statement as a warranty, quite apart from the lack of intention to contract and the absence of consideration, as emphasised by Lindley L.J. at 103.

[50] *Supra*, n. 49.

[51] See Chap. 4 *supra*, pp. 86–87.

[52] See Chap. 3 *supra*, pp. 46–47 and Chap. 4, pp. 79–80.

tee will claim under the Act; if it does not he will have to fall back on the common law claim.

The most extensive step towards a degree of rationalisation in this area of the law has occurred in New Zealand in the Contractual Remedies Act 1979.[53] The Act has its origins in the 1967 Report of the Contracts and Commercial Law Reform Committee on *Misrepresentation and Breach of Contract*. No action on the Committee's recommendations was taken at the time, but the Report was revived in 1978 and the Act followed soon afterwards. Its object is to reform the law relating to remedies for misrepresentation and breach of contract. Section 6 follows the general recommendation of the Committee that the best solution to the problems posed by the existence of the various categories of pre-contractual and contractual representation was to treat them all as contractual promises. Thus, section 6(1) provides as follows:

6. Damages for Misrepresentation

(1) If a party to a contract has been induced to enter into it by a misrepresentation, whether innocent or fraudulent, made to him by or on behalf of another party to that contract—

(*a*) He shall be entitled to damages from that other party in the same manner and to the same extent as if the representation were a term of the contract that has been broken; and

(*b*) He shall not, in the case of a fraudulent misrepresentation, or of an innocent misrepresentation made negligently, be entitled to damages from that other party for deceit or negligence in respect of that misrepresentation.

Previously, the position was that damages were only available if the representee could prove fraud, negligence, breach of a collateral warranty or breach of a collateral contract. An effect of the section is that the representee does not have to prove negligence nor, provided he has perpetrated a misrepresentation, can the representor avoid liability in damages by proving reasonable grounds for believing his statement to be true. Thus, to borrow Professor McLaughlan's use of the example of the *Howard Marine* case,[54] if the case fell under section 6 all the hirers of the

---

[53] See Dawson and McLauchlan, "The Contractual Remedies Act 1979" (1981); McLauchlan, "Contract Law Reform in New Zealand: the Contractual Remedies Act 1979" (1981) 10 J.L.S. 284.

[54] [1978] Q.B. 574. This discussion ignores the problems posed by the exclusion clause in the case. See (1981) 10 J.L.S. 284 at 286.

barge would have to prove would be that the statement as to capacity was untrue and they relied upon it.

The term "misrepresentation" is not defined in the Act, repeating the omission of the English Act, but it appears to be intended to bear its common law meaning of "false statement of existing or past fact."[55] As under the English Act this raises the question whether the new statute affects the remedies for actionable non-disclosure, and it may require a fairly broad interpretation from the courts in order to avoid the retention of the pre-Act law for cases of non-disclosure.

Of especial significance, however, is the assimilation of pre-contract representations to contractual promises. Awarding expectation losses in the case where the statement made is merely a representation which induced the contract rather than being a statement which is a term is certainly controversial and, not surprisingly, split the Committee.[56] It is certainly true, as we have seen,[57] that the distinction between the case where the representor is regarded as having accepted responsibility for the accuracy of his statement and the case where he is not so regarded is an extremely difficult one to make, but it may be questioned whether the continued effort to make such a distinction is better replaced by an arbitrary assumption that expectation losses are always appropriate in such cases. Such an approach seems unduly simplistic, and, as one commentator has noted, "it may be that the maligned Misrepresentation Act 1967 (U.K.) had correct policy objectives and was unfortunate only in its detailed drafting."[58]

A further aspect of the strategy of the Contractual Remedies Act is to provide a code which governs the right to cancel a contract for misrepresentation, repudiation or breach. Cancellation for misrepresentation, which is designed to replace the pre-Act remedy of rescission, is available, according to section 7(4);

if, and only if—

(a) The parties have expressly or impliedly agreed that the truth of the representation or, as the case may require, the performance of the stipulation is essential to him[59] or
(b) The effect of the misrepresentation or breach is, or, in the case of an anticipated breach, will be,—

[55] 1967 Report, para. 13.3 cited in Dawson and McLaughlan *op. cit.* n. 53.
[56] See Dawson and McLaughlan *op. cit.* n. 53, pp. 33–34.
[57] *Supra*, pp. 97–105.
[58] Reynolds (1982) 12 V.U.W.L.R. 199 at 200, reviewing Dawson and McLaughlan.
[59] *i.e.* either party to the contract.

(i) Substantially to reduce the benefit of the contract to the cancelling party; or

(ii) Substantially to increase the burden of the cancelling party under the contract; or

(iii) In relation to the cancelling party, to make the benefit or burden of the contract substantially different from that represented or contracted for.

This right will be lost, according to section 7(5), if the representee, with full knowledge of the misrepresentation, has affirmed the contract.

Where a contract is cancelled the court has extensive powers to grant relief under section 9, which may include vesting in either party the property that was the subject of the contract (section 9(2)(a)) and directing one party to pay to the other such sum as the court thinks just (section 9(2)(b)). In considering whether to make an order under the section, the court must have regard to a number of factors, including the terms of the contract (section 9(4)(a), the extent to which any party to the contract was or would have been able to perform it in full or in part (section 9(4)(b)) and any expenditure incurred by a party in or for the purpose of the performance of the contract (section 9(4)(c)). The guidelines in s.9(4) are regarded by Professor McLaughlan, as

"given the multifarious range of situations the court is empowered to deal with, too vague and likely to prove extremely difficult to apply . . . the solution *cannot* be to leave it to the court to decide what is just on the facts of each individual case and thus make the law more uncertain than ever."[60]

This brief review of aspects of the Contractual Remedies Act illustrates some of the problems that may attend attempts to reform this area of the law. It also demonstrates the extent to which the law of misrepresentation is linked to the law of contract and the fact that reforms of the law of misrepresentation cannot be considered in isolation.[61] Indeed, the implications of any radical reform of the law of misrepresentation for the law of contract, tort and equity are such as to daunt most, if not all, would-be

---

[60] *Op. cit.* n. 53, p. 292.

[61] It should be noted that the Contractual Remedies Act forms part of a series of extensive reforms of the law of contract in New Zealand (see also, the Illegal Contracts Act 1970 and the Contractual Mistakes Act 1977), which also exemplify the strategy of furnishing the courts with wide remedial powers and a broad discretion to apply such powers.

reformers. If it is accepted, as it surely must be, that the general law of misrepresentation cannot be reformed and simplified at one fell swoop, reform within the context of a general review (perhaps a reforming codification) of the law of contract may be feasible, though, as the New Zealand example shows, the balance between flexibility and certainty is, as always, extremely difficult to maintain.

Appendix

THE MISREPRESENTATION ACT 1967

(1967, c. 7)

1. Removal of certain bars to rescission for innocent misrepresentation.

Where a person has entered into a contract after a misrepresentation has been made to him, and—

- (*a*) the misrepresentation has become a term of the contract; or
- (*b*) the contract has been performed;

or both, then, if otherwise he would be entitled to rescind the contract without alleging fraud, he shall be so entitled, subject to the provisions of this Act, notwithstanding the matters mentioned in paragraphs (*a*) and (*b*) of this section.

2. Damages for misrepresentation.

(1) Where a person has entered into a contract after a misrepresentation has been made to him by another party thereto and as a result thereof he has suffered loss, then, if the person making the misrepresentation would be liable to damages in respect thereof had the misrepresentation been made fraudulently, that person shall be so liable notwithstanding that the misrepresentation was not made fraudulently, unless he proves that he has reasonable ground to believe and did believe up to the time the contract was made that the facts represented were true.

(2) Where a person has entered into a contract after a misrepresentation has been made to him otherwise than fraudulently, and he would be entitled, by reason of the misrepresentation, to rescind the contract, then, if it is claimed, in any proceedings arising out of the contract, that the contract ought to be or has been rescinded, the court or arbitrator may declare the contract subsisting and award damages in lieu of rescission, if of opinion that it would be equitable to do so, having regard to the nature of the misrepresentation and the loss that would be caused by it if

the contract were upheld, as well as to the loss that rescission would cause to the other party.

(3) Damages may be awarded against a person under subsection (2) of this section whether or not he is liable to damages under subsection (1) thereof, but where he is so liable any award under the said subsection (2) shall be taken into account in assessing his liability under the said subsection (1).

3. Avoidance of provision excluding liability for misrepresentation.

[If a contract contains a term which would exclude or restrict—

(a) any liability to which a party to a contract may be subject by reason of any misrepresentation made by him before the contract was made; or

(b) any remedy available to another party to the contract by reason of such a misrepresentation,

that term shall be of no effect except in so far as it satisfies the requirement of reasonableness as stated in section 11(1) of the Unfair Contract Terms Act 1977; and it is for those claiming that the term satisfies that requirement to show that it does.]

4. Amendment of Sale of Goods Act 1893.

. . .

5. Saving for past transactions.

Nothing in this Act shall apply in relation to any misrepresentation or contract of sale which is made before the commencement of this Act.

INDEX